AN INSIDE LOOK AT

NAPA
VALLEY

This book was produced by
Copyright Studio, Paris, France, in collaboration with
Color Print Graphix, Antwerp, Belgium, and
Atomium Books, Wilmington, Delaware.

Original concept and project coordination
Jean-Paul Paireault

Project coordination in California
Mona Abadir, Lightwater Concepts Inc., Sausalito, California

First published in the United States by
        Atomium Books Inc.
        Suite 300
        1013 Centre Road
        Wilmington, DE 19805

Printed in Belgium by Color Print Graphix.

First U.S. Edition
ISBN 1-56182-026-1
2 4 6 8 10 9 7 5 3 1

Beyond The Grapes

AN INSIDE LOOK AT

NAPA
VALLEY

DAN BERGER
RICHARD PAUL HINKLE

Photography
ERIC SANDER

atomium books

TABLE OF CONTENTS

INTRODUCTION

The phrase "wine country" has come to mean one thing to Americans: the Napa Valley. The small region from Yountville to Calistoga was neither the first of this country's winegrowing regions nor has it ever been the largest. But it has been fortunate enough to have been the recipient of some good luck, a touch of magic, and it happens to produce some of the best wine in the state, if not the world. Its wines have won a number of timely awards, and, not incidentally, it has adopted some pretty effective public relations. All this combines to place the Napa Valley No. 1 in the minds of Americans, who feel this is the spiritual center of American wine.

It didn't hurt, of course, that Frank Loesser's popular musical *Most Happy Fella* was a Broadway hit following its May 3, 1956, opening. It ran for 676 performances and wowed audiences with the engaging aria by the star of the show, an aging vintner by the name of Tony, who asks youthful Rosabella to be his wife and make him "the most happy fella in the whole Napa Valley."

That romantic play, by itself, may not have brought an immediate wave of development to the Napa Valley, but it surely gave Americans a hummable tune that carried a message: Napa was wine country.

And certainly there is no question that Napa's climate zones — from wind-raked Carneros in the south to sun-baked Calistoga in the north — are ideal for many varieties of the Vitis vinifera grape. That fact was clear as early as the late 1880s, when wine production in this green belt filled the tranquil valley that was also home to prunes and cows. Many other areas can boast sublime climate and long genealogy, too. Indeed, in the early days of winemaking in the United States, attempts were made to grow grapes and make great wine in diverse regions. One of the first serious attempts began in Virginia, with Thomas Jefferson. His failure never dampened his belief that great wine some day would emanate from American soil. There were other early tries, too — in Ohio, New York, Wisconsin, New Mexico, San Diego, and Los Angeles.

Yet it was the combination of the soil, climate, and exposure found in Napa that provided the perfect setting. By the turn of the century, as other regions still struggled to make wine against the rigors of harsh winters and searing summers, Napa was a rising star. Author Frona Eunice Wait wrote that 142 wine cellars existed in Napa County in 1889, and their numbers were growing. Though few of their wines were considered in the same breath as those of the great growing regions of the Continent, Napa was filled with an enthusiastic spirit that was killed only by the advent of Prohibition.

The spirit of adventure that originally built Napa into a great winegrowing region — and that rebuilt the valley after the Repeal of Prohibition — was born from the old West's traditions, such as barn raisings and quilting bees. It is a spirit that was embodied in the efforts of a single man, perhaps the monumental figure of the Napa Valley's earliest days — Charles Krug.

Krug was the pioneer wine grower in the Napa Valley. He used the first mechanical press and built the first commercial winery of any size in the county. It would have been easy for him to establish a monopoly and keep others out, but instead he encouraged fresh viticultural development, unworried about competition. He offered his expertise and even personal funds to the cause of local development. Jacob Beringer learned winegrowing under Krug; Karl Wente was Krug's "cellar boss" in the 1870s. Both went on to found great wineries of their own. Clarence J. Wetmore (brother of Cresta Blanca's Charles Wetmore) was apprenticed at Krug. So were John C. Weinberger, William W. Lyman, and Emil C. Priber, all of whom opened wineries of their own nearby. In the latter days of the last century, Frona Eunice Wait wrote of Krug that he was "a man whose name has been associated with every venture for the promotion of the industry throughout the state, from its inception to the present, giving a lifetime and a fortune to the work."

Sadly, during the 1880s and into the 1890s, California's vineyards were ravaged by the root louse phylloxera. The resulting financial strain on Krug and his operation put him into debt, and he never was able to wipe it out in his lifetime.

Another important pioneer of the area was the first white settler in the valley: a Missouri Indian fighter by the name of George Yount. He claimed a 12,000-acre Caymus land grant from the Mexican government and became a friend and protector of the local "Digger" tribes

— the Ouluke, Caymus, Conahamanas, and Miacomus.

Yount settled north of the town of Napa in 1836 and planted orchards and vineyards, the first one in 1838. By 1860, he was making 5,000 gallons of wine a year. Yount gave a part of his ranch for the site of a town, first called Sebastopol. After his death the town was renamed Yountville, in his honor.

One of the most colorful and controversial of the founders of Napa Valley towns was Sam Brannan, who set up a gold miners' supply camp ten miles north of St. Helena. Brannan brought in mining supplies, charging exorbitant prices, and made such a fortune that he decided to found a town. Local legend says that the naming of the place was accomplished late one evening after Brannan, a notorious drinker, had consumed a filling dinner and a plethora of libations. Brannan arose, unsteadily, prepared to announce that he would turn the little town of hot springs and mud baths into the Saratoga of California. However, because of his condition, Brannan is reported to have said he would turn the place into "the Calistoga of Sarifornia," and the name stuck.

In the years following the Civil War, wine evolved from farming adjunct into industry as people like Krug and Jacob Schram, a teacher and a barber, elevated their hobbies into businesses, turning whimsy into art and creating excitement for the region. Robert Louis Stevenson, after visiting with Schram in his hillside estate, called the wine "bottled poetry" and noted that "the stirring sunlight and the growing vines and the vats and bottles in the cavern made a pleasant music for the mind."

Another industry pioneer, Hamilton Walker Crabb, arrived in Oakville, planted his To Kalon Vineyard ("the boss vineyard," as *he* translated it from the Greek) and became the valley's largest grape grower by 1880, producing some 360,000 gallons of wine. Crabb experimented with more than 400 different varieties of grapes. (Nearly a century later the To Kalon Vineyard was solely Cabernet Sauvignon and owned by Robert Mondavi, one of the industry's most innovative winemakers.)

In the early 1870s, W. C. Watson planted a 70-acre vineyard at Rutherford and named the estate Inglenook, a Scottish term for a cozy corner. A meticulous sea captain, Gustav Niebaum, eventually transformed Inglenook into the template for all quality wine operations in the area. By bottling wines under his own label, he took the first step in identifying the Napa Valley to a public eager to praise American wines.

By coincidence, the two decades following 1870 and the two decades following 1970 were the greatest in terms of growth in the Napa Valley. The massive stone structures of Inglenook, Greystone (the 20th century home of The Christian Brothers), Chateau Chevalier, and Chateau Montelena were erected in the first wave of wine growth. The one design that differed was the classic Rhine House of the Beringer family, with its handsome stained-glass windows. Among the early edifices were also Tiburcia Parrott's Miravalle (now called Spring Mountain Winery), the elegant Far Niente, and the sturdy wooden, pumpkin-orange edifice of Eshcol Winery, now owned by the Trefethen family.

Prohibition was a blight to the wineries, but for a curious reason the growing of grapes actually increased through the 13-year "noble experiment." The law permitted the head of a household to make wine for his or her own consumption, and home winemaking spurted. The nation, which had produced the equivalent of 45 million gallons of wine in 1919, produced grapes for 150 million gallons by 1930. One of the busiest families during this period was the clan of Cesare Mondavi, based in the central San Joaquin Valley. Sons Robert and Peter worked long hours packing Zinfandels and Alicante Bouchets for home winemakers in the east.

Many wineries survived through Prohibition by making sacramental and medicinal wines. The most successful was Beaulieu in Rutherford. The Wente Brothers in Livermore, to the south, actually bonded their winery in the midst of Prohibition as "Beaulieu Vineyard No. Two."

Prohibition ended in 1933, and large cooperative wineries ruled the valley in the turbulent months and years that followed, but the move of The Christian Brothers, the Mondavis, and the Martinis to the Napa Valley gave the revived viticulture some grace and quality appeal. During the war years, there was only scant attention to quality wine. Except for the work done at Inglenook and at Beaulieu Vineyard (the latter run by French-trained, Russian-born Andre Tchelistcheff) and some efforts at Krug and Martini, super-quality wine was not really a major part of the Napa wine scene. Most wineries continued to market wines called Sauterne and Chablis (often the same wine out of the same tank!). Generics were dominant, and sweet wine was as important as dry. Slowly the Mondavi family, which moved into the Krug facility, and the Martinis, who operated two wineries south of St. Helena, made greater strides toward truly high-quality wine.

That happened only after international wine marketing expert Frank Schoonmaker encouraged wineries to follow the lead of Beaulieu and Inglenook (and, later, Krug and Martini) and bottle wines with varietal designations. Rebirth was slow. For roughly the first 0 years after Prohibition, Napa remained little more than an agricultural zone with as many walnuts and sheep as grapes.

Then the spirit that existed in the 1880s began to return. By the 1950s, Napa still had fewer than two dozen wineries, but the biggest statement was being made by tiny, mountainside operations such as Mayacamas, owned by the Taylors; the McCreas' Stony Hill, and Lee Stewart's Souverain, on the other side of the valley. These craftsmen made unique wines, aging them in small barrels and giving them needed time in the bottle. They reduced crop levels to get more intense flavors from the grapes.

Two of the early pioneers were Joe Heitz, an enologist from U.C. Davis who had worked alongside Tchelistcheff at Beaulieu, and Myron Nightingale, who made wonderful wine at Cresta Blanca. Both later went on to fame — Heitz at his own operation and Nightingale at Beringer.

It wasn't until the mid-1960s, however, after brothers Robert and Peter Mondavi had a falling out over the way Charles Krug should be run, that the rebirth of the Napa Valley really began. Robert left Krug, irate that the winery wasn't moving forward as fast as he wanted, and used his brashness to obtain the funds to build his own winery at Oakville in 1966.

To put Napa's recent expansion into perspective, consider that when Mondavi built his Oakville winery in 1966, it was the first new Napa Valley winery of any size since Repeal in 1933.

Mondavi sensed the spirit of artistry — of dedicated grape growing and creative, science-based winemaking — that was afire in the eyes of dozens of his younger neighbors. He not only made the wines himself in the late 1960s, but he was a tireless trouper, going from Rochester to Raleigh, from Brownsville to Boston, to sell his wine. And his genuine enthusiasm caught on with the people. Napa was his sermon and he preached so tirelessly that people at first remembered the message better than the man or his wines.

In 1971, recalls Robert's son, Michael Mondavi, after five solid years of promoting their products, Michael was the honored guest at a winemaker dinner in New York. He was proud that now, at long last, the Mondavi name was a household word. "I'll never forget it," he says. "The host of the function introduced me as Michael Montovani."

Grape growing and wine collecting had not yet become symbols of status, yet Dr. Bernard Rhodes and his wife, Belle, and Robert Adamson and other friends bought vineyards in Napa and planted superb grapes. They even imported wine from Europe for the small coterie of wine lovers who were as avid as they were.

By the early 1970s, wine fever was gripping dozens of wealthy men with a dream. They came from all walks of life: from billboard advertising (Bruce Markham) to auto repair shops (Jack Cakebread), from the pilot's seat of an airliner (Tom Burgess) to the dentist's drill (Pete Minor). And they brought with them the spirit of quality that had been so long the quest of Mondavi and Tchelistcheff and Heitz and McCrea and Stewart and Nightingale and Martini.

In the 25-year period from 1965 to 1990, Napa re-grew out of the ashes of Prohibition, from a dozen wineries to 20 times that. It was the quality of the wine and the quality of life that generated the mania to live here and make wine. Wealthy entrepreneurs were still eager to make a mark here, even though every one of them was aware of the odds — odds that included such significant stumbling blocks as recession, drought, labor-cost increases, new taxes, neo-Prohibitionist attacks, warning labels, fears of liability lawsuits, high marketing costs, lower and lower tax incentives, bizarre laws in 50 different state bureaucracies that made marketing a nightmare, and threats from developers.

Yet they took all of this because of one thing: the rural, peaceful, vineside lifestyle. That was one of the main reasons for the gnawing desire to live here.

"It's sort of like the Champagne district here," farm advisor Keith Bowers once noted. "It's a relatively isolated area and the people work closely with one another. These people see each other at church on Sunday, at school functions, at community gatherings, and in the valley's technical group. That closeness fosters a supportive kind of competition, where everyone learns more quickly by their mistakes."

That last remark unveils one key to the Napa Valley's success. The competition here is more philosophical than cutthroat. Those already established here fight the newcomers seeking to move in beside them, feeling there are already too many folks making wine. But once a new winery is built and making wine, the old-timers seem to want the newcomers to succeed — because that benefits the reputation of the Napa Valley, which in turn benefits them.

Moreover, winemakers are friendly with each other. It's not uncommon to see them lunching together at Tra Vigne or grabbing a hamburger at The Spot. They share the latest information about barrels, presses, and yeast strains, and the latest technical data from the University of California at Davis (U.C. Davis) or Fresno State. They help each other in times of need, lending motors and hose fittings in times of crisis.

By the early 1980s, the valley was nationally and internationally recognized as one of the finest growing and winemaking regions on earth. And with that acclaim came the hordes to feast upon the flavors of the land. The tasting rooms (set up to lure newcomers to wine) brought tourists in by droves, filling narrow, two-lane Highway 29 with a flotilla of cars. Before long, the crowds were more than anyone had anticipated. Rather than widen the road and encourage even more tourism, the wineries sought to scale things back. By the middle of the 1980s, there was fear that more wineries would pollute the lifestyle that the residents coveted — and that benefited the grapes and the wine.

Politics then entered the fray. Growers and winemakers, who for decades had been at each other's throats because of business ("they don't understand us," was a common cry on both sides of the line), fought over the precise definition of a winery. Some said all you had to do was sell wine and that made you a winery. Others said you had to crush the grapes, not simply sell someone else's wine along with aprons and pot holders.

Meanwhile, increasing development in the southern half of the county — most of it housing — increased the population of the county and tilted the voting base. That threatened to give the power to the non-agricultural majority, newcomers by and large, who might pass regulations that would have a negative impact on winemaking.

The issues created a curious coalition. The number of wineries was approaching 300 in a county that had just 31,000 acres of grapes and little more acreage that could be practically planted. And that, as much as anything, got the growers and wineries to agree that something must be done.

In the election of 1990, the voters approved a measure that would remove the development of Napa Valley land from the political sphere — formation of an "agricultural preserve" that limits the way a landowner can divide and sell property. Backed by both wineries and growers, the measure was a rare point of agreement. It set the tone for the excitement of the last decade of the 1900s, which everyone was sure would be calmer than the first nine decades. *DB and RPH*

ACACIA WINERY

Acacia Winery sits alphabetically and serendipitously at the top of most wine lists. Founders Mike Richmond and attorney Jerry Goldstein say they chose the name in 1979 so it would be easy to spell, and based it on some trees in the area. The winery sits on a slope in the Carneros district, looking south over low vine plants to the northern reaches of San Francisco Bay.

"We originally thought of doing Chardonnay only," recalls Richmond, who grew up in Texas. He had meandered across the country via bicycle — working ore boats on the Great Lakes and picking apples in Washington —

before finding a short-term home and a long-term education as sales director at Freemark Abbey (where he had a hand in developing their famed dessert wine, Edelwein).

"But others were making great Chardonnays, and we didn't feel honestly that we could do any better than they were already doing. We considered Cabernet, but the same objection raised itself. Then we took a closer look at Pinot Noir, figuring that maybe we could make that better than anyone else. You see, Pinot Noir was still pretty much the bastard child. Very few people were taking it seriously. People weren't using new barrels; they wouldn't

The sun sets with gold and amber colors over the northern reaches of San Francisco Bay, here called San Pablo Bay. The bay is clearly visible from the winery, at the foot of low, rolling swells of vine rows.

pay extra for the best grapes. So we decided to give Pinot Noir our best effort."

That gamble paid off. Another did not. In the mid-'80s the Acacia crew decided to spin off a second winery, based on the Bordeaux mold, to produce Cabernet Sauvignon and Sauvignon Blanc. While the concept might have been sound, the economics weren't — at least at that time. When the smoke cleared in mid-'86, Acacia was back to its Burgundian theme . . . and owned by Chalone, Inc.

Chalone is the corporation that operates the Chalone, Edna Valley, and Carmenet wineries, in addition to having ties with

Along with Pinot Noir, Chardonnay is a focal point at Acacia. As Chardonnay fruit ripens, the berries change from tiny, green, bitter pinpoints to large, round, almost translucently yellow goblets of sugar and acidity — ready to be made into wine.

Château Lafite Rothschild and a vineyard in Washington State.

"Things have been a lot calmer here since Chalone bought us," says winemaker Larry Brooks, who used to sell Toyotas ("lucrative, but no challenge") and is now an avid bicyclist. "It's been the end of our financial worries, which takes some pressure off, and allows us to concentrate on production, with only limited on-site public relations and sales. Most of the headaches, and all of the upper financial stuff and national sales, are routed through the corporate offices in San Francisco."

The largest part of getting the production job done — especially as it relates to making quality Pinot Noir — lies in forging close grower relationships. "All of our Pinot Noir is grown within walking distance of the winery," notes Brooks. "Buck Bartolucci, Jim St. Clair, Ira Lee, Dave Lund — these guys stay close to what we're doing in the winery. They come in and help during the crush and come taste with their families.

"A winery is not a separate entity, surrounded by vines. A winemaker has to be in the vineyards if he's going to make decent wines. We work very closely with our growers, and if there's a problem with the fruit we feel that it's our fault. You see, we want these people to be working with us 20 years from now." *RPH*

The Carneros District has shallow, hard soils and low relief. The land is composed of youthful marine deposits, and is not very fertile — which is good for growing grapes, as vines need to be stressed somewhat to grow the best-quality fruit for wine.

S. ANDERSON VINEYARD

The story of the S. Anderson winery begins in the mid-1960s. Stan, a Pasadena dentist, was friends with Donn and Molly Chappellet and Jamie Davies of Schramsberg, who had moved to the Napa Valley from the Los Angeles area to become winery owners. A home winemaker, Stan found that idea too intriguing to pass up. He began looking for land in Napa in 1968 and two years later bought a 50-acre ranch just east of Yountville. Vineyards were planted and grapes sold until the winery was founded in 1979. The first wines released commercially were not sparkling, but still, Chardonnays.

S. Anderson also makes a top Cabernet Sauvignon. The winemaker for the still wines since 1989 has been Gary Galleron, partnered by Carol Anderson, Stan's wife. Carol is also the champagne winemaker, while Galleron also makes the Cabernets for the famed Grace Family Winery.

But sparkling wine is the wine S. Anderson has become famous for. It all started after Stan realized that the cooler climate at his vineyards might be appropriate for the production of sparkling wine from Chardonnay as well as a table wine. "The style we go for in sparkling wine is for fuller body, one that emphasizes a lot of fruit," says Stan. The richer style of sparkling wine has appeal for many people. But not content with an all-Chardonnay type of wine, Anderson began also making one blended with Pinot Noir. First released under the Tivoli label, it became so popular that the Andersons couldn't keep up with demand.

It was the Tivoli label which permitted the Andersons to market wines priced a little lower than the rest of the S. Anderson line. That prompted them to expand more rapidly than they had intended, explains Stan's son, John. By 1991 the Tivoli line had grown to about 30 percent of the winery's volume,

In front of a hospitality room at the S. Anderson Vineyard is a trellis system supporting climbing roses. Roses often are used as decorative flowers at wineries because they are sensitive to mold and can signal to the winemaker that a potential problem for the grapevines exists and needs attention.

The Stags Leap region of the Napa Valley also produces some fully ripened Chardonnay grapes, though it is better known for its Cabernet Sauvignon. Under winemaker Gary Galleron, the S. Anderson Vineyard will focus on Cabernet Sauvignon from the area in the 1990s.

setting them on target to become a 25,000-case winery by the turn of the century.

"We're not expanding too quickly, however," says John Anderson. "We're still a small, family-owned winery." Indeed. The production room is so small that, on bottling days, it's crowded wall to wall with workers.

The focal point of the winery is the cave Stan had dug into the hillside, where the barrels of wine age. The idea behind caves as a medium for wine barrels is economically sound.

For one thing, digging a cave costs less than constructing a new building. Also, no air conditioning system is needed because the temperature stays constant in an underground cellar. Without air conditioning (which removes moisture from the air), the cave has a humid environment that minimizes the amount of evaporation from the barrels, which can be as much as a five percent loss of wine per year.

Anderson's sparkling wines have improved since 1986, when Roger Viron was hired as a consultant for the project. Of all of his sparkling wines, Anderson is most intrigued by the rosé, which they began making in the mid-1980s. *DB*

Adjacent to the Chardonnay grapevines that Stan Anderson and his family use to make both still and sparkling wine, under the S. Anderson and Tivoli brands, is a patio that the family uses for social events and for unveiling new releases.

BEAULIEU VINEYARD

Railroad tank cars have often been used to transport wine. The French-American Wine Co. was the name used by Georges de Latour around 1898, when he was manufacturing cream of tartar from the tartrate crystals scraped from the insides of wine tanks. His original plant was in Healdsburg, Sonoma County.

The Napa Valley had a well-established reputation by the time a short, stocky, French chemist purchased 120 acres of orchards and wheat fields just north of the Niebaum place in 1899. The man was Georges de Latour, and his legacy would include some of the most memorable Cabernet Sauvignons ever made in California.

He was born in Bordeaux in 1856 and studied chemistry at the Ecole Centrale in Paris. He came to San Francisco in 1883, the year the Brooklyn Bridge opened. Putting his chemistry to work, de Latour went to work in the gold fields. In 1888 he began the manufacture of baking powder from cream of tartar, and so came into contact with the wine business. He toured the wineries to obtain argols (the crude form of tartar that forms as a crust, or

deposit, in wine tanks) and eventually established factories in the wine centers of Healdsburg, San Jose, Fresno, and Rutherford.

When he acquired the Rutherford property his wife christened it "Beaulieu," the beautiful place. Georges and Fernande loved beauty. They became patrons of the arts, maintained flowered, formal gardens, and were widely renowned as providers of "lavish but sincere

hospitality." President Herbert Hoover, Sir Winston Churchill, and visiting European nobles were guests at their San Francisco and Rutherford homes. The de Latours also made annual visits to France. On one visit, in 1924, their daughter Helene married winegrower Marquis Galcerand de Pins.

The winery, founded just after the turn of the century, produced notable wines from the beginning. In 1915 de Latour bought the Seneca Ewer Winery across from his home. Later enlarged, it remains the central core of Beaulieu today.

Curiously, the winery was put on a financially solid footing during wine's darkest hour in America — Prohibition. (Though Georges was fond of saying, "The shortest road to ruin is slow horses, fast women, and wineries!") Through the friendship of San Francisco's Archbishop Patrick Riordan, de Latour kept the winery open as a supplier of altar wines. Additionally, at Prohibition's demise he had on hand a stock of well-aged table wines that rushed Beaulieu to the front during the confusion of post-Prohibition winemaking. Reported Ernie Pyle in 1939, "Wine in the making is something alive and human to Georges de Latour. It is as human as a member of his family and must be treated as such. Winemaking is an art and a noble career."

The doughty Frenchman secured the future of Beaulieu in 1937 when he went to France to select a successor to retiring enologist Leon Bonnet. At the Institut National Agronomique in Paris, Professor Paul Marsais recommended a young Russian research enologist. André Tchelistcheff began his career at Beaulieu the following September, a career that would last over 40 years and make him the most widely revered winemaker in America.

Georges de Latour died in 1940. He was accorded, says wine historian Leon Adams, "the greatest funeral held in San Francisco in that decade, at which four archbishops presided." Fernande operated the winery until her death in 1951, when the estate went to her

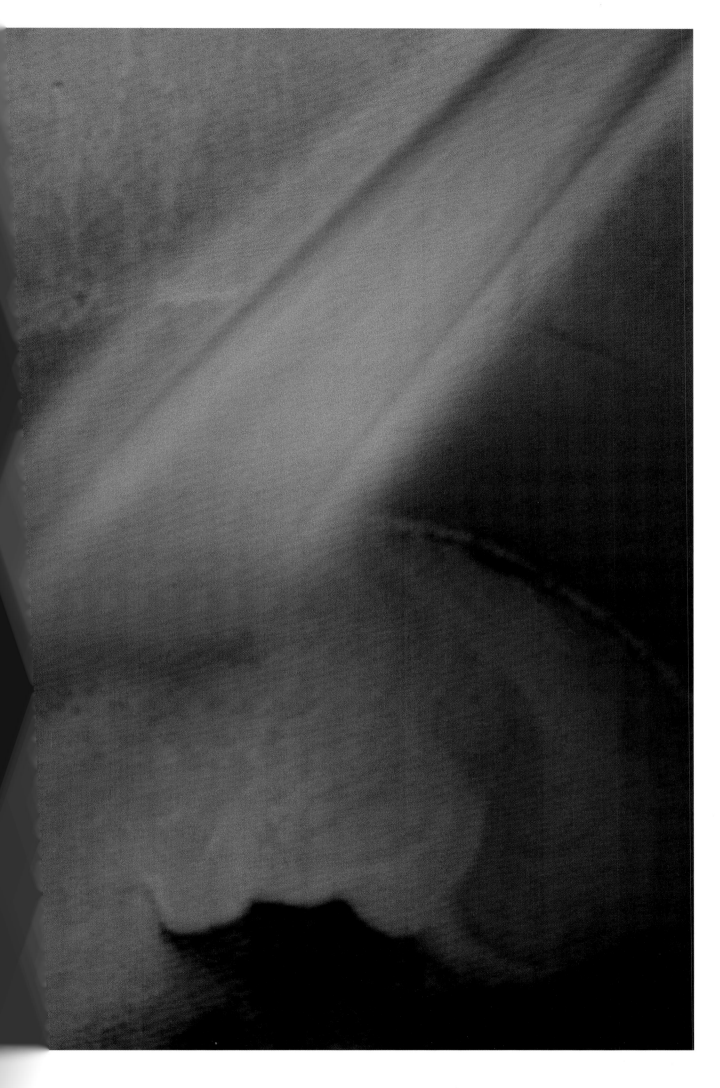

Winemaking is an art, they say. Here the spray of warm red fermented wine must against
the cold blue-gray stainless-steel tank edge literally turns to a work
of abstract art.

daughter. Helene de Pins sold the winery and four of the Beaulieu vineyards to Heublein in 1969. She retained the original estate, with its sunken formal gardens, and the Cabernet Sauvignon vineyard (BV No. 1) that continues to produce Beaulieu's justly famed Georges de Latour Private Reserve Cabernets. The original winery, across the street from the main building, was leased to Heublein for the production of sparkling wines.

Still, Cabernet Sauvignon is the heart and soul of Beaulieu. This is the direct result of Tchelistcheff's phenomenal success with Cabernets made from grapes grown in what he calls "the Rutherford dust." Though he could not convince de Latour to limit his production to Cabernet alone — "Why am I making starlets when I could be making stars?" he would cry — he did obtain a separate cellar where the wine could be aged two years in American oak and two years in the bottle prior to release.

The year of de Latour's death saw the release of Beaulieu's first Georges de Latour Private Reserve Cabernet. From the 1936 vintage, it sold for the then outrageous price of $1.50 per bottle. Today Private Reserves go for more than $25 per bottle, and older vintages command hundreds of dollars per bottle. It is no accident that over half of Beaulieu's vineyards are planted to Cabernet in the Rutherford

A "cellar rat" pumps red wine must — the fermenting juice — over the "cap," a nearly solid, accumulated mass of grape skins, seeds, and pulp. The infusion of oxygen is helpful in extracting the most flavor from red grapes, but would be destructive in the production of most white wines.

and Oakville districts and that nearly half of the winery's production is of that varietal.

The late Marquise Helene de Pins, who headed Beaulieu after her father's death, once recounted her own introduction to that first Private Reserve, the 1936 Cabernet. "My father opened this still very youthful bottle of wine — this must have been in '38 or '39 — and the wine's aroma exploded into the room. He told me, 'I want you to taste this new wine now, because I'm growing old and I may not be here to drink it with you. Taste it. This is the wine I've been trying to make all my life, and I'm certain that it is going to be the greatest in Beaulieu's future.'"

The 1989 Georges de Latour Private Reserve Cabernet Sauvignon rests in American oak barrels before being bottled. The notation at the bottom informs when the wine was last racked — drained off its sediment — from one barrel to another.

Beaulieu's Reserve Cabernet offers, in a sense, an enigma. It breaks a couple of the currently faddish "rules" of great winemaking. First, the wines are solely Cabernet, admitting no addition of Merlot, Cabernet Franc, Malbec, or Petit Verdot "for complexity." Second, they are aged exclusively in the "crude," verboten American oak, which supposedly gives only harsh flavors to the best Cabernets.

The rule it does prove is, "If it ain't broke, don't fix it." That Beaulieu Reserves require no fixing was amply proved by a vertical tasting of vintages from 1941 to 1986 at the 1990 Napa Valley Auction. If the '41 was on the ripe side, with spicy caramel, cassis, and chocolate flavors, the '45 was still youthful, with brittle bell pepper, green olive, coffee, and cassis. The '58 was (along with the '70) the highlight of the evening, with its vibrant anise, cherry, berry, and bell pepper fruit and long, silky texture.

The '70, as expected, remained a lively powerhouse, packed with coffee, bell pepper, olive, and cherry fruit fairly bursting with freshness. The younger vintages also showed promise, especially the '86 — the 50th anniversary vintage — with its black currant and cedar nose and rich, thick, berry and cherry fruit in the mouth. *RPH*

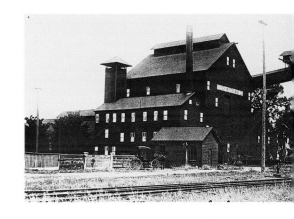

Georges de Latour used this winery at Rutherford near the turn of the century for his French-American Wine Co. Not long after, the facility was renamed Beaulieu Vineyard.

BERINGER VINEYARDS

As exciting and as active as Beringer's present is, it also has a long and fascinating history. It began with the brothers Beringer, from a winemaking family in Mainz, on Germany's Rhine River. Frederick was educated in Paris, then sailed to New York, and in 1866 started a malt-producing business, a venture that would provide the finances for the winery.

Jacob, five years Frederick's junior, was then learning the cooper's and winemaker's trades in Mainz and Berlin. He, too, came to New York, then moved on in 1867 to St. Helena, where he became cellarmaster for Charles Krug. While still in Krug's employ, the popular young man purchased 215 acres called "the old Hudson place" (the Hudson House is now home to Beringer's School for American Chefs) and began planting vines. The year was 1875: America was preparing to celebrate its first centennial and St. Helena was incorporating.

"Los Hermanos" was the sobriquet given German brothers Frederick and Jacob Beringer by friend and neighbor Tiburcio Parrott. The name survived "the brothers" to become a trademark of the winery they built.

In 1877 Jacob hired 100 Chinese to begin the work. Nearly 1,000 feet of tunnels were

Beringer's jewel is the Rhine House, begun in 1883 by Frederick Beringer and built in the image of the family's ancestral home in Mainz, Germany. Rhine House today houses several tasting areas, including the Founder's Room at the head of the main staircase, where older vintages and Reserve wines are poured.

chiseled out of the mountainside by the laborers, "working with picks and shovels and carrying the debris outside in small woven baskets." The winery itself was built of massive, native stone, and measures 40 by 104 feet. The second story was built watertight, caulked regularly, and could be flooded to a depth of several inches without a leak. Grapes crushed on the third floor were fed by gravity to the second floor for fermenting, and then to the first floor for barrel aging.

By 1883 the winery was sufficiently established for Frederick to join his brother in St. Helena. His first task was to begin work on a

The 17-room Rhine House contains one of the largest collections of stained-glass windows in northern California. This pair at the main entry depicts the brothers Beringer, Frederick and Jacob, in Renaissance costume.

home that would resemble their 17-room ancestral home in Mainz. The foundations and ground floor were cut from native stone and the building framed with California redwood. The wainscoting, staircases, and mantelpieces were of ornately carved white oak ordered from Germany.

Intricately patterned floors were cut from oak, mahogany, and walnut. The leaded glass windows were crafted in the Bay area and eight ornamental fireplaces heated the elaborate house. Tiburcio Parrott was so impressed that he ordered the same architect to construct an identical mansion for himself a half-mile up the hill at his Miravalle estate, now Spring Valley Winery (which has since become famous as the setting for TV's *Falcon Crest*).

"Uncle Fritz," as Frederick was known to his friends, helped to found the high school, the creamery, and a savings bank in his adopted community. When he died of Bright's disease in 1901, the *St. Helena Star* lauded his "steadfastness to his friends. He was liberal, kindhearted and true, such a man as wins his way into the affections of all." Jacob died in 1915.

Beringer remained open during Prohibition to produce sacramental and medicinal wines and brandies, giving credence to the winery's claim of being the oldest continuously producing winery in the Napa Valley ("every vintage since 1879"). At Repeal, the 600,000-gallon winery employed 36 people.

In January of 1971 the Beringer heirs sold the winery to Nestle, Inc. The global Swiss food company promptly hired veteran winemaker Myron Nightingale and set aside a substantial amount of money to replant vineyards, replace worn cooperage, and build a sparkling new production facility. Nightingale presided over the construction of the modern winery, placed great emphasis on the uniqueness of the several Napa Valley vineyard locations, and extended his pioneering on botrytised wines (started at the old Cresta Blanca).

His successor is Ed Sbragia, a third-generation winemaker, who has effortlessly continued the steady improvement of Beringer wines, particularly the Reserve Chardonnay and Reserve Cabernet Sauvignon, which today stand at the head of the class. "It's easy if you get good grapes," says Sbragia, sounding very

The caves in the hillside behind the Rhine House were chiseled by Chinese laborers who had returned to San Francisco after working on the Transcontinental Railroad. The carved oak ovals depict harvest scenes and various vinous deities.

much like Nightingale's reincarnation. "As a winemaker, especially with reds," says Ed, "I tend to allow the wine to show itself before I jump in and do something.

"Wine isn't made by recipe. You go out and look at the fruit, and taste it, and you make an educated decision as to how to make the wine this year from these grapes. A lot of winemakers have been fermenting wines, even reds, at lower temperatures, but I prefer warmer fermentations. Some like to clean up the juice a lot prior to fermentation, but I'd rather go in dirty so that the wine can relate itself to the fruit it came from." Which is how you get wines of character.

It also helps to have great grape sources, acquired and carefully tended over the years by viticulturist Bob Steinhauer. The Gamble Ranch, at Oakville, is the home of Beringer's Barrel Fermented Chardonnay. The nearby Hudson Ranch Chardonnay goes to the Reserve wine. State Lane, near Yountville,

offers a prime component for Cabernet from small, intensely-flavored berries. Chabot Vineyard, at the foot of Glass Mountain, provides dense, minty, Cabernet fruit, and the Home Vineyard, on the lower reaches of Spring Mountain, yields Cabernet fit for the Reserve program. And up north in Knights Valley (actually within Sonoma County), volcanic soils are good for Sauvignon Blanc and Cabernet.

Noting the importance of appellations, the pedigree of fine wines, Beringer has been bodaciously bold in seeking out and acquiring new properties throughout California. Under its corporate umbrella, Wine World, Beringer entered into partnership with Champagne Deutz to produce fine sparkling wines in San Luis Obispo County, rescued Chateau Souverain from its grower turmoil, snatched Estrella River from familial malaise (luring winemaker Chuck Ortman and his label, Meridian, for that Paso Robles plant) and snared Italian Swiss Colony's exquisite Alexander Valley vinelands.

With all the hustle and bustle, Beringer remains one of the most accessible wineries for visitors, who thrill at the elm-lined highway out front, the hand-hewn tunnels, the hand-carved oak ovals, and the intricate and intimate tasting rooms in the glittering Victorian jewel that is the Rhine House. *RPH*

Behind sturdy wrought-iron gates lie rare and dusty wine treasures from decades ago. Beringer boasts of making wine each vintage since 1879. Prohibition was a difficult period, but Beringer made sacramental wines to keep the winery and its attendant vineyards in shape for Repeal.

Jacob Beringer (left) and his older brother, Frederick (right), were as popular in the Napa Valley as they were successful.

BOUCHAINE VINEYARDS

Bouchaine sits near the northern edge of San Francisco's expansive bay, a "chateau" quality winery housed in the near ruins of the old concrete and redwood Garetto Winery — built in 1931 and bought by Beringer for storage in 1951.

Founded in 1981, Bouchaine had gone through a series of ownership and winemaker changes before settling down in 1986, when John Montero was named winemaker and DuPont heir Gerret Copeland bought out nearly all of the limited partners.

Through it all, the steadying influence — if a redheaded Irish lass could ever be so describ-

ed — has been President and CEO Eugenia Keegan. "After graduating from Berkeley, I attended law school at Boalt Hall," says the dynamic Keegan. "That lasted one quarter. It's a neat education, and I love the way lawyers think, but the day-to-day job . . . no way." Her dark, penetrating, blue eyes are laughing. "I worked in banking, which I really hated, then worked as a production assistant for a film company in L.A. But the environment there was too seductive, too superficial, too lacking in sincerity."

Keegan returned home to Sonoma County, where she spent some years with Joe Swan ("I really learned how to taste wines from Joe") and

Sturdy end posts anchor vine row trellises at Bouchaine Vineyards, the closest winery to San Pablo Bay. Bouchaine is actively assessing a variety of Pinot Noir clones to determine which work best with the land and the winery's style.

Hop Kiln Winery before hooking up with the fledgling Bouchaine in 1982. "I especially like the agrarian part of wine," she says. "My job is much like the one I had as a production assistant: get things organized, get us into the black, make things a little better, and above all make it fun. Life doesn't mean much if it isn't fun, right?!"

A big part of the fun is making and representing fine wines, and Bouchaine has been fairly consistent in that department, from early winemaker Jerry Luper to present-day winemaker John Montero, whose curly locks and inquisitive eyes remind one of Harpo Marx. Montero

Built as the Garetto Winery in 1931 in anticipation of the end of Prohibition (then two years away), the concrete and redwood facility was later used by Beringer Vineyards for wine storage until Bouchaine was founded in 1981.

has an inquisitive mind, and that's the key to the extensive Pinot Noir investigations being made at Bouchaine.

"We like Carneros Pinot Noir, let there be no mistake about that — it's really fruity; but we want a little more spice, a little more of that earthy character," he says by way of introduction. "You should note, too, that it was Francis Mahoney, at Carneros Creek Winery, who really did the pioneering work here on Pinot Noir clonal selections."

In 1988, Montero gathered bud wood from five excellent sources: Lazy Creek (a tiny Mendocino winery), Hanzell (the fine Sonoma Valley estate), Chalone (at the Pinnacles, in Monterey County), Pommard (a Burgundy clone, taken from an Oregon site), and Joseph Swan (in the Russian River Valley). The year after they were budded to mature vines, the first experimental wines were made. "The Pommard clone really had a lot of spiciness, with teak and mahogany, and is almost a complete wine by itself," observes Montero.

A beer brewer at home, with his wife Roberta Manell (who works at Duckhorn Vineyards), Montero also has a great love for Gewurztraminer, garnered while working at Navarro Vineyards. So, about 1,000 cases of a dry, green apple Gewurz has recently been added to the Pinots that make up the bulk of Bouchaine's 25,000-case annual production. *RPH*

Handsome wrought-iron gates guard the entrance to Bouchaine Vineyards. Originally called Chateau Bouchaine, the winery is known for buttery, balanced Chardonnays and chewy, black-cherry-filled Pinot Noirs.

BUEHLER VINEYARDS

John Buehler Jr. is irreverent and honest when speaking about his winery. Asked why John Buehler Sr. chose to buy this 200-acre ranch on the east side of the valley, John simply says: "My dad needed a tax shelter and I needed a career."

John Buehler Sr., a West Point graduate, spent 20 years in the Army Corps of Engineers and left as a full colonel to become a vice president of the Bechtel Corporation in the San Francisco area. In about 1972 he began looking for a tax shelter. Farming was a good investment because of tax benefits available then. "So my dad bought land here," explains John Jr. "It was

while I was up here that I realized I always had agrarian tendencies. Or, as I used to say, growing up Catholic, I drank such bad altar wine as a kid that it was inevitable I would try to find out where the good stuff was made."

Buehler had 63 acres to plant — much of the land sloped with excellent drainage. He felt red wine grapes were best for the area because of the warmth of the region, and believed most white wine grapes wouldn't mature properly. So he planted Cabernet Sauvignon and Zinfandel, almost equally split between the two. John Jr., however, liked white wines as well as red; but, iconoclast that

The Buehler Winery is not located on the well-traveled roads, but rather is in Conn Valley. It can be reached only by driving up a country lane through a cathedral of towering trees and then over a hill into the tiny valley, hidden from the crowds. "It's not the end of the world, but you can see it from here," says John Buehler.

he is, he refused to plant the variety everyone was gaga over, Chardonnay. Instead he chose to plant Pinot Blanc.

In 1978, after the grapevines were planted and flourishing, John Sr. finally was persuaded by his son to establish a winery. Some 800 cases were made that year. The first Cabernet was highly regarded by some collectors; a large bottle of it commanded a top price at the Napa Valley Wine Auction. Buehler was off and running. Still, fame didn't multiply for the Buehlers the way it might have. One reason was that the wonderful Pinot Blanc the winery made wasn't fat and rich enough for the con-

In front of the Buehler home sits a Japanese Buddha, which John and Lisa inherited from Lisa's father, John Harold Dollar. He was once owner of Dollar Steamship Lines that operated in the Orient. To the Buehlers, the Buddha represents the peace they have found in Conn Valley.

sumers who had grown used to buttery, almost sweet, Chardonnays. Buehler's Pinot Blanc was a stylistic wonder, an excellent example of the variety treated with delicacy, but it never caught on.

Because sales of red Zinfandel were slow, Buehler turned to making a white Zinfandel. It was really a rosé in disguise, and the wine was one of the best made in California. But it still didn't sell as well as a Cabernet.

When Heidi Peterson Barrett joined Buehler as winemaker in 1983, all the wines improved markedly. Buehler's production rose steadily in the 1980s, based on demand for the excellent White Zinfandel. Eventually, Buehler was making 20,000 cases of White Zinfandel, with the red wines accounting for another 10,000 cases and the Pinot Blanc for about 2,000.

Heidi, who married Bo Barrett, winemaker at Chateau Montelena, left Buehler in 1987 to do consulting work and spend more time at home. Then, in 1990, Buehler discovered that his Pinot Blanc vineyard was infected with phylloxera, the devastating root louse that can destroy a vine quickly. Calling it a blessing in disguise, John decided to replant the vineyard with another variety. Meanwhile, John and his wife, Lisa, and their four children run this ranch with the joy and delight most unbecoming a tax shelter. *DB*

The first three tanks installed at Buehler in the late 1970s, when the winery was founded, were outside. Later, as Buehler expanded, all fermentation tanks were installed inside the new winery building.

BURGESS CELLARS

Burgess Cellars sits more than 1,000 feet above the Napa Valley floor on a shelf in the foothills. The original building, since expanded by Tom and Linda Burgess, was constructed more than a century ago.

One of the quietest wineries in the Napa Valley is the small, professionally run Burgess Cellars of Tom and Linda Burgess. One reason for the lack of national acclaim of this property is that Burgess's handsome redwood and stone winery is located out of the mainstream, four miles east of the Napa Valley's busy tourist road, Highway 29.

Another is that Tom Burgess and his winemaker, Bill Sorenson, have never sought the limelight, preferring instead to make wines of consistent quality without much fanfare. There are no extraneous oak flavors to muck up the Napa Valley's indigenous fruit. The wines are not extractive brutes that confuse the issues of balance and grace. And Burgess doesn't demand a ransom for these wines.

The winery itself was built in the 1880s and

the vineyard planted on nearly vertical soils by the Rossini family. The property was bought in 1943 by Lee Stewart, a Napa pioneer, who made excellent wines through 1970, when he retired. The winery then went through another owner before it was acquired by Tom and Linda Burgess in 1972.

Burgess had been an Air Force jet and corporate pilot who sought a less strenuous life in winemaking. But the Napa Valley was, in the early 1970s, just entering a period of unprecedented growth and Burgess became part of that dynamic scene, which kept Tom busier than he had anticipated.

Fortunately, he hired as his winemaker one of the most talented men around, but a man even quieter than himself. Sorenson had graduated from Fresno State University's viticulture and enology program, where he later operated that school's experimental winery.

Twenty acres of the 70 that the Burgesses farm is Cabernet Sauvignon, located at the winery. Over the years the Cabernet Burgess called Vintage Selection was one of the most intense, prototypical Napa Valley Cabernets around, rich with herbal fruit, loaded with blackberry backbone and tannins, and ageworthy. In the late 1970s, Burgess eliminated his "regular" Cabernet and began making only a single Cabernet, called Vintage Selection. However, it was made the way the former Vintage Selection wines were made, and it was just as rich and potent.

The Chardonnays of Burgess are another big, bold statement. The wines, made from grapes off Burgesses' own Triere Vineyard, located in the cooler southern portion of Napa Valley, are barrel fermented and normally loaded with extract and concentrated flavors. These are not wines for the faint of heart.

One of the most stunning wines that Sorenson fashions each year is his marvelous, claret-style Zinfandel. The grapes, which come from the home property and the Burgess's Ink Grade vineyard, yield a combination of elements, starting with a blackberry and raspberry fruit quality, but the wine usually carries with it a pepperiness, especially in the aftertaste, that pleads to be consumed with pasta arrabiatta or puttanesca.

Burgess is not a fast-growth winery, though it did grow from 12,000 cases in 1973 to 30,000 cases in 1990 — the capacity of the winery. Never one to toot his own horn, Burgess nonetheless gets credit from his neighbors for his professional manner and the consistency of his wines. *DB*

The original construction of what is now Burgess Cellars was done by the Rossini family. A descendant of that family is Marylouise, who married Hanns Kornell, producer of sparkling wines in a winery in the Calistoga area of the valley.

The vines on the Burgess home property, including these Cabernet vines, were planted on sloping land with excellent drainage. The result is deeply concentrated flavors in the wines, but normally at the expense of a tiny crop.

CAIN CELLARS

You can understand tentative start-ups by new wineries. After all, there are thousands of other wineries out there and tens of thousands of wines competing for shelf facings, wine lists, and cellar slots. There's enough pressure to give anyone pause.

Yet the road to success is not paved with pauses, but by the yellow brick of confidence. Joyce and Jerry Cain have shown drive and confidence enough to secure their position in a hectic, roiling marketplace. Their vineyard produces exceptional fruit, the winery fine wine, and the setting is almost unparalleled. The ranch is located nearly three miles up Langtry Lane, out past Fritz Maytag's York Creek Vineyard, on a southeastern aspect of Spring Mountain.

"This used to be the McCormick Ranch, 542 acres of cattle and sheep," says Joyce Cain as we walk around the winery faced with native rock and with green canvas awnings over the windows, offering vistas from the swells of the Pacific to the snows of the Sierras. "We're only the second owner," adds Jerry with a laugh. "The McCormicks owned it from 1840 to 1980. We've owned it ever since!"

In terms of grapes, the ranch was virgin land. "We have planted Cabernet Sauvignon,

Winery and entertainment wings enclose a courtyard reminiscent of the Spanish haciendas that once dotted the dry, leonine-summer hillsides of California. The buildings are faced with native stone and set off by green canvas awnings.

Cabernet Franc, Merlot, Malbec, and Petit Verdot. We're doing the whole Bordeaux route here — blending the five Bordeaux varieties — so much so that our red wine is called, simply, 'Cain Five.'"

The concept of making a non-varietal red blend of those varieties is plenty sound. Ask Robert Mondavi (Opus One) or Joseph Phelps (Insignia). Great red wines do not have to be called Cabernet Sauvignon. If they are distinctive enough, their proprietary names will suffice for knowledgeable buyers.

The primary goal with the Cain Five is to have continuity in the flavor impression, to

have no gaps from the first taste to the finish. That means the mouth feel, the body, the texture, how the tannin works with the wine. Cain wants smooth, fine-grained tannins. You might not have that in any of the component wines, but blending wine is like working a jigsaw puzzle: even though you don't have it in the parts, you can still work toward it in the finish.

One reason that Cain Cellars works is that Joyce and Jerry are builders by nature. Jerry turned his UCLA electrical engineering to real estate construction in Palm Springs, while Joyce's forte is architectural and interior design. "Both Joyce and I are self-made people," reminds Jerry. "Once we started building here, an architect was superfluous, because Joyce could translate the design better for the engineers and draftsmen. She learned by doing. And she has one special quality: she designs from the inside out, placing function before form. Thus, by the time you get to the outside, it's simple!"

The design of Cain Cellars demonstrates that ability nicely, from the harmonies of the native stone exterior and the fine redwood trim work inside, to the expanse of the free-standing ceiling of the barrel cellar. If function came first, form did not end up a sacrificial lamb. *RPH*

CAKEBREAD CELLARS

Jack Cakebread really never intended to get into the wine business, but the thought of it was always there in the back of his mind. "My grandfather used to buy jug wines from the old DiMartini winery in Contra Costa County," Jack recalls. "We used to ride over in the Model-T Ford, and he'd buy three or four different kinds, and then we'd get home and he'd blend them to make the best wine."

Jack's career began with a family business. His father had opened an auto repair shop in 1927 in Oakland, and Jack worked there from 1939 until 1950. He flew B-47s for the Strategic Air Command from 1951 to 1955, then returned to the family garage.

However, Jack had always been an avid photographer and student of Ansel Adams's work, and early in the 1970s, he was hired by a

publishing company to do some photography work for a book on wine. This got him traveling through the Napa Valley, and he became intrigued by the industry. He and his wife, Dolores, loved the lifestyle they saw, so they bought a small parcel of land on Highway 29, just north of the Robert Mondavi Winery.

Their winery was founded in 1973, at a time when the Napa Valley had few tourists and no glitzy hype. It was thus not much of a chore for Jack to continue operating both the garage and the winery. However, over time, as Cakebread wines gained more national and international acclaim, Jack and Dolores, the main sales force, were stretched awfully thin.

In 1978, things eased up on the Cakebreads when their youngest son, Bruce, graduated from U.C. Davis's department of viticulture and enology and joined the winery as winemaker. Bruce's wife, Rosemary, also a U.C. Davis graduate, was interested in sparkling wine and went to work for Mumm's Napa Valley operation.

In 1986, middle son Dennis Cakebread came to the winery as chief financial officer, and three years later, Jack and Dolores — by now coping with the pleasant burden of worldwide fame and rising sales of their wines — sold the garage.

"It just got too difficult to do everything," recalls Jack. "Doing everything" in the small winery literally meant getting his hands wet. Often during harvest Jack would be washing barrels and during bottling he'd be in the cellar.

By 1988, after Bruce and Rosemary had a baby daughter, Mia, the family decided to add Rosemary to the staff to handle such chores as weigh tags and winery record-keeping. Karen, the wife of son Steve, indirectly aided the family project by working for the company's distributor in Singapore.

The Cakebread style of wine has always been wine that ages well in the bottle — more classical than many later wineries adopted. The Chardonnays have been hard and lean, some said austere, early in their life. The fruit was classic Chablis graced with just the barest amount of oak treatment. The Sauvignon Blanc has the grand melony components of the variety, reminiscent of the Loire, but with a note of lemon and earth when young. The wine seems to age nicely, gaining traces of green chili as it goes. The Cabernet Sauvignon has also often best been seen later than earlier, being on the hard side when released. However, the wines have grand underpinnings of fruit, leaning on black cherry and cassis. *DB*

Although some wineries are switching over to high-tech materials, such as space-age rubber bungs (stoppers) to keep air out of the wines, Cakebread still uses the traditional wooden bungs for the barrels that hold the Chardonnay, Cabernet Sauvignon, and Sauvignon Blanc.

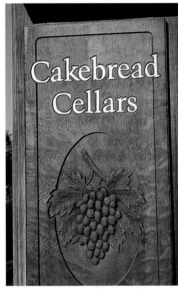

A hand-carved redwood sign sits out on Highway 29, in front of the small tasting room, beckoning visitors to sample the wines of Jack and Delores Cakebread and their children.

CARNEROS CREEK WINERY

At the foot of Milliken Peak is Carneros Creek Winery. "Carnero" means ram or male sheep in Spanish, and the Carneros district was once home to hordes of the woolly beasts. But now grapevines populate much of this cool, southern Napa Valley district.

Carneros Creek originally made a name for itself with sturdy, ram-like, thick Zinfandels and Cabernet Sauvignons from Amador County's Esola and Eschen Vineyards. Thus, the stout ram's head on its label may be considered doubly appropriate. However, the ultimate goal of partner/winemaker Francis Mahoney has always been to produce elegant Carneros district Pinot Noirs and Chardonnays, with character akin to the French Burgundies he is so fond of.

Carneros Creek Winery began its evolution in 1971 when Mahoney's partners, Balfour and Anita Gibson, owners of Connoisseur Wine Imports in San Francisco, needed to make just

enough wine to maintain the winery license that had come with the store. (Anita has wine in her genes; she is the great-granddaughter of Elias J. "Lucky" Baldwin, who produced medal-winning wine from the 1,200-acre vineyard at his famous Santa Anita Ranch in Southern California.)

The winery was constructed next to Carneros Creek in 1973 and expanded in 1978. Pinot Noir is its centerpiece. Mahoney knows he has the right climate and rocky, well-drained soil, and he's brought together the right mix of Burgundian tradition and modern equipment. The last element he needed to make the quintessential California Pinot Noir was the right vines.

That quest for the right vines became an ongoing clonal selection trial, set up behind the winery, run in conjunction with U.C. Davis. One and a half acres there are planted to 20 different clones of Pinot Noir. Each is planted in three soil zones.

Jacketed stainless-steel tanks stand out in back of Carneros Creek Winery. By control of the temperature during fermentation, more fruitiness can be retained in the finished wine. The tanks can also be used to cold stabilize wines, chilling them to near freezing to settle out tartarate crystals.

Milliken Peak is little more than a low hill behind Carneros Creek. Most of the Carneros is flatland, rising slowly on the northern edge of San Francisco Bay, here called San Pablo Bay. Pinot Noir and Chardonnay are the grape varieties grown most in the Carneros, but Merlot is catching on rapidly.

"Each year we'd vinify 15-gallon batches from each clone," says Mahoney in wonder at the colossal effort he's put into the research. "As the years wore on, a pattern began to emerge. It wasn't that one clone or the other was winning, but that different clones demonstrated different desirable characteristics. We finally selected six of the clones as being the most promising, and planted them as we expanded the vineyard to 65 acres."

The culmination of that research was the release, in 1990, of the Signature Reserve Pinot Noir. A case of the first release, from the 1987 vintage, went for $1,400 at the Napa Valley Wine Auction. "The Signature Reserve is the fullest expression of all we've learned," assesses Mahoney. "Its strawberry and cherry flavors combine with those of pepper and spice in a subtle interplay that continues to evolve for more than an hour after you uncork the bottle."

The Signature Reserve complements Carneros Creek's other two Pinot Noirs: Fleur de Carneros is a fresh, young wine with easily accessible fruit; the Los Carneros Pinot Noir is mature and full-flavored, made in a traditional style. "I don't think we've solved the mystery of Pinot Noir, but I think we've peeled away several intriguing layers of the mystery and we've found a style that will endure." *RPH*

CASA NUESTRA

The purple juice of ripe red grapes cascades out of the old hand-operated basket press Gene and Cody Kirkham employ to separate juice from solids at their homey Casa Nuestra vineyards, north of St. Helena on the Silverado Trail.

Born and raised in San Francisco, Eugene "Gene" Kirkham studied law at the University of California's Boalt Hall, and spent part of the Vietnam years providing legal services for California Indians. He then earned a Fulbright Scholarship to study the effects of European law on the Maori tribesmen of New Zealand.

On his return, Kirkham practiced law in San Francisco, but found the cityscape unsatisfying. "My family had had a summer home in Oakville since 1958, so I knew the Napa Valley," says Gene, dressed comfortably in dusty blue jeans and a blue work shirt, his equally dusty brown-and-gray hair and beard in mild disarray. "In 1975 my wife, Cody, and I made the break, buying this vineyard.

"You had to see it to believe it. There were

six acres of Chenin Blanc, four acres of Napa Gamay, and four acres of Grey Riesling. I must have learned something about grape growing. We only got 25 tons the first year. Now we're getting over 40. We actually made some wine from the Grey Riesling in 1979. We called it 'The Green Torpedo,' because the corks blew off when the green bottles were left in people's car trunks on warm days!"

Chenin Blanc *is* Casa Nuestra ("Our House," in Spanish). "If I were starting off in the wine business today, there's no way I would have a vineyard. I can buy Chenin Blanc much cheaper than I can grow it. In fact, I'm not sure I'd even have a winery. I was talking to a California *négociant* who sold 200,000 cases a year, and asked him, 'Where's your winery?' He said, 'Winery? Are you kidding?' He just buys wines in bulk, hires a winery's bottling line, sends the wines to a warehouse to be shipped, and collects his money." In contrast, Gene's winery is a gray, 1,000-square-foot, concrete-block building situated next to an ancient peach orchard. Honey is a hobby with Kirkham, hence the beehives hidden behind the peach trees.

Kirkham gets grumpy over restaurant and retail customers who require a full-time sales effort just to stay on his wine lists, but gets absolutely irate over consumers who don't trust their own palates. "It's amazing how little confidence people have in their own sensory judgments," he says in wonder. "These are the same people who have very definite opinions as to which ice cream flavors they'll touch. It's as if a gold medal gives them permission to like a wine.

"At a charity event once, I was pouring a Chenin Blanc of ours that had won a gold medal at the San Francisco Wine Competition, and a second Chenin Blanc of ours that was somewhat sweeter. I asked people to taste them side by side and tell me which one they preferred. But they were all very reluctant to do so, to the point of being apologetic about their preferences. If I had been selling berry pies, that wouldn't have been a problem."

Berry pies do not carry the same aura of mystery and romance. "It's nice, because we do have a wonderful product," says Cody, who grew up a block away from Gene's home in San Francisco. "You know, it just happened that this place had grapes. If it had had prunes when we bought it, we might be selling prunes or making prune juice. How do you think Casa Nuestra Prune Juice would sell?" *RPH*

The Kirkhams'
battered basket press,
which would be
relegated to museum-
piece status in most
other wineries, stands
in humorously stark
contrast to this surreal
backdrop.

A weathered wooden
sign copies Casa
Nuestra's label, with
its huge, old oak tree,
the winery's founding
date (1980), and the
proud reliance on
Chenin Blanc — a
variety hardly headed
for any Hall of Fame
but sure to please the
willing palate.

CAYMUS VINEYARDS

The Napa Valley, for all its worldwide reputation as "California's Wine Country," still speaks loudest when it's speaking Cabernet Sauvignon. And Caymus Vineyards, more than any other property, remains a prototypical example of what Napa does best.

Founded in 1971 by Charlie and Lorna Wagner, Caymus started out not as an elite winery bent on competing with the Latours and Lafites of Bordeaux, but simply as a family farming operation.

Charles Wagner Sr., Charlie's father, originally bought this ranch in 1906 to grow grapes and prunes, a common pre-Prohibition combi-nation. In 1941, Charlie and Lorna bought 73 acres nearby that would eventually become the Caymus winery site.

In California's second wave of winemaking excitement, in the early 1970s, Charlie and *his* son, Chuck, decided to make wine under the label Caymus. The name comes from the Indi-an tribe that lived on the first land grant follow-ing Mexican rule.

The winery's plan was to make Cabernet, one of the best grape varieties growing on the property. But the senior Wagner also wanted to make wines from estate-grown grapes — Ries-ling, Chardonnay, and Pinot Noir. The winery

The new Caymus winery production facility is complete with the most modern of wine-making equipment, a far cry from the earliest days when the Wagner family made wine in a small, barn-like facility adjacent to their home.

would purchase grapes to make Zinfandel and Sauvignon Blanc.

Starting with an excellent 1972 Cabernet made from the home ranch, Caymus launched a string of Cabernets unequaled for consistency and depth of flavor. One reason for that was the source of the grapes: the fruit growing on the Wagner ranch, midway between the Silverado Trail and Highway 29, gives Caymus's Cabernets their classic aroma.

The estate-bottled wines have always showed a depth of cherry/chocolate fruit with a Napa Valley exclusive, an herbal note that seems a bit like tarragon and sage with a trace

Demand for Caymus Vineyards' stunning Special Selection Cabernets, regardless of the vintage, has become so heated that wine merchants lucky enough to get even one six-bottle case trumpet it as a trophy equivalent to the bagging of a white rhino.

of green tea. They provide the newcomer to Napa Valley wines with the most perfect example of what the valley does best with its best wine. Caymus's Cabernets evoke the character of the land more consistently than any other winery's wine.

The sweetness in this wine comes from a winemaking threesome that has become widely respected in the valley. Randall Dunn, who joined the winery in 1975 to work the crush, had a background in chemistry. During that harvest, he became enamored of making Cabernet. Father Charlie and son Chuck followed the system they had in place before Dunn came, but Dunn added nuances. He stayed on after that harvest and joined the effort to make the Caymus wines.

Dunn and the Wagners eventually made an impact on the grape growing and winemaking ventures of Grace Family Vineyard and The Terraces, owned by Wayne Hogue.

Dunn left Caymus in 1979 to make wine under his own label, and Chuck, the founder's grandson, took over as winemaker.

Winemaking is important. But Caymus's fruit is critical to the success here. Before, during, and after Dunn, Caymus's Cabernets were excellent and improved almost every year. The 1974 Caymus Cabernet was — and still is — remarkable, and the 1985 Special Selection was a stunning achievement, topped in the decade only perhaps by the 1986, with even greater promise for later vintages.

The Special Selection wine was produced starting in 1975, but the so-called "regular" (Napa Valley) bottling, more widely available, is often a better example of classic Cabernet. The Special Selection wine usually needs a decade to be fully enjoyed.

Caymus's estate Cabernets may be tracked closely because Caymus uses nothing but the Cabernet Sauvignon grape, no blending varieties. This makes the wine more definable as a Cabernet Sauvignon and makes for less variation, less extraneousness of flavor.

Chuck Wagner has improved the wines across the board. Zinfandels are packed with a spice and delicate jam-like fruit quality. He has also greatly improved the style and quality of the Sauvignon Blanc. (Chardonnay and Riesling eventually were dropped.)

But Cabernet was such a big part of the Caymus story that demand for it outstripped the winery's grape supply. So in 1984 Caymus introduced a third Cabernet to its line. Called Napa Cuvee, it contained only five percent of Caymus's own fruit; the rest was bought from neighbors. Chuck then blended in a small amount of estate-grown St. Macaire (a rare Bordeaux variety). The result was as spectacular a success as the estate wines.

By 1987, however, Caymus decided to winch back to just two Cabernets, one called Napa Valley and the other Special Selection. The latter had risen in price to $50 a bottle and even at that price, demand was so high that the wine was on allocation.

"Two times a year we had severe arguments over which wholesalers were going to get how much wine," explains Chuck. "Also, it was less confusing to have two wines than three. And starting in 1987, the purchased grapes going into the Napa Cuvee were so close in quality to our own grapes that there

A flower garden and ancient, gnarled oak trees give grace to the grounds surrounding the Caymus tasting room, which is located just east of Highway 29 where Highway 128 splits toward the Silverado Trail.

wasn't a great deal of difference between them. We felt a 'Napa Valley' wine would be simpler for everyone, rather than having two wines priced so similarly."

The Napa Valley wine contains between 15 and 25 percent of Caymus's own estate grapes, as well as 20 percent mountain-grown fruit including some from high-altitude Atlas Peak to the east and some from the neighbors of Spottswoode, on the other side of the valley.

So now, instead of just 1,000 to 1,500 cases of the Special Selection per year, Caymus has about 2,000 cases of it, as well as 18,000 cases of the Napa Valley-designated wine. Most of Caymus's Cabernets are aged in French oak barrels, between a quarter and a third of them new. A small portion is aged in French-coopered American oak. Longer aging of the Special Selection in oak shows the Wagners' faith that these wines will age.

The depth and richness of Caymus's Cabernets over the years has given them the life and the punch to last in the bottle for well over a decade. With few exceptions, they are amazing testimony to superb fruit and courageous winemaking. *DB*

Caymus Vineyards' shaded, flower-graced, hacienda-style tasting room is located midway in the Napa Valley, at a point where Highway 128 forks. The red wines are clearly in demand, but a recent improvement in the Sauvignon Blanc has prompted interest in it.

After decades of storing wine barrels in a tiny, cramped building, in 1990 the Warners finally built a modern warehouse, adjacent to the tasting room and offices, that will accommodate all the barrels the winery uses.

CHAPPELLET VINEYARD

Donn and Molly Chappellet fill virtually every room in their spacious, window-filled hilltop home with flowers — both fresh and dried — that are grown in a plot near Molly's famed vegetable garden.

When Donn and Molly Chappellet and their children moved to the Napa Valley from Los Angeles in 1967 to found this winery bearing the family name, less than three dozen operations dotted the hills and plain, almost all of them old-timers. For Chappellet was only the second new winery to be built in the Napa Valley since Prohibition ended.

But the Chappellet property became one of the least visible. The striking pyramidal structure is situated high atop a tor on the eastern flank of the valley, on remote Pritchard Hill, in a crevice below the zenith. From here you look down on Lake Hennessy and the Conn Dam.

It's a spot that Donn knew would be hard to farm because of the steeply canted hillsides, but terracing was not an unheard-of idea. Indeed, some of the greatest vineyards in the world are

on this sort of well-drained soil. Of the property's 120 acres, more than 40 percent are on terraced land and the remainder is sloped to yield true mountain flavors from the vines.

Chappellet is a winery that focuses on estate-grown grapes, and thus features a delicate style of wine because of the lean, angular tastes one gets from grapes yielded by the stony soil.

At the start, Donn wanted to make a wine that was little toyed-with, so the Chardonnay was handled very little. This permits the wine to have as its main fruit interest the various clones of Chardonnay. It is aged in French oak barrels, only a small portion of which are new, so the fruit shows through — but only after the wine has been in the bottle for a couple of years. Chappellet Chardonnays are among the longest-lived in the state, with a marvelous expansiveness creeping into the wines at age 15, quite atypical for most California Chardonnays.

Chappellet Cabernet Sauvignons and Merlots also show the character of the soil and exposure, and seem to demand some time to smooth out. The astringency of the early wines is hard on youthful palates, yet merely aerating the wine helps to unveil the tones of the fruit.

The winery's Chenin Blanc became a stylistic model for the variety in California and is reminiscent of some of the more classical Loire wines.

In 1989, the winery reached 25,000 cases in annual production and two of the six Chappellet children came back to the fold. Cyril, who had worked for a venture capital company, returned to the winery to become marketing director. He then hired Alexa, his younger sister who had been in the sportswear business, to be the winery's director of sales for Southern California.

Molly Chappellet is a major factor in the winery, too. Her huge garden encircles one side of the rambling Chappellet home and is the starting point for dinners known around the valley. This fits the Chappellet goal: to match the wine with food.

Donn, a quiet man who left the Los Angeles area and a thriving food-vending-machine business to establish Chappellet, is also involved in this food-and-wine pairing business. He makes a hellacious wine vinegar from a starter that began life during the 1906 San Francisco earthquake. Salads hereabouts are not mild-mannered things. *DB*

The cant of the roofline gives the winery at Chappellet a dramatic appearance, especially as sunlight filters through the skylights illuminating the winery offices that sit above the action at the apex of the walls.

Chappellet sits well above the floor of the Napa Valley. Its terraced vineyards force the grapevines to struggle for nourishment. It is this viticultural milieu that produces tiny crops and keeps the picking bins less-than-full at harvest time.

CHATEAU MONTELENA

A solitary, pine-covered hillock stands at the base of hulking Mount St. Helena, where mountain streams form the headwaters of the Napa River. Atop the rise one discovers a curious juxtaposition of architectural philosophies: against the hillside is a stone winery of 19th century "French Chateau" design; just beyond is a small lake, the nucleus of an oriental park replete with red-lacquered pavilions, weeping willows that flirt with the breeze, and a five-ton, dragon-eyed Chinese junk.

But there is no conflict among the wines that come out of Chateau Montelena, brought suddenly into the glare of publicity by the 1976 Paris tasting that raised the flag over the winery's 1973 Chardonnay.

Montelena Chardonnays are not like the big, fashionably husky Chardonnays consumers have come to expect from California, yet they invariably possess rich texture, full fruit, and a touch of oak.

"I would say that comes from the fruit," says winemaker Bo Barrett, whose wife, Heidi Peterson, also makes wine. "If you start with properly grown, mature grapes, you can develop a full-bodied Chardonnay. Richness, those layers of depth, come from blending wines from different vineyards. If you were making

This red-lacquered bridge extends over the man-made lake at the foot of the solitary hillock atop which sits the stone winery. The lake is the center of an oriental park created by Chinese engineer York Frank, who acquired the property in 1958.

the wine from one vineyard, it would be hard to get the same depth, richness, and complexity."

Indeed, Montelena draws from three vineyards for its Alexander Valley Chardonnay, and from five for its Napa Valley Chardonnay. Montelena has also installed 15 acres of Chardonnay in its 100-acre estate vineyard, which arcs around the winery hillock.

"The stretch just north of Tubbs Lane is a lot cooler than you might think," reminds Barrett. "Our days are warm, but it really cools off at night, with the marine breezes coming up Knights Valley and down the slopes of Mount St. Helena."

A pair of old basket presses pose below the stone facade of Chateau Montelena, one of the great fortress-like wineries constucted more than a century ago by Napa Valley's premier winery architect, Hamden W. McIntyre, the Vermont native who also built Inglenook and Greystone Cellars.

Chateau Montelena was founded just over a century ago by tycoon Alfred J. Tubbs, who made his fortune selling rope to whaling fleets. Once a state senator, Tubbs purchased the 275-acre estate, north of Calistoga, in 1880. Two years later he had the fortress-like winery notched snugly into the hillside. The rear and sides, from three to 12 feet thick, are of native stone hauled from the vineyards. The facade is of imported cut stone, with battlements and turrets, and you half expect Sir Lancelot to coming riding up behind you.

Having gone to France to secure his French architect, Tubbs returned for grape cuttings and a French winemaker, Jerome Bardot, who gave Chateau Montelena a solid reputation. Prohibition brought an end to Tubbs's dream; the winery lay dormant for 60 years until a partnership of James Barrett, Laura Barrett, Lee Paschich, and Ernest Hahn recreated Montelena.

Though it was the Chardonnay that brought Montelena its initial fame, Cabernet Sauvignon is the foundation upon which its future lies.

"The old winemakers used to say that great wines are made in the vineyard and finished in the cellar," notes Bo Barrett, who loves to fly airplanes in his spare time. "Though we respect tradition, we have never tried to make a copy of Bordeaux here. We like the ripe fruit, big body, and finesse we're getting." *RPH*

A pair of swans grace the oriental park's lake, which boasts red-lacquered pavilions, weeping willows that flirt with the breeze, and a dragon-eyed, five-ton Chinese junk. The winery was founded in 1882 by State Senator Alfred Tubbs.

THE CHRISTIAN BROTHERS

The Christian Brothers' aging cellar, where former winemaker Tom Eddy experimented in the mid-1980s with a méthode champenoise sparkling wine. The name of the product would have been Greystone, but when Heublein acquired the winery, the super-premium sparkling-wine project was terminated.

Winemaking began in the Napa Valley in the middle of the last century. However, the modern history of the Napa Valley really began when the industry started to reawaken from its Prohibition slumber in the early 1930s. And that coincides with the modern era of The Christian Brothers, one of the Napa Valley's oldest wine operations, now under the control of a multinational corporation.

The history of The Christian Brothers' winery operations actually dates back to 1879, shortly after wine began being made in Northern California, when the lay religious teaching order of the Roman Catholic Church (called The Brothers of the Christian Schools) purchased land in Martinez, southeast of the Napa Valley. In 1882, the brothers — who had taken vows of poverty, chastity, and obedience — made a few experimental wines and sold some to their neighbors. Over the next few years a small amount of wine was made at the Martinez winery and was sold mainly to the church and to physicians for medicinal purposes.

By the onset of Prohibition in 1919, the Martinez winery was one of the few in California with a history of making sacramental and medicinal wine. So Prohibition didn't affect the winery as much as it did other operations.

However, the city of Martinez was growing and encroaching on the spiritual training facility for the young brothers, so a new novitiate was needed. In 1930, the brothers bought the old Giersberger Winery northwest of the city of Napa, in the hills. A monastery was constructed there and the facility was renamed Mont La Salle, in honor of St. John Baptiste de La Salle, who had founded the order 250 years before.

By the end of Prohibition in 1933, only a tiny handful of the hundreds of wineries that existed before had survived. With the public eager to buy wine again — this time legally — the wines of The Christian Brothers, which were in the winery's cellar for sacramental sale, became available. But because the Mont La Salle property had been expensive, the brothers were saddled with debts, so for the next few years they couldn't afford to do much to improve the winery or fund any marketing until they gained national distribution for their wines.

In 1937, the brothers' fortunes changed radically when they met Alfred Fromm, a German-American importer and marketing expert. They agreed to a 20-year marketing deal which brought stability to the marketing of the wines, permitting The Christian Brothers to become a nationally famous brand.

Meanwhile, the wines of the brothers improved markedly with the assignment of a 25-year-old brother by the name of Anthony George Diener as wine master in 1935. Known as Brother Timothy, this former high school chemistry teacher had a keen palate and brilliant blending techniques, which improved the brothers' wines and made them broadly appealing. Brother Timothy's impact on California wines, like that of his counterpart, Andre Tchelistcheff, is incalculable.

In 1941, the brothers began to make a small amount of brandy, and again Brother Timothy's sensitive palate provided the direction. The brothers' brandy eventually became the most profitable item in the line, and a product o

The Christian Brothers' Greystone Cellar, north of St. Helena, was one of the Napa Valley's major tasting-room attractions until it was closed in the 1980s because it wasn't earthquake-safe. The building was strengthened, however, and reopened in 1988.

remarkable consistency. Revenues from the sale of wine and brandy were intended to raise funds for support of the schools sponsored by the brothers. The order grew rapidly over the years, with the brothers funding more than 1,600 schools around the world, teaching more than 100,000 students.

Mont La Salle remained the home of the brothers as well as the winemaking facility, but other wine production facilities were added over the years. A plant at Reedly in the San Joaquin Valley was acquired in 1945 and five years later the Greystone mansion was bought. This great building, sitting on a rise just north of the town of St. Helena, housed the barrels of aging wine and became the facility in which the brothers entered the champagne business. Greystone also became a major tourist attraction: by the 1980s it attracted more than 300,000 visitors each year.

In 1965 The Christian Brothers renewed its contract with Fromm's company (by now Fromm and Sichel) for 20 years. By the following year the brothers owned five winemaking facilities including a newly constructed winery south of St. Helena that was designed to be one of the world's finest, and at the time the Napa Valley's largest, winemaking facility. The brothers had also acquired more than 1,200 acres of prime Napa Valley vineyard land, which was

Hundreds of thousands of visitors tour Greystone each year, where tour guides tell of the founding of the winery, of the period during Prohibition, and of the rebirth of the industry in the 1960s with the explosion of interest nationally in premium varietal wines.

farmed by Rollin Wilkinson, one of the industry's most respected vineyardists.

Through those years, all The Christian Brothers' wines were non-vintage blends. Brother Timothy's philosophy was that blends of newer wines, with their rougher tannins and greater fruit, and a small portion of carefully aged older wines, with their burnished, mellow textures, were the best wines to market because the consumer could then be guaranteed not only a consistency of style, but also a wine ready to consume with little bottle aging necessary. And the wines were remarkable for their lovely textures and prototypical flavors.

However, in the mid-1970s fashions were

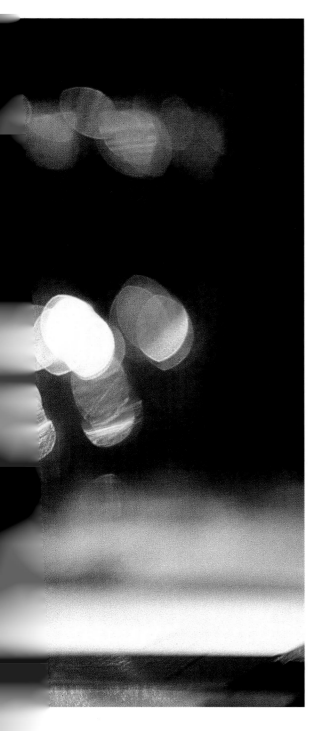

changing and vintage-dating was seen by some consumers and wine writers as a mark of quality. After a number of internal discussions, the winery began making vintage-dated wines. In 1983, when Brother Timothy reduced his activity with the winery and Tom Eddy came in to handle winemaking, The Christian Brothers expanded its vintage-dated wine program significantly, and won numerous medals at major wine competitions. Meanwhile, their brandies had become important in the marketplace: and by the 1980s brandy represented about 80 percent of the company's revenues. The Christian Brothers and E. and J. Gallo were neck and neck for the lead in national brandy sales, both with excellent products.

It was The Christian Brothers' brandy that interested Heublein Inc., the Connecticut-based beverage company that was owned by Grand Metropolitan of England. In 1989, in a deal valued at more than $200 million — the largest winery sale in U.S. history — Heublein acquired The Christian Brothers. The deal permitted the brothers to take the profits from the sale of their vineyards and winery and continue to fund their schools for decades. Brother Timothy, who had been active with the winery for 54 consecutive years, retired upon the sale of the property. *DB*

Underneath the first level at Greystone is a series of caves dug into the hillside. The caves, which are naturally cool, need no air conditioning and thus are perfect for the aging of barrels as well as premium sparkling wines, as shown here behind a rock wall.

The Christian Brothers owned hundreds of acres of top Napa Valley vineyard land, which was one of the attractions the property had for Heublein when it acquired the winery from the brothers. That deal, valued at more than $200 million, added to Heublein's already vast holdings in the Napa Valley.

CLOS DU VAL WINE COMPANY

It is no surprise to anyone that Bernard Portet's Clos Du Val Cabernet Sauvignons are as melodies rising from the rich Bordeaux symphony. Though he works with an orchestra of Napa Valley vines, his baton is decidedly French. Bernard is, after all, the oldest son of Andre Portet, the *regisseur* (technical director) at Château Lafite-Rothschild for more than 20 years.

Born in Cognac, Bernard studied at Toulouse and Montpellier, taking degrees in agronomy, engineering, viticulture, and enology. After his schooling, he further developed his vinous "ear" working in Bordeaux before moving on to the challenge of orchestrating winegrowing in California.

"I came to California quite by accident," admits Portet in his cellar, set along the southeastern edge of the Napa Valley north of Napa. "In 1970 I was asked by John Goelet to study possible château projects in France. When the costs proved exorbitant, he asked me to make a study of the best grape-growing areas of the world. His goal was to make top-quality wines, particularly Cabernets, that would rival the best of Bordeaux."

Portet spent two years investigating every continent. In Australia he found what would

Clos Du Val's yellow buildings glint in the strong California sunlight. The year Bernard Portet arrived, the vineyards were deluged with rain. But he still managed to draw from the rained-upon vintage one of the best Cabernet Sauvignons in the state — a feat to make any father proud, but especially his!

eventually become Clos Du Val's second wine-growing project, operated by Bernard's brother, Dominique Portet, under the name Taltarni, in Victoria. In Chile he met Helia, who later became his wife. "Chile was lucky for me," Bernard laughs, "but at the time it was too unstable politically to begin such a venture, even though very fine wines are produced there. Napa, finally, became our first choice."

Portet's ability was immediately displayed as he drew forth one of California's finest Cabernet Sauvignons from the much-rained-upon 1972 vintage, an otherwise dismal year for that late-ripening variety.

Clos Du Val President Bernard Portet was born and educated into wine in France, and came to the Napa Valley in 1972. Originally he intended to return to his homeland, but Portet finds Napa's ambience and wine-industry people so appealing.that he and his wife, Helia, plan to stay.

The wines of Clos Du Val invariably display great depth and character, be they whites — Chardonnay and Semillon — or Portet's reds, the Cabernets, Merlots, Pinot Noirs, and Zinfandels. The last, though made in Bordelais fashion, are made of sterner stuff. "Zinfandel can handle more tannin than Cabernet can," assesses the slender, curly-haired Portet. "Cabernet needs lower alcohol, so I try to make it rounder, more complex; balanced, but not big."

Clos Du Val is, aesthetically, a rather austere winery, a functional facility which doesn't pretend to be a showplace. Set against the eastern foothills, it is nearly surrounded by the Chimney Rock Golf Course. The golf course once boasted the regulation 18 holes, but it is a sign of the times that land is more valuable for hand-tended, wine-grape bearing vines than for fairways and manicured greens. Which is why nine holes were removed some years ago in favor of small grape trees.

Better than 140 acres of Clos Du Val Cabernet Sauvignon, Merlot, and Zinfandel extend northward from the winery's cypress and magnolia-lined driveway toward the rocky prominence of Stags Leap, which gives this sub-region its name.

The early and continued successes of Clos Du Val led, as they often do, to expansion. In

1980, 105 acres of a Carneros holding were planted largely to Chardonnay and Pinot Noir. In 1988 Clos Du Val acquired the Chardonnay house of St. Andrew's, just three miles to the north on the Silverado Trail. "St. Andrew's fits our 'estate' mold," says Portet, "and the Chardonnays grown there have an earthy aspect peculiar to the vineyard that surrounds the winery, so they're quite different from our Carneros Chardonnays. The only thing it lacked was good marketing, and we already had a good marketing organization in place."

As Clos Du Val and Bernard have grown comfortable with one another — and as long-time assistant, Algerian-born and Montpellier-trained Krimo Souilah, has taken over much of the day-to-day winemaking chores — Bernard has been given the luxury of time to devote to certain of his vinous "causes." One of these is the ignorance of and inattention to Semillon in the U.S. When Americans think of Graves, or other White Bordeaux, they think first or exclu-sively of Sauvignon Blanc, yet most blends there rely more on Semillon than the white Sauvignon.

Bernard doesn't beat around the bush. "I prefer Semillon to most Chardonnays," he says with a studied nonchalance. "Semillons can be such rich, silky wines, very complex, and they can be consumed so much sooner than most Chardonnays. But the retailers won't sell them. They won't even try. And you ask a restaurateur to put Semillon on his wine list, and he says he doesn't have room! All he has to do is expand his Sauvignon Blanc section a lit-tle. Call it 'Sauvignon Blanc, slash, Semillon.' What's so tough about that?"

Portet feels that his best wine would be an equal blend of Semillon and Sauvignon Blanc, but is realistic enough to realize that the market-place continues to be resistant to such propri-etary blends. "Semillon, by itself, ages a bit too fast. It oxidizes, and turns into honey. Without Sauvignon Blanc it gets too fat, too weighty. The

An "aerial" view of Clos Du Val's tasting room. Wines are tasted at the L-shaped counter (right and top). The door at the upper left looks into the cellar. The gift-shop side of the tasting room offers poster artist Ronald Searle's offbeat view of the world of wine.

best wine, with our Semillon and our Sauvignon Blanc, is invariably a fifty-fifty blend."

Though Bernard once thought of retiring to France after his winemaking career here, he has since altered his future outlook. "I like it here," he says quietly, evenly. "My family is growing up here, the people are very nice, and this is a nice place to live. The more I work here, the more work I see ahead of me. Here. I have no thoughts, even, of retirement." Which is a nice way to live.

Portet particularly appreciates the quality of the people that the wine industry tends to draw. "Americans are very generous people. When I came here, I spoke only 'school' English. Yet I got tremendous support from everybody. People were very helpful, and nobody tried to put rods in my wheels.

"In 1973, when we were short of tanks, Hanns Kornell lent us some. That goes on all the time here. And there is a tremendous sharing of information, information that would be closely kept in any other business. Robert Mondavi has been pulling the Napa Valley behind him for years. People you don't even know help you and give you straight answers. The attitude seems to be, 'If we keep helping each other, we'll all survive the onslaught of development.'" *RPH*

A vineyard worker harvests fruit with a curve-edged knife that can slice a finger as easily as a vine stem. Skilled workers can pick more than a ton of fruit a day. Picked into 30-pound lug boxes, that's a lot of boxes, any way you look at it.

The front facade of Clos Du Val. The tasting room is housed in the forward half of the south wing (right). Another building was erected years ago behind this facility, when the winery's success demanded expansion.

CLOS PEGASE WINERY

The development of the Napa Valley as a fine winegrowing region occurred first and above all because the wine was great. Worldwide recognition and the glitz and hype of star status came later.

A few wineries that now sport exotic buildings and use Madison Avenue advertising agencies may seem to embody the antithesis of what the valley was founded upon. Others have creative and expensive edifices but are more substance than form; Clos Pegase is one of these.

Not even a decade old, Jan Shrem's striking winery, just south of the town of Calistoga, is one of the new breed of California wineries that look more like a museum than a place to convert grape juice into wine. Constructed in controversy, Clos Pegase is now accepted as

qualities, but for the sublime qualities he knew it could have. He believes wine is an art form and a way of life to so many cultures around the world, and that it deserves its own museum.

Shrem wanted to build a winery that was itself an architectural masterpiece. So he staged a nationwide contest to find an appropriate design. Entries came from some of the most famous architects in the world, and the winner was noted Princeton architect Michael Graves.

The unusual design of the building, with its columns and towers, is certainly atypical, not like the barn-like images that come to mind when thinking of a Napa Valley winery. Nor is it a "château" in style, like some wineries in France. In fact, said a number of Shrem's neighbors, it was so exotic that it was a tourist attraction. That sparked an immediate outcry. Some said it existed more as a museum and they wanted restrictions placed on it. Moreover, when Shrem sought permits to expand the facility, there was more opposition.

But most of the brouhaha died down once the locals realized that Shrem was a beneficent neighbor whose real goal was not to create a neon-lighted tourist center, but to make great wine and to protect the vines and the lifestyle of the valley.

The style of wine Shrem chose to make in this palace of art was one of true delicacy and taste — wines of charm, not wines of power. The Clos Pegase wines are the work of a craftsman, winemaker Bill Pease. A quiet, poetic, contemplative man, Pease keeps his wines delicate by managing the vineyards in such a way as to develop character rather than deep and exotic flavors.

one of the Napa Valley's most intriguing and integrated "concept wineries."

Shrem and his wife, Mitsuko, were the visionaries who saw winemaking as part of art and who hoped to integrate the art forms into a single facility. Shrem, a book publisher and an art collector, wanted to place wine among the other art treasures of the world, and to have it viewed not just for its more mundane

"With only 150 years of viticulture as opposed to the hundreds, if not thousands, of years of grape growing in Europe, our soils are much more fertile and we must farm accordingly," says Pease. He points out that it takes more work to make a wine of delicacy than to make one of raw force.

Jan Shrem's tastefully appointed office is decorated — as is the entire winery — with paintings and sculptures. The interior of Clos Pegase has become one of the Napa Valley's most attractive wineries, with hundreds of museum-quality artworks and artifacts.

One method he employs to make the wines delicate is to keep the growth of leaves down and the development of the grapes on an even keel. This means that the vines have been stressed early in their lives, by withholding water at certain times. "The idea is to not let them develop root systems." The more growth the vine experiences below ground, Pease explains, the more the growth of leaves is encouraged above ground. And there must be a balance of leaves to grapes for the proper maturity of the fruit.

To make their white wines with more delicacy, Shrem bought land in the Carneros region, far to the south, in the coolest growing region in the county. There, grapes ripen more slowly than in other areas and retain their naturally high acids longer.

The Clos Pegase style in the red wines intrigued the wine community from the start. Delicate yet ample fruit flavors dominated, but inside a package that was relatively crisp and aimed at long-term aging in the bottle. Pease's first successes were with Sauvignon Blanc. He also made a stylish Chardonnay from Carneros fruit, a lean and delicate Merlot, and a handsome, balanced Cabernet Sauvignon.

The style of wines at Clos Pegase is, in part, a product of the Shrems' desire to make wine that goes well with food. That coincided with the

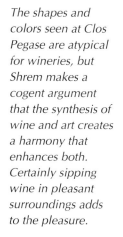

The shapes and colors seen at Clos Pegase are atypical for wineries, but Shrem makes a cogent argument that the synthesis of wine and art creates a harmony that enhances both. Certainly sipping wine in pleasant surroundings adds to the pleasure.

feelings of the first consultant to the project, the esteemed winemaker Andre Tchelistcheff, who began working with Shrem even before construction of the winery had begun. By 1986, when the winery was built, the style for the red wines had already been set into stone. (Tchelistcheff's picture used to adorn a wall in Shrem's office.)

Stone was firmly at the heart of another concept behind Clos Pegase: an extensive series of underground caves in which the wine would be stored and in which some of the Shrems' art would be displayed. Using the talents of respected cave-digging specialist Alf Burtleson, they hacked out a network of high-ceilinged caves covering 20,000 square feet.

On the surface, Clos Pegase has the trappings that make it seem more form than substance. For months after the structure was completed, the controversy it generated was all anyone in Napa talked about. In time, the great sense of style behind the Shrems' winery and their wines became clear enough for others to admire.

Completed in 1990, it is one of the most extensive wine cave networks in the country and nearly matches the 23,000 square feet of the winery above. The caves were wired for special lighting and coated to prevent mildew. Then into the caves Shrem placed a literal museum dedicated to his personal fine art collection. Art dating back five centuries is exhibited: pre-Columbian drinking vessels, reproductions of sculptures from the Louvre, and ancient vineyard implements.

The selection of Pegasus as the namesake for this winery wasn't accidental. Greek mythology says that Pegasus, the winged horse, planted his hoof and thus created the fountain of Hippocrene, the sacred Spring of the Muses. The fountain irrigated the vines, which created abundant fruit to make wine. It was wine that was drunk by the poets, who were thus inspired to create art.

The design on the Clos Pegase label that Shrem chose is a reproduction of the classic work *Pegasus* by Odilon Redon. Other works of art appear on Clos Pegase labels from time to time, some on wines of the "Hommage" series, paying homage to a great artist. The artists have included Salvador Dali and Jean Dubuffet. And in each case, the work pictured is in the Shrem collection. *DB*

CONN CREEK WINERY

Occasionally the persona of a winery changes in mid-course when the ownership switches and the new owners decide that things should be done differently. Such is the case at the Conn Creek Winery. Founded in 1974 by Bill and Kathy Collins, it was later sold to the wine division of a tobacco company and today is making better and more consistent wine.

The Collinses founded Conn Creek when they leased the Ehlers Lane winery — a century-old stone building north of St. Helena. Both Bill and Kathy had viticultural backgrounds and wanted to have a Cabernet in their line of wines, but they owned no Cabernet Sauvignon vineyards then. So they sought to buy wine in the open market.

The first two wines released under the Conn Creek label, Cabernets from the 1973 and 1974 vintages, were stunning wines that gave Conn Creek immediate star status in the Napa firmament.

The '73 Cabernet was produced from grapes grown in Dick Steltzner's Stags Leap ranch, to the south; the '74 was from grapes off the Eisele Ranch, to the north, a vineyard that later was to gain fame for Cabernets made by the Joseph Phelps Winery.

Andre Tchelistcheff, the most influential winemaker in California history, joined Conn Creek as a consultant in the late 1980s to help turn that winery around. In 1991, shortly after his 89th birthday, Tchelistcheff resigned from all his consulting work (except Buena Vista) to return to his emotional "home," Beaulieu Vineyard.

Both of these wines had been made at Lyncrest Winery by Lyncrest's winemaker, John Henderson. When Lyncrest went out of business, the Collinses bought both wines, still in barrels, from Lyncrest and hired Henderson to be their first winemaker.

However, their small winery never again matched those wines in quality. The source of grapes changed just often enough to make for a wine style that varied. Although Conn Creek made good wines in the latter 1970s and into the '80s, the public never could get a handle on what the house style was.

Things didn't change until 1986, when the

Stimson Lane's acquisition of Conn Creek precipitated a spurt in investment for the winery . The company not only added new winemaking equipment, but redesigned the tasting room, adding a room where older vintages would be stored.

Collinses chose to sell the property to Stimson Lane, the wine division of the United States Tobacco Co., which also owns Chateau Ste. Michelle and Columbia Crest wineries in the state of Washington as well as Villa Mt. Eden in the Napa Valley. Stimson Lane then made a series of changes to renovate and upgrade Conn Creek, including signing contracts for top grapes.

But the key move in Stimson Lane's plans came when the firm asked Andre Tchelistcheff, the dean of California winemakers, to head the new winemaking team at Conn Creek and to coordinate with new winemaker Jeff Booth. Tchelistcheff, then in his late 80s, had been consulting for Stimson Lane for two decades, mainly at its Ste. Michelle property. Booth continued to experiment by buying grapes from various sources, but he and Tchelistcheff chose to release only those blends that showed true greatness and represented a consistent style.

Starting with the 1986 vintage, Conn Creek Cabernets have been designated Napa Valley Barrel Select and Private Reserve, the latter being produced only in those years when the quality is exceptional. Merlot, too, is made only when the fruit is good enough to make the wine as a varietal. Also in the line are a stylish Sauvignon Blanc and a gutsy, richly flavored Zinfandel. *DB*

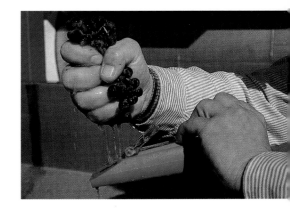

Winemaker Jeff Booth, a disciple of Andre Tchelistcheff, joined Conn Creek Winery in 1986, after the winery was acquired by Stimson Lane, and immediately began to make an impact on the style of wine being made there.

COSENTINO WINERY

Just north of Mustard's Restaurant — on the west side of Highway 29 — is one of the Napa Valley's newest wineries, Cosentino, which opened its double doors to the public in 1990. If the building evokes a sense of déjà vu, that's because it is pretty familiar to wine buffs, having been pictured on Mitch Cosentino's label years before it was ever constructed.

"We designed the winery back in 1985, and began putting it on our labels before we were able to begin construction," reflects the youthful owner/winemaker.

While it might appear that Mitch moved north just to escape Modesto — "the town wasn't big enough for the both of us," he jokes, (referring to the hilarity of his 12,000-case winery juxtaposed against the 60-million-case production of Ernest and Julio Gallo) — it was really more a matter of logistics. "Mostly, we needed to be closer to our grape sources," he says, "and it will give us more respect and attention from the world wine community. No matter how many awards we won, you just don't get the same attention unless you're in the North Coast.

"Being closer to our grape sources gives us greater control over our winemaking, which was the main reason for the move. Another

Cosentino is a curiosity in that this building existed on the winery's label long before it ever had a physical presence. The design was used on Costentino labels in the late '80s; the real winery opened in 1990.

thing I've discovered is that it also enhances my ability to find new grape sources, just by being here. We've found a new Cabernet Franc vineyard — they came to us — and a couple of better Chardonnay sources, too."

If his labels are a bit on the drab side, artistically speaking, Cosentino nonetheless has a flair for marketing and unquestionable talents as a winemaker. He distinguishes his finest Chardonnays and Cabernets by proprietary names, "The Sculptor" and "The Poet," respectively, and has been a leader in the development of the "Meritage" movement (a designation for top flight Bordeaux-blend wines, red and white).

Owner-winemaker Mitch Cosentino started out in radio and television broadcasting. Here, he's "punching down the cap" of a red wine fermentation — pushing the skins and seeds down into the must to gain further extraction of flavor and tannin.

"We want our wines to be known for themselves, and not so much for varietal makeup or for appellation of origin," says Cosentino. "Our best Chardonnay is called 'The Sculptor' because a sculptor takes his medium and shapes it into an artistic work. And we use 'The Poet' for our Meritage wine, our red Bordeaux blend, because a poet takes the dictionary — all the words and all his feelings — and creates a work of a single focus that remains open to many interpretations."

As good as the Cabernets are, Cosentino's Merlot is really the star of his vinous show — with its penetrating black currant fruit — despite the sudden attention to, and competition within, that category. Consultant, collector, and wine broker Charles F. Mara (Syracuse, New York) is particularly taken with Cosentino's reds: "The kid is on fire," says Mara with fervor. "He's the next Dunn. He has no vineyards, but he's a real magician. His Merlots and Cabernets are killer material, with marvelous complexity."

Though we don't like to think that these things make a difference — wines should speak louder than labels or locations — it's a dead-cinch bet that you'll be hearing a lot more about Cosentino wines now that they're happily ensconced in their new Napa Valley home. *RPH*

Like most thoughtful winemakers, Mitch Cosentino sets aside a portion of each year's production for a wine "library." Monitoring a wine's life over decades provides clues on how to improve wine quality and longevity.

CUVAISON

uvaison is a winemaking term that refers to the frothy, at-first clear juice that ferments on grape skins, extracting color. It makes for brilliant purples in young red wines, turning by shades from ruby to garnet to a mature brick red, with hints of brown in older wines. The term gives a clue to Cuvaison's active, bubbling, changeable history.

At Cuvaison's founding in 1970, an astounding variety of wines was made in a quartet of stainless steel fermenters, huddled against the hillside under the cover of friendly oaks, then barrel aged in a former farmhouse that can only charitably be described as "rustic."

Subsequent sales — first to a publishing company, then to the Schmidheiny family from Switzerland — brought vast change to Cuvaison. First, a handsome, new, mission-styled winery was erected. A small retail room was built in the same style (just below the winery), where an oak-shaded patio is equipped with picnic tables for visitors.

The character of the wine went through a series of pendulum swings, from the broad, eclectic tastes of the winery's founders to the formidable, hillside beasts carved out by Philip Togni, who had made wines all over the world. Then, as John Thacher slid into the winemak-

These two stained-glass winery windows are the models for Cuvaison's labels. The left window represents Chardonnay, the right Cabernet, though Cuvaison is also known for excellent Merlot and is seriously dabbling in Pinot Noir.

er's seat and the Schmidheinys named Manfred Esser president, the identity of Cuvaison began to come into sharp focus.

Several factors contribute to the dramatic change. A large chunk of Carneros (400 acres) was purchased for vineyard in 1979. Thacher brought a more graceful style to the wines. Esser brought an aggressive marketing attitude to bear. And the number of wines was trimmed to three: Chardonnay, Cabernet, and Merlot.

Thacher first came to Cuvaison in 1977, starting out as a "cellar rat." That means hauling hoses, cleaning out tanks, washing barrels, and doing everyone's bidding. It also means

Sturdy metal gantries secure the small oak barrels stacked five high in Cuvaison's barrel cellar, which stands immediately behind the main winery. The winery sits on a low rise of the Silverado Trail at the corner of Dunaweal Lane, just south of Calistoga.

learning the basic values of winemaking. If Thacher is a vastly different stylist than Togni, he learned valuable lessons. "The main thing Philip taught me was attention to detail," recalls the soft-spoken Thacher, an avid fisher, hiker, and camper. "You can't compete in the premium wine business without it."

It is never enough to make great wines, for they must also be brought to the attention of the public. That's Esser's challenge. "I was very excited when the Schmidheinys approached me in 1986," says Esser, who had previously sold the German Pieroth line by means of personal, home, and office wine-tasting sessions.

"Cuvaison had nearly everything in its favor to become one of the great wine estates of California. It had the 'deep pockets,' what we call in Europe 'patience capital.' It had a great new vineyard in the Carneros. It had a talented winemaker. The only thing Cuvaison lacked was effective and aggressive marketing."

Esser gets frustrated with the roadblocks wineries place before the public. "Look at what most wineries put on their back labels," he grumbles. "They put the Brix of the grapes, the pH and total acidity of the wine. That's not what the consumer is interested in. He wants to know two things about a wine: one, how does it taste, and two, what kind of food does it go with. That's it!" *RPH*

The Swiss flag, flying alongside Old Glory, represents Cuvaison's Swiss ownership. The winery, originally built by a pair of scientists, has grown substantially through several ownership changes.

DE MOOR WINERY

Despite one of the finest locations — tourist-wise — in the tourist-laden Napa Valley, De Moor is hardly the most demonstrative of wineries. There are neither waving flags nor flashing neon signs to lasso passing wine lovers. Only the unusual geodesic structure of its tasting room lures more than the usual attention as you pass Mustards Grill's packed parking lot a mile north of Yountville.

Yet there are reasons for stopping at De Moor. Those reasons go beyond the grassy picnic area surrounded by a tiny Chardonnay vineyard, and the well-equipped tasting and retail room under the dome. They are the same reasons for going out of your way to stop at any winery: the wines.

The winery's first recognition came not from its wines but from its unique design. Built in 1976 as Napa Cellars by Charles Woods, both winery and tasting room (really only a table in the, well, one can't say corner . . .) were originally housed under the dome, cramped by oak barrels and five 1,500-gallon Yugoslavian oak uprights.

De Moor has changed hands twice, the last time in 1990 when it was bought by the Tokyo firm Sky Court Napa Corp. Their immediate

A new trellis all but hides the original geodesic-dome winery, a tiny facility that has been expanded twice. The truncated pyramid behind the dome was the first addition, and even that has been enlarged and restructured.

plans are to upgrade the winery's barrel program, add to the landscaping, and explore marketing and distribution possibilities in Japan.

Wineries are judged by their wines, not by their architecture or owners. At De Moor the wine is in the hands of winemaker Aaron Mosely, who came to work for Woods back in January 1980. For Mosely, it was a roundabout sort of homecoming. Born in Napa in 1944, he had grown up in St. Helena, where his father managed a dairy.

"After high school I joined the Air Force," says Mosely with a grin. "I wanted to be a

Originally built as Napa Cellars, De Moor took its present name from the winery's third ownership group, a French family. Today De Moor is owned by Tokyo's Sky Court Napa Corp., but retains the demure, quiet manner it has always possessed.

pilot, but came up a little short on their height requirement. So I became a jet engine mechanic. But I did get my private license after I left the service."

After spending some service time in Germany, Mosely snuck sideways into wine. "I came back home and took a crush job at Charles Krug. George Vierra (then at Krug, now owner of Merlion Winery) liked my work and gave me books on winemaking to read in my spare time. I even set up a small wine lab at my house.

"Winemaking seemed to come easy to me. I spent some time working for Mike Grgich at Chateau Montelena, and when he left I knew that I had better get a degree if I wanted to advance. So I attended Fresno State by day and worked at United Vintners' Madera plant at night. About every fourth week, I'd have breakfast Saturday morning . . . and sleep until Sunday night!"

Though De Moor's winemaking focus is on Cabernet Sauvignon and Chardonnay, at least as far as volume is concerned, Mosely seems to take special pleasure in working with both dry (table) and late harvest (dessert) styles of Sauvignon Blanc. "The sweet dessert wine we make, Fie Doux, is great stuff," enthuses Mosely. "We could sell a thousand dollars a day of it out of the tasting room on weekends — if we could keep it in stock!" *RPH*

A tractor kicks up a small plume of dust as it slowly works its way down the vine row. As any good winemaker will tell you, most of what can be done to improve wine quality has been done — or not done — by the time the grapes hit the crusher.

DIAMOND CREEK VINEYARDS

There are people out there in wine-collector land who will say that Diamond Creek Vineyards is one of the greatest wineries in the world; that its sole product, Cabernet Sauvignon, is long-lived and wonderful; and that no amount of money is too much to spend on a bottle. Others would say that Diamond Creek Vineyards makes a Cabernet Sauvignon that is so hard and tannic it will never develop classic flavors, but that nonetheless it is enjoyable when it's young because of the intensity of flavors.

That last characteristic — intensity — is the one no one disputes. Nor does anyone dispute the fact that this property is a tribute to Al Brounstein's dedication to a single goal — super-premium wine. It took Al and Boots Brounstein a decade of hard work and lean living to see their first wine and it took another decade before the world recognized what they were doing.

Today, Diamond Creek Cabernets are acclaimed for their density of fruit, powerful aromas, and that omnipresent tannin. The wines are monumental, to be sure, and reflect three different soil types.

There are only 20.7 acres of vineyard planted here, halfway up Diamond Mountain. If you look carefully, you can see the three soil types

To those who say there is no blue food, one look at the gondolas of grapes at Diamond Creek as they come in from the field dispels that notion. The uniqueness of the Diamond Creek Cabernet Sauvignon grapes is legend among wine collectors.

slanting on three triangular slopes of land that all come together at one point.

Red Rock Terrace, north-facing, is the most prominent of the three vineyards. The soil is redder than the other two, indicating a higher iron content. The seven-acre Red Rock Terrace produces a slightly more refined kind of Cabernet (if the word "refined" can in any way be used to describe any of the Diamond Creek wines). The wines from this parcel of land tend to be ready to consume a bit earlier than the others.

Volcanic Hill is the eight-acre parcel that faces south. The land here is gray in color, looking like decayed chalk and lava, with

To extract the color from the grape skins, Diamond Creek uses a broom-like metal device to punch down the cap of skins that forms at the top of each tank. The richness and power of Diamond Creek wines is often gauged in auctions, where the wines command top prices.

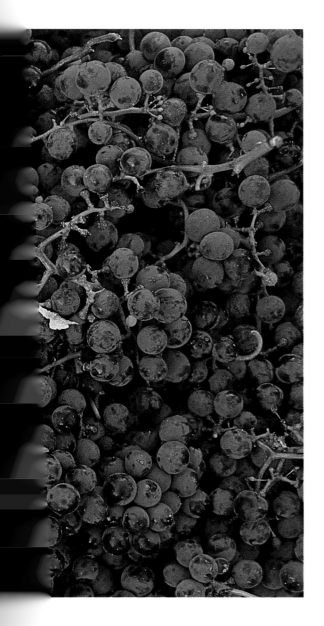

crumbly and caked soil. This vineyard gives the densest, darkest wines, "my Château Latour," says Brounstein. The drainage is better than in the other two vineyards and the vines, struggling to survive, yield deeper fruit.

Gravelly Meadow appears to be larger than the others, but that's an optical illusion. It's only five acres, and faces east. The soil here is a dull, brownish beige with dark brown to black earth mixed in. This vineyard yields harder wines than the other two. Brounstein feels they are earthier and longer-lived than others.

Al and Boots moved here in 1968 when Al sold his over-the-counter drug warehouse in Los Angeles after a 19-year career. On the 70 acres there was no house, no vineyard. The couple planted the hidden acreage that year. The real estate people had projected the property would yield 40 acres of grapevines. But the hilly land held less than half that. Only in the last few years, with the Brounsteins adding 10 more acres, has the total been over 20.

To finance their desire to make premium wine, Al turned to wine sales and other odd jobs, for the vineyards didn't yield a cash-flow profit until the late 1970s. Today many collectors go gaga to get a few bottles of Al's wines, even though prices are high. One wine, a tiny lot of 1987 Cabernet, was released for $100 a bottle. It sold out in a day. *DB*

Al and Boots Brounstein built a tiny man-made lake at the base of the mountain that separates their three unique vineyard sites, and created an island that may be reached by a tiny footbridge.

DOMAINE CARNEROS

Attention to detail is mandatory if one is going to make great sparkling wine. This is because making wine by the slow *méthode champenoise*, developed in the Champagne district of France, is actually two separate fermentations.

The first fermentation turns the grapes into a tart, essentially undrinkable wine; the second fermentation, in which more yeast and cane sugar are added to the bottle, creates the bubbles.

Thus the winemaker must be aware of tiny details because fermentations can go awry. And attention to detail is the hallmark of Eileen Crane, who heads up Taittinger's California operation, Domaine Carneros.

Domaine Carneros is one of the newer sparkling-wine ventures of the dozen set up in California by European investors. It is also one of the most beautiful. From Highway 121 passersby can see the winery's chateau, a majestic, 18th-century-style structure set on a hillock. Domaine Carneros is never going to be a very large winery in terms of total sparkling-wine production. But even on its opening day visitors were guaranteeing the venture's success.

When Claude Taittinger of France decided

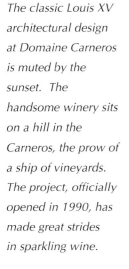

The classic Louis XV architectural design at Domaine Carneros is muted by the sunset. The handsome winery sits on a hill in the Carneros, the prow of a ship of vineyards. The project, officially opened in 1990, has made great strides in sparkling wine.

nearly a decade ago to establish a sparkling-wine property in the southern end of the Napa Valley, in the Carneros region, he had only an idea what style of wine he wanted to make.

Crane gave form to that idea. Hired in 1987 as general manager and winemaker for Taittinger's Domaine Carneros property, Crane prefers to make wine of true delicacy, a bit different from the rather bold style of wine Taittinger makes in Reims, France.

Taittinger and partners spent approximately $9 million building the property and giving it the framework for making great wine. But it was Crane, who made wine at two other Cali-

The success of Domaine Carneros was in the air even before the winery's opening day. Nearly $9 million was spent giving the winery the framework to produce great sparkling wine and an 18th-century-style building that is one of the most beautiful in the Napa Valley.

fornia sparkling-wine wineries before this, who filled in the picture and infused life into it.

The concept at Domaine Carneros, Crane says, is to make sparkling wine that best reflects the character of the cool Carneros region where the grapes are grown, which means making a wine of grace and finesse. Is this better than other sparkling wines?

"You don't compare a Picasso to a Renoir," she says, adding that what she is attempting to create neither compares nor contrasts with Taittinger's French Champagnes. She says her wine will ideally be compared only with other California sparkling wines.

She points out that few sparkling wines are made in California exclusively from Carneros fruit, despite the Carneros region's suitability for classic sparkling wines.

This is Crane's third position in the wine business. In each of her two previous ventures, at Domaine Chandon and at Gloria Ferrer, she worked with Carneros fruit. When she arrived at Domaine Carneros in mid-1987, she made immediate changes. For example, when she was hired the winery intended to use small harvesting bins. Crane chose a slightly larger but equally shallow bin better suited for her purposes.

Domaine Carneros's vineyards were developed in 1982 by Jim and Steve Allen, owners

The foyer of the winery, adjacent to the hospitality room, is graced with a blue and white rug that is an American interpretation of an oriental rug found in the lobby of the Hotel Crillon in Paris. Crane saw the original, photographed it, and had a duplicate made. The interior of the winery, crafted by local artisans, is in the style of Louis XVI.

(with their families) of the Sequoia Grove Winery further north in the Napa Valley. The Allens, in partnership with Peter Ordway, planted 100 acres in Carneros, 60 to Chardonnay and 40 to Pinot Noir, with the idea of making either sparkling wine or varietal wines from those grapes.

A few years later, the brothers approached Kobrand Corp. and Kobrand offered Taittinger the opportunity to join in the partnership that would become Domaine Carneros. Ordway and the Allens contributed the vineyard land to the venture in exchange for a percentage of the project, and a joint partnership was formed. Construction of the chateau began November 15, 1987, and the facility opened its doors to the first visitors on August 2, 1989, offering for tasting a first release of a sparkling wine Crane had made at a neighboring facility.

That wine set the tone for what Domaine Carneros would attempt to do: that is, make a wine that shows utter finesse. Nothing will be overplayed. Crane points out that the "yeasty" quality some people like in a French Champagne actually comes not from the method of production per se but from the long aging of the wine in the bottle at the winery. That characteristic is possible to achieve in California, she notes, but it cannot be accomplished instantaneously. It can be developed if the wine is aged in the winery's cellar for a long period of time, with the wine constantly in contact with the yeast, *en tirage*, gaining character.

The first wine from Domaine Carneros achieved much in terms of fruit and delicacy without a great deal of the yeasty components. Instead, there was fruit from Chardonnay and richness from Pinot Noir, but the wine also had the delicate balance to age handsomely, on the cork, in cool cellars.

"I'm not looking for an intellectual experience alone," says Crane. "The most important thing is that the wine has to be a sensual experience."

For the first few years, she says, Domaine Carneros is focusing on making a non-vintage blended wine, though experimentation was begun early into making a Blanc de Blancs from Chardonnay grapes. That could appear as a vintage-dated product in time.

The tasting room at Domaine Carneros is one of a new breed of civilized settings, avoiding the Disneyland or supermarket atmosphere that pervades so many of the north county's wine tasting rooms.

Visitors to Domaine Carneros park in a lower parking lot and walk up a series of marble stairs to the chateau's patio entrance. Inside, local artisans have re-created a French drawing-room atmosphere, with hand-carved wood panels, brass railings, and the aura of another time, another place. Classical music emanates from hidden speakers as tasters sit down at tables for a glass of Domaine Carneros. *DB*

One reaches the Domaine Carneros facility by walking up a marble staircase. On the top landing, visitors may stroll around a balustrade surrounding the building and look at the vineyards undulating into the horizon.

DOMAINE CHANDON

There was no one to ride horseback through the valley shouting, "The French are coming! The French are coming!" Even so, there was a considerable stir among the winegrowing establishment at the 1973 announcement that a prestigious, French Champagne company had purchased 1,200 acres of prime vineland in Yountville, the bay-cooled Carneros, and on steep hillsides of Mount Veeder.

The company was Moët-Hennessy, a Paris holding company made up of Moët & Chandon, Mercier, and Ruinart Champagnes, Hennessy Cognac, and Dior perfumes. They had several reasons for looking to California. First, they saw an escalating demand for sparkling wines in the world market. Second, the French district of Champagne, due to restrictive appellation-of-origin laws, had almost nonexistent growth potential. Third, their premier winemaker, Edmond Maudière, had tasted a broad selection of Napa Valley wines and judged them suitable for the Moët style.

The fourth generation of a family of Champagne makers, Maudière produced his first sparkling wine at age five. "Delicacy is the main quality of fine sparkling wines," says Maudière, who flies airplanes and helicopters for sport.

Rows of huge "gyro-pallets" take the place of several people in delicately moving dying yeast cells down to the neck of each bottle. The bottles will then be frozen so that the "plug" of yeast can be expelled from the bottle before corking and shipping.

"Then lightness. When I first came in 1972, we bought 600 bottles of what we thought were the best sparkling-wine-oriented still wines here. We blended those wines, fermented them, and five months later tasted them as sparkling wines. I had to mentally adjust their sugar/acid ratios because they had been initially fermented as still wines. But it was very exciting. That was when we knew we could produce great sparkling wines in the Napa Valley."

An experimental vintage was conducted in 1973 at Trefethen Vineyards, with Maudière testing a dozen Napa Valley varieties, from Green Hungarian to Colombard. While there

had been little doubt that Chardonnay and Pinot Noir would predominate the blend of Chandon's primary offering, the question was what other varieties might prove beneficial to the blend. Pinot Blanc turned out to be thoroughly compatible, so much so that nearly 75 acres at the Mount Veeder and Carneros ranches have since been planted to that variety. Later, the French variety, Pinot Meunier, was also added to the list.

Chandon's Napa Valley Brut (labeled "Sparkling Wine" and not Champagne) is the company's flagship, accounting for two-thirds of all sales. Chandon's second sparkler is the berry-fruited Blanc de Noirs, made only from Pinot Noir. Chandon Reserve is a creamy Brut *cuvée* that has its secondary fermentation solely in magnums and is aged on the yeast four years. None of the wines is vintage dated, as Maudière follows the French practice of holding back 15 to 30 percent of the wines from each harvest, to be blended back into future *cuvées* for stylistic consistency.

A silky aperitif wine is produced from press wine. "Panache" is made from fresh Pinot Noir juice that is blended with a pot still brandy (itself distilled from Pinot Noir) to create a wine of 18 percent alcohol (and more than eight percent residual sugar) that resembles a *ratafia de champagne* or a Pineau des Charentes.

Master winemaker Edmund Maudière assesses a glass of Domaine Chandon Sparkling Wine out in the vineyard, where the whole process starts.

A teenage member of the French underground during World War II, Maudière flies helicopters for fun today.

A sign, a lake, and a bridge form the entryway to Domaine Chandon's wine museum, restaurant, and winery. The museum shows how sparkling wines are made, from vineyard to glass, and the restaurant boasts excellent cuisine and a full Napa Valley wine list.

Though Moët produces wines in Argentina, Brazil, Germany, Austria, Spain, and Australia, Maudière considers the Napa Valley wines he oversees superior to all but those of Epernay. "We didn't expect the Napa Valley wines to age as well as they do," he notes. "We thought they would oxidize more quickly, but they don't. They also have much better balance than we expected."

Though Maudière jets out to California several times a year to monitor things, the real winemaking responsibilities fall to Dawnine Sample Dyer.

A biology student who first came to work at Chandon in 1976, Dyer is skilled at all the winemaking techniques, and is a most effective taster. This is the key to blending, which lies at the heart of fine sparkling wines.

"I spent some time working with U.C. Davis on a new 'flavor wheel,' adapted specifically to describing the flavor characteristics of sparkling wines," says the dark-haired Dyer.

"We added some characteristics that came from the winemaking side of things and expected to delete a lot of the fruit characteristics. But that didn't happen. It's just that, with sparkling wines, the fruit characteristics are there at a markedly lower intensity level."

Domaine Chandon was one of the first California wineries to open its own, on-premise restaurant. "We did have the restaurant in mind when we built the winery, but not for the reason we use it today," notes winery president John Wright, a Wesleyan University graduate who got hooked on wine during an Army stint in the Rheingau and Moselle. "In those days, you could not charge for on-premise wine tasting unless you had a restaurant — one serving warm food at regular hours. Sparkling wine, with its luxury tax, is too expensive to give away."

Chandon's French owners decreed that the restaurant had to be of the highest quality, and so it was, from the day it opened in 1977

Domaine Chandon

(when Chandon's first wines were released) to rave reviews, full seatings, and reservations that had to be booked up to a month in advance! "We had no inkling that that would occur," exclaims Wright. "As it happened, people would come to the restaurant having no idea whatsoever that there was a winery connected to it!

"I travel a lot, and there are still places I go where our restaurant's reputation exceeds that of our winery. It took us three years to get any kind of regular tourist flow to the winery." It was only in the late '80s that the restaurant began to show the occasional profit.

"The restaurant's primary purpose is to expose and educate people to wine in a setting of fine food. The kind of food we prepare requires a ton of people, and we're not willing to compromise its quality by cutting staff or having two seatings a night. Our customers like to linger, knowing that their table is theirs for the night. We accept any losses as public relations expense . . . worth every penny."

Chef de Cuisine Philippe Jeanty, who has been a fixture since opening day, may be French-trained, but has no qualms about offering sushi, herb-smoked salmon, and wild mushrooms along with more traditional French items. *RPH*

Dawnine Sample Dyer takes responsibility for winemaking at Domaine Chandon. Not only does she stand out as a talented professional and a successful woman in California's wine industry, but she and her husband, Bill, are one of the few married couples in the world in which both partners are winemakers.

While Domaine Chandon employs mechanical means (gyro-pallets) to settle wine yeasts into the neck of the bottle, it also uses people in the old-fashioned method of riddling (where each bottle is given a quarter-turn each day on an A-frame riddling rack). An advanced method, using alginate beads to trap yeast cells, is also being tested.

DUCKHORN VINEYARDS

The reputation for Merlot and Cabernet Sauvignon that Duckhorn Vineyards has gained in the last decade and a half is remarkable. The wines — dark and dense — have won major tastings, sell out rapidly, and command attention on restaurant wine lists.

Yet the style of wine that Dan and Margaret Duckhorn have fashioned, under the direction of winemaker Tom Rinaldi, is rather surprising when one considers that the company that owns Duckhorn Vineyards (the St. Helena Wine Company) produces only a small amount of the fruit off its own tiny acreage in the Napa Valley. The bulk of the fruit, including the wine

from the famed Three Palms Vineyard, is bought from more than 20 growers around the valley. That, one might think, would make for wines that change each year, at the whim of the growers. But their reputation for fairness and their loyalty to Dan and Tom, combined with long-term contracts, assure the supply of top-quality grapes well into the 1990s.

Rinaldi makes a bold statement with his red wines mostly because the grapes (Cabernet Sauvignon and Merlot) come from hilly places like Mount Veeder and Spring Mountain, and from Spottswoode, which has itself made some stunning red wines under that label. In recent

Duckhorn has only 6.9 acres of grapevines on the home ranch, growing the white wine varieties Sauvignon Blanc and Semillon. All the grapes for the rest of Duckhorn's wines — including its world-famous Three Palms Vineyard Merlot — come from other ranches.

years, Rinaldi has also experimented with fruit from the cooler, flat Carneros.

The Duckhorn story begins in 1976. Dan had been a manager of Crocker Associates, handling that banking family's investment in a vineyard consulting and grapevine propagation business located on the Silverado Trail, north of St. Helena. When a slump in grape prices hit in 1975, and the Crockers decided to sell, the Duckhorns and four other families acquired the land and Dan and Margaret moved north to run the property as a winery.

"I just became enamored of this industry and thought it would be a great place to live

The Duckhorn winery was built in 1978, but its many oak doors give the winery an older look and feeling. Additions to the winery in 1981 gave winemaker Tom Rinaldi the added size he needed to expand production.

and raise a family," says Dan. Soon five more families bought into the company, making the firm a "partnership" of ten families. Duckhorn had no delusions about making back the investment overnight, but getting rich was not what this project was all about. It was more about lifestyle.

"Our intention was to never get really very big," he says. "Margaret was a school nurse, and in 1976 I became a consultant to Heublein." Being a consultant to that huge corporation gave Dan another view of the industry. He later became one of the most active supporters of movements aimed at protecting the valley's agricultural heritage from incursions by development.

The winery's initial crush in 1978 was 28 tons — about 1,600 cases of wine. Production later increased to more than 400 tons.

Despite its image as a red-wine winery, Duckhorn is known to connoisseurs for also making a delightful Sauvignon Blanc and a stylish Semillon (under its second label, Decoy).

In 1989, Duckhorn began making a Pinot Noir that features fruit from the famed Sonoma-Cutrer Vineyard, which long has been synonymous with top-quality Chardonnay. This wine is sold under the name Obsidian, reflecting the type of rock found on Glass Mountain, a historic Indian site that overlooks the winery. *DB*

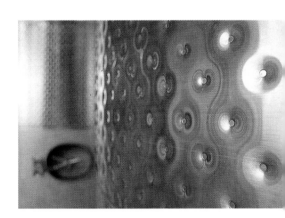

Despite a strong national reputation and excellent distribution, Duckhorn Vineyards remains a small winery, with only 25 stainless-steel tanks used for storage and fermentation. Dan Duckhorn hopes a Pinot Noir project will give the winery another wine that collectors will love.

DUNN VINEYARDS

Saying to a wine collector that you just got a bottle of Dunn Cabernet is like saying you just won the lottery. The name is magic. It represents the epitome of dense, mountain-style Cabernet Sauvignon — powerful wine that evokes thoughts of Latour.

Randall Dunn is surprised by accolades like this one. He is a quiet fellow who developed his reputation as a fine winemaker while at Caymus Vineyards. In 1979, while still at Caymus, Dunn leaped into history with the first of a string of Cabernets made from fruit grown on Howell Mountain, on the eastern edge of the Napa Valley.

Within two years, collectors in the know were scurrying to buy bottles of Dunn's wine at any price. Demand is now so high that half of it is sold to mailing list customers.

Still, controversy surrounded the Dunn wines in the late 1980s. There was a feeling they were so hard and tannic that they might never become drinkable. Dunn said in 1990, "I don't think any of them are ready to drink yet. The '79 and '80 still need another five years."

Dunn recognizes the long-lived nature of his wines, and tries to ensure that they will age well by sealing the neck of each bottle in French sealing wax, protecting the cork from

Barrel-aging caves under the winery at Dunn Vineyards on Howell Mountain were completed in December 1989. The underground storage keeps the barrels at a constant temperature and prevents evaporation of the wine. Dunn had contractor Russell Clough dig the caves for him, and the result is stunning.

air. It's a time-consuming method of adding a capsule to the top of the bottle, and Dunn is one of the few wineries in the world that does it for table wine.

The Dunns created this winery more from hard work than cash, for they had no deep financial backing. Randy did the mechanical and electrical work; he used old dairy bins to hold juice; and it took him a decade before he invested in a computer. Until then he and his wife, Lori, hand-addressed all the envelopes for their mailing list clientele.

Dunn's vineyard on Howell Mountain consists of only five of the 55 acres of land he owns

The caves at Dunn were designed with a small chamber at one end. Randy and Lori Dunn intend one day to enclose the chamber with a door and turn the room into a private hospitality area in which they can stage small dinner parties.

2,000 feet up, but it generates about a third of the wine he calls Howell Mountain. The other two-thirds of Dunn's Howell Mountain Cabernet comes from two local growers. For obvious reasons, Dunn declines to say who.

But he is pleased to say that he makes his Howell Mountain Cabernet entirely from Cabernet Sauvignon grapes; that he uses a Montrachet yeast (which some winemakers fear) to ferment the juice; and that he uses exclusively French oak barrels for the aging, which takes two and a half years. That's about it — all in a winemaking facility that is anything but high-tech.

"There is no mystique about what goes on up here," he says. "Winemaking's just like cooking; you gotta taste it and then make it so it tastes like what you think it should taste like." So before making a final blend, Dunn tastes constantly for months. And then, he says, "The fact is I am so sick of the wines after they're bottled, I never taste them until six to eight months after."

Regarding the use of the controversial Montrachet yeast to ferment, Dunn says, "It can produce hydrogen sulfide, so you can't let the stuff sit around on the lees, because it does start to stink. But if you're careful with the wine, it's excellent."

Despite the acclaim his wines get, Dunn never sought fame. To this day, he says, "We keep the gate locked on weekends." *DB*

Some of the Cabernet vines on Howell Mountain turn a dramatic red color soon after the harvest is completed. Dunn Vineyards, as with many mountainous vineyard properties, gets only a small crop of grapes each year, but they are grapes with intense flavor.

FAR NIENTE WINERY

The restoration of Far Niente, built by John Benson in 1885, is a gift to the Napa Valley wine community like no other. The winery has a tastefully luminescent beauty that is unrivaled. The job done by Oklahoma horticulturist Gil Nickel is as complete and pure a restoration as has ever been done on an old California winery.

There is a touch of irony involved, for the meaning of the Italian phrase from which the winery's name and motto are derived is at loggerheads with the mode and mood of the winery itself, both originally and now. The motto is "without a care." The full phrase is *dolce far niente* ("sweet to do nothing"). There may be sweetness at Far Niente, as expressed by the occasionally produced Dolce (a botrytised Semillon and Sauvignon Blanc blend), but plenty is happening.

Like many who come to wine for its aesthetic pleasures, Gil Nickel, a classic auto collector and racer, navigated a tortuous path along the route. His grandparents helped lay out the streets of Muskogee, Oklahoma, where Gil was born. Though Gil studied guided-missile physics at Baylor University and Oklahoma State, his agricultural interests eventually brought him back to the family firm, the Green-

Owner Gil Nickel holds an Imperial of Far Niente Cabernet as he sits on one of his many restored racing cars, his opulently restored winery for once serving as mere background. Trained in guided-missile physics, Nickel is an active competitor in classic auto races.

leaf Nursery, one of the largest wholesale nurseries in the country. But even that proved too confining, so he turned the business over to a partner and set off for other pursuits. He opened a travel agency and a few restaurants, became involved in oil and gas drilling and real estate, and even thought of becoming a winegrower.

"I found a beautiful old Victorian townhouse on San Francisco's Nob Hill," says the solid, blue-eyed, blond-haired Nickel. "It had a fabulous old wine cellar, with a steel vault door and a few pieces of winemaking equipment. I audited a few courses at [U.C.] Davis,

The meaning behind the name Far Niente *stands in almost ludicrous contrast to the energy and expense given to meticulous restoration and construction at this exquisite wine estate. The motto, in Italian, translates to "without a care."*

made some home wines — my first Chardonnay took first place at the Napa County Fair — and tried to find the best places to grow Chardonnay and Cabernet Sauvignon."

He homed in on the west side of the Napa Valley, on an Oakville bench (next door to Martha's Vineyard and Mondavi's Reserve blocks) that grows some of the finest Cabernets anywhere. The winery itself — little more than an empty shell when Nickel found it in the late 1970s — rests on an elevation slightly above the valley floor, carpeted thick with vines as far as the eye can see.

"It is an interesting coincidence," muses Nickel, "but Benson also lived on Nob Hill in San Francisco, his vocation was real estate and mining, and his avocation, like mine, was horticulture. In fact, it was Benson who, before the turn of the century, imported the cork oak trees from Portugal that still stand on the winery property."

Nickel's restoration of what Benson had built was a tremendous project. Extensive stone work on the two-foot-thick walls was carried out by Eugene Domenichelli, who had learned the art as a young man from an elderly Italian stonemason. Rotted fir timbers were replaced, extensive tunnels (now 15,000 square feet) were excavated by Alf Burtleson ("probably the first new wine cave in the valley since the turn of the century"), and new slate floors were laid in the first and second levels — the working part of the winery.

The third level — which houses offices, lab, and living quarters — was floored with varnished oak planks, whose screws were plugged with wooden dowels, as is done with ship's decking and is appropriate for the expert sailor that Gil is. The building's cupola, with its almost unrestricted valley view, was remodeled as an office. A circular staircase of oak, with its hand-carved banister, descends from the crow's nest of an office to the Great Hall, headed by an eight-foot fireplace, ringed by antique wall lamps, and anchored with oak tables large enough to seat 50 for dinner. The elegant chandeliers are from the old Seattle Opera House.

In 1989 and 1990, tunnel specialist Alf Burtleson excavated 15,000 square feet of new caves — using an English coal mining machine — under the knoll behind the main winery. At the center of this labyrinth of caves is an octagonal wine library room, with a 30-foot dome ceiling. Curiously, the cave additions do not add to Far Niente's production capacity, but only allow for longer aging in barrel, not to mention easier access to the more than 1,000 barrels.

Glorious as the slate-roofed structure is, Far Niente the winery stands or falls on its wines. Gaudy wine label aside (one must admit that it has grown on us through the years, despite its extravagant use of color on parchment), the Chardonnays annually tend to show

The newest aspect of Nickel's thorough restoration of this 19th-century jewel is extensive barrel-aging caves, which add more than 15,000 square feet of wine storage space. The winery, built in 1885, featured the archway to a cave that had been designed, but never built.

the same butter and pineapple fruitiness capable of enduring a fair amount of bottle age.

The Cabernets are rich wines that will live for decades, fragrant with violets and blackberries in the nose, filled with bell pepper and iodine in the mouth. These are classic Oakville-Rutherford Cabernets that will secure the winery's reputation if it never makes another wine.

Winemaker Dirk Hampson, a native of Portland, Oregon, has been at Far Niente since 1982. After taking his degree in enology at U.C. Davis, Hampson went to Europe, where he worked at Schloss Vollrads in the Rheingau, with the Burgundian *négociant* Laboure-Roi, and at Bordeaux's famed Château Mouton-Rothschild. "The European experience was

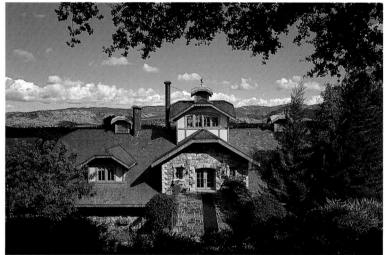

Far Niente, built by John Benson in 1885, has been unstintingly and faithfully restored by Oklahoma nurseryman Gil Nickel. The stone structure, which looks out over the sea of vines just north of Yountville, is on the National Register of Historic Places.

extremely valuable for me," says the lean Hampson. "In school, you learn winemaking by the numbers, which has nothing to do with making great wines. And here, I have the luxury of making only 'reserve' wines. If it doesn't fit our style, it goes down the drain or we bulk it out!"

While Dirk is quite serious about the quality of his wines, the quality of his sense of humor is pretty good too. "I like to laugh when I work, and the big auctions get far too serious," he says. "So, one year Larry Maquire, our marketing guy, and I decided to make up barrel-fermented wine cooler to put in the Napa Valley Auction. We put it in a six-pack, Gil came up with the name Dos Okies, and the bidding started out at eighty-nine cents. But it was for a good cause, the hospitals, and it finally went for $2800!" *RPH*

Winemakers employ cooperage, large and small, to age their wines. Small barrels, with a greater surface area in relation to the volume of wine stored, impart tannin and oak flavor quickly to wine. Upright oak tanks give up their extractives more slowly and sparingly.

FLORA SPRINGS WINE CO.

The base of the Mayacamas Mountains, which frame the western edge of the Napa Valley, has some excellent conditions for growing fine wine grapes. The soils up on the benchland that look east into the valley are perfect: they are lean and well-drained. The weather is temperate, warm enough to fully ripen the Cabernet vines, yet not so warm that it causes them to get overripe. This is partly because the sun sets behind the hill earlier than it does for west-facing vineyards, cooling the soil off sooner and ripening the grapes more slowly.

It was here, in the early 1880s, that a handful of small wineries popped up during the birth of fine wine in the United States. A decade later many of the vineyards were devastated by the root louse phylloxera. But today family-operated Flora Springs Wine Co. has its vineyards and winery on this ideal soil. And here winemaker Ken Deis makes some of the Napa Valley's best wines.

The winery was founded in 1978, nearly 100 years after the property was originally developed. The first winery on the site was called Rennie Brothers, and was a handsome two-story stone structure owned by James and William Rennie of Scotland. They made table wine until 1888, when they moved to Fresno to

The temperate climate of the western Napa Valley foothills is evident, not only in the annual ripening of the Cabernet vines, but in the profusion of lemon and orange trees that grow at the edge of the property and give fruit to the families here about six months out of the year.

make sherry and port, which had become all the rage in the United States. The Rennie winery was sold to a San Francisco banker and for the next few decades, through Prohibition, no wine was made at the property.

In 1933, Louis M. Martini, quietly preparing for the end of Prohibition, bought the Rennie property and used it to make sherries and to age a number of vintages of fine wines.

In 1977, Jerome Komes, then president of Bechtel Corporation, and his wife, Flora, bought the Rennie winery as well as the adjacent Brockhoff Winery, which had been built in 1885.

As Flora Springs was being developed, some of the poorer soils were chosen for Merlot, which appears to give best results in conditions in which the vine struggles. Visitors to Flora Springs are greeted by signs showing which variety is planted where.

Jerome, Flora, son John, and daughter Julie sought simply to sell their grapes to existing wineries. Soon the Komeses had planted more than 400 acres of fine wine grapes in five of the best locations in the valley, and were selling grapes to neighboring wineries. As the wineries recognized the high quality of the grapes they were getting from the Komes ranch, the family realized what it had.

In 1978, John Komes and his sister, Julie Komes Garvey, began making wine in the old Rennie winery, which was renovated and renamed Flora Springs. The Brockhoff winery, also renovated, became a home for John and Carrie Komes, who are principals in the Flora Springs winery. Julie's husband, Pat, a viticulturalist, took on the farming chores.

Winemaker Deis came in 1979, and constantly sought better styles for his wines. The Sauvignon Blanc, for example, was originally intensely grassy, almost vegetal. By 1989 Deis had developed a way of growing the grapes and making the wine that avoided the vegetal elements in exchange for a wine more in the style of Graves. Deis's Chardonnay also took on more depth and richness. The Cabernet Sauvignon, always rich and concentrated, led to the development of the winery's proprietary red wine, Trilogy — one of the first super-premium red wines in California to be blended from the classic Bordeaux varieties. *DB*

A worker carries a lugbox of Cabernet Sauvignon back to a waiting truck for the one-minute ride to the Flora Springs winery crushing pad. The Komes vineyard property off west Zinfandel Lane is within shouting distance of the winery.

FOLIE À DEUX WINERY

Playful, fanciful minds are at work here at Folie à Deux, the small winery that sits 300 yards back from Highway 29, beyond the Freemark Abbey complex on the northern edge of St. Helena.

"Our name refers to a psychiatric diagnosis that describes a fantasy or delusion shared between two closely related people," explains proprietor Evie Dizmang who, along with her psychiatrist husband, Larry, founded the winery with 150 cases of Dry Chenin Blanc and 80 cases of Cabernet Sauvignon in 1981.

"Life in general, and wine in particular, should have a playful aspect, especially when the two are put together," adds Evie, a clinical social worker. "It takes a bit of craziness to start a small winery. When we bought the 21 acres here, in 1974, it was a dilapidated sheep ranch, with high weeds, auto bodies here and there, and a quarter-acre of Petite Sirah at the base of the knoll from which the owner made 'Louie's Red.'

"The house, which is now our tasting room, was prison gray (it's now yellow), with stucco plastered on over redwood. Larry

An old basket press and crusher-stemmer stand silently in front of the older farmhouse that once sheltered Folie à Deux's founding family, the Dizmangs. Today, winemaking has been removed to a newly dug cave in a low hillock behind the house, which is now an office and retail room.

decided that we had to plant the vines ourselves, so that we could one day sit back and say, 'I did that.' So, instead of hiring someone to do it in four weeks . . . it took us four years."

The little yellow house actually housed barrels, not to mention the Dizmang family, in the early years, before a larger home could be built ("that also took us four years!") on the north-facing slope. Further on around the knoll, a series of tunnels has been excavated for barrel aging. At the end of the tunnel is a metal sculpture of the winery's logo — mirror-

Adding a twist to man's millennia-old seduction by the fruit of the vine is the hallmark of Folie à Deux. The winery's motto: "Share the fantasy."

image twin dancing girls, resembling a Rorschach ink blot — executed by Santa Rosa sculptor Sharon Desidere.

The fanciful theme extends to winemaking. Folie à Deux makes a highly unusual sparkling wine, called Fantasie, so unusual as to be justly called unique. "Well, it's 60 percent Chardonnay and 40 percent Muscat Canelli," begins winemaker Rick Tracy. "It is a *méthode champenoise* champagne, and it's finished nearly dry, so it's not like an Asti Spumante. We originally made it entirely of Muscat, but wanted a little more complexity, so we added the Chardonnay. We want the flavor of the grape, but we also want the complexity you get from yeast aging, so it gets at least a year on the yeast." Fragrant with the Muscat fruitiness, the wine is full in body, but nicely round in the finish.

"The winery motto is 'Share the fantasy,' and everybody is open to new ideas here. We made a Petite Sirah in '86, and Merlot in '88, and a Zinfandel in '89. We even toyed with making a port from Zinfandel and Petite Sirah. We would have called it Petite Port!"

At Folie à Deux you see how sharing a delusion has grown into magnificent obsession, the making of varied and interesting wines. Anybody willing to suspend conventional wisdom can share the fantasy — and the wine — with these wickedly wonderful folks. *RPH*

FORMAN VINEYARDS

"I couldn't make wine unless I grew my own grapes," says thoughtful, bespectacled Ric Forman, who ensured his reputation in the early '70s as Sterling's original winemaker, fresh out of school. "I enjoy being in the vineyard every bit as much as I do being in the winery. When grapes are just 'delivered' to you, it's so cold. In a way, it's like having a test-tube baby — you didn't get to be involved in the fun part!"

Forman began to formulate what he wanted for his own operation while still at Sterling. "Sterling had gotten too big," he remembers, "to the point where I couldn't really maintain control over both vineyards and winery. So I began looking for a place to settle.

"In 1979, I was looking at a place. At first, it seemed like nothing more than a goat hill. But in a clearing above the trees, there was this incredible gravel. 'This is it!' I said to myself. Much of it was forested, but there were old grape stakes everywhere. And when we tried to drill a couple of wells, the driller got nothing but gravel for sixty feet. This stuff has the consistency of sugar after cultivation, and is so well-drained that I can drive a tractor in here 24 hours after a heavy rain. You walk in it and you never get mud on your boots!"

Ric Forman's newly dug cave is well suited to the barrel aging of wine. A constant temperature is an energy plus, and good for the wine, but more important is a constant and high relative humidity, which markedly reduces ullage (evaporation loss).

Forman bought the property, and planted rootstock right away, later budding them to Cabernet Sauvignon, with a smattering of Merlot, Cabernet Franc, and Petit Verdot. "Being in the vineyard is so important, because good grapes will make you a hero every time. Besides, if you know what goes on in the vineyard, you'll know what to do in the winery."

A native of Oakland, Forman developed his penchant for chemistry as a young man, nearly destroying his family's home when a flask of distilling material blew up in his face. "The whole process of fermentation fascinated me," he recalls. "I worked at Stony Hill and

Ric's home and office rest atop the main cellar and production area. A swimming pool adjoins the patio on the opposite (north) side, and a west-facing deck overlooks Napa Valley proper to the left.

Mondavi while working on my master's. Sterling came in 1969. I liked the international feel of what these people had in mind, and I liked the idea of starting a new winery on my own, from the ground up."

While he was at Sterling, Newton, and Charles Shaw, where he consulted before devoting full time to his own winery, Forman particularly distinguished himself by making Sauvignon Blancs capable of wondrous aging in the bottle.

"With my Estate Cabernet, I'm aiming at the elegance of a Château Latour," notes Forman. "I'm also buying some Chardonnay to make a Meursault-styled wine, a big, classic white wine. I'm keeping things small because I need to do everything myself, and still have a little time for other things. I like to travel. Europe. The Sierras, just to rest and look at the beauty of it all. I like to read: an occasional mystery or two and the old classics, the stuff I never got to read in college. I was too deep into chemistry to read Steinbeck and Dickens.

"I've never been real good about being told what to do. I don't like to be 'owned' by anybody, but I don't want to have only one thing going, either. That's too frightening. I like to work by myself, and I'm convinced that if I can do my work out of love and enjoyment, and not out of duty, my wines will be better and I will be better." *RPH*

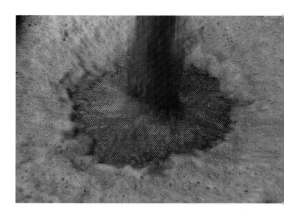

Red wine must is pumped over grape solids to increase extraction. Forman's red is mainly Cabernet Sauvignon, seasoned with Merlot, Cabernet Franc, and Petit Verdot — all grown in his small estate vineyard.

FRANCISCAN VINEYARDS

You'd be right to think that Franciscan Vineyards had some serious spiritual connections for, as a winery, Franciscan has died and been reborn more times than Lazarus. In 1975, a heart monitor would have shown nothing but a flat line. Clinically dead.

If that sounds overly dramatic, recall that the winery was founded in the early '70s by a group of San Francisco investors who saw only stars. And red ink. They erected a magnificent redwood-faced edifice and, with their first crush in 1973, made nearly 300,000 gallons of wine. Nary a drop was sold before the venture had to be completely reorganized with the infusion of Canadian capital. The 40 shareholders of the new group lasted scarcely a year before bankruptcy was declared.

The corpse was taken at crush in 1975 by Colorado developer Ray Duncan and winemaker Justin Meyer. Together they charted a more realistic course. They started by selling off the uneven inventory at fire-sale prices, many of the wines going for a dollar a bottle under the now-defunct "Friar's Table" label.

Under Huneeus, Franciscan has been almost entirely rebuilt. While aesthetics are nice -- including the humorously huge "Rutherford Bench," and oversized redwood bench near the fountain that mocks the arguments over the appelation of the same name -- Franciscan has been renovated in both vineyard and winery.

In August 1979, Duncan and Meyer sold Franciscan, along with their Alexander Valley and Oakville vineyard holdings, to the Peter Eckes Company. (By then, Duncan and Meyer had founded Silver Oak Wine Cellars, a winery devoted to Cabernet Sauvignon. Only.) A German company, Eckes makes and distributes spirits, liqueurs, and juices. They had the wisdom to bring in, as partner, one of the country's finest marketing minds, Agustin "Cucho" Huneeus.

"We have been deluding ourselves for a long time by thinking that every variety can be grown in every part of California," says the Chilean-born entrepreneur. "If we look ahead ten or 20 years, wine marketing — because it is such a low-margin business — is going to be based almost entirely on varietal wines, general appellations, and specific vineyard appellations."

Attention to specific appellations has been the key to Franciscan's resurgence. "If we look ahead ten or twenty years, wine marketing is going to be based almost entirely on varietal wines, general appellations, and specific vineyard appellations," argues Huneeus.

Huneeus cut his wine teeth at Chile's Concha y Toro, then joined Seagram when Chilean companies were nationalized. In 1977, in California, he bought Noble, a top bulk-wine producer, leveraged that into the ownership of Concannon Vineyards in Livermore — selling both prior to settling in at Franciscan.

One of his first priorities at Franciscan was to lure winemaker Greg Upton from Concannon. Blond and fair skinned, Upton studied aerospace engineering before straying into a wine class at U.C. Davis. "Winemaking is easy," says Upton disarmingly, "if you're willing to work. If you're willing to oversee each step. If you're there, tasting the wine often, you can react before a small problem becomes a big problem."

Under Huneeus, Franciscan has acquired Mount Veeder, a small hillside Napa Valley estate; become a partner in a Chilean winery (Errazuriz Panquehue, sold here as Caliterra for obvious reasons); and in 1990 added a 270-acre vineyard property along the Silverado Trail in Rutherford. Franciscan no longer needs prayers, for it is blessed with workers. *RPH*

FREEMARK ABBEY

The old stone cellar at Freemark was built by wine pioneer Antonio Forni, who started construction in 1899 and finished about seven years later. Stone provides excellent insulation, which is especially important during the warm days of summer.

F reemark Abbey, like Franciscan, has never had any connection with the cloistered life. The name actually came to the property late in its history, derived from the names of the owners who purchased the winery in 1939: Charles *Free*man, *Mark* Foster, and Albert M. Ahern (nicknamed "*Abbey*").

The site of the winery had survived a long and variegated history by the time it acquired its religious-sounding name. The first vines were probably planted in 1875, on land acquired from Charles Krug in 1867, by Captain William J. Sayward. A crusty sea captain, he built the lighthouse at Cape Flattery (at the far western tip of Washington State) and survived the sinking of his ship, the wheat-loaded Sequilla, in an 1863 Atlantic storm — without losing a single hand. Sayward later sold the

probably began construction of the present stone structure in 1895, completing it ten years later. He also discovered a distant and untapped market for his wines in the Italian stone masons who quarried marble and granite in Barre, Vermont.

The building had a succession of owners after Prohibition began until it was revived and renamed by the Aherns of Santa Monica. The Aherns produced, for a time, a full line of wines and were successful with a line of "varietal" grape jellies.

In 1965 the property was purchased from hotelman Ben Swig — who had acquired the closed winery only two years earlier — by Lester and Barbara Hurd. They moved their candle factory and retail store into the upper level, then leased the lower level to a partnership of growers, who re-established the name and essence of Freemark Abbey.

The group was led by Charles Carpy, whose grandfather had operated the Uncle Sam Wine Cellars in Napa nearly a century before. The partners included Carpy, former tax lawyer William P. Jaeger, consulting winemaker Brad Webb, grape grower Frank (Laurie) Wood, investment banker/grower John M. Bryan, World Affairs Councilman Richard G. Heggie and local real estate man James C. Warren. (Many are also partners in Rutherford Hill Winery.)

Freemark's winemakers, under the guidance of legendary partner/consultant Brad Webb — Webb was the first to isolate and understand the malolactic bacterium — have produced substantial wines from the beginning. Leon Adams, writing in *The Wines of America*, described Freemark's 1968 Cabernet as "the first California red wine I have thus far tasted that I might have mistaken for a good vintage of Château Margaux."

In 1973 then-winemaker Jerry Luper created Edelwein, a lush, honeysuckle, *beeren-auslese*-styled Johannisberg Riesling that kindled the interest of California winemakers in sweet botrytised wines. Freemark's subseque

26-acre vineyard to John and Josephine Tychson. After her husband committed suicide (the weak, sickly Dane was dying of tuberculosis), Josephine went ahead and built the Tychson Winery in 1886 — likely the only American winery built by a woman in the 19th century.

Phylloxera forced her to sell the redwood winery, which later came to Antonio Forni, who rechristened it Lombarda Cellars. Forni

The winemaking team at Freemark Abbey has always shown a strong preference for using Nevers oak, both for Chardonnay and Cabernet Sauvignon. The feeling is that Nevers oak is softer and intrudes less upon the fruit.

winemaker, Larry Langbehn, expanded on that theme with Rieslings of varying residual sweetness, designated as Sweet Select, Edelwein, and Edelwein Gold (the sweetest).

Carpy is the glue that holds things together at Freemark. A big fellow, he's as friendly and self-effacing as your favorite Labrador retriever. And if Tommy Lasorda's veins flow Dodger blue, then Chuck Carpy's assuredly pump Napa Valley Cabernet red. "My dad was a San Francisco banker/property manager before he retired to St. Helena, where I was born in 1927," says Carpy. "He loved kids, and spent his retirement coaching the local youngsters after school was out." That commitment is still honored by Carpy Field, St. Helena's public athletic grounds.

Chuck Carpy's winegrowing genes come not from his father, but rather from his namesake grandfather who, near the end of the Civil War, came to California from Bordeaux "quite without financial resources, but with youth, good looks, a fine physique, and first-rate native ability," says wine historian Ernest Peninou. By the year of the American centennial Charles Carpy had hooked up with San Francisco wine merchant Charles Anduran; the pair purchased the Uncle Sam Cellars at Fourth and Main in Napa City. Carpy later owned a winery in San Jose and the famed Greystone Cel-

The main tasting room at Freemark Abbey, here set for an elegant dinner. The folks at Freemark have always been hospitable, whether the tasting is of barrel samples in the cellar or of finished wine in these lovely, sumptuous surroundings.

lars (now part of The Christian Brothers) before becoming a banker in San Francisco.

Today's Chuck Carpy got his start as a grape grower after taking an agricultural economics degree from U.C. Davis and an M.S. from Montana State. "I bought my first piece of property in 1961. I had to clear the trees, remove the weeds, and level it all, so I didn't get it planted until 1964."

If Carpy is the glue, R. Brad Webb is the bridge from winemaker to winemaker. As Langbehn once noted, "Brad was there to hold my hand, to bridge the gap between the theoretical, the practical, and 'The Freemark Way.' That means an analytical style. If a wine turns

Winemaker Ted Edwards grew up with agriculture and studied for wine at U.C. Davis. "You have to know where you are going to get your grapes, because that's where the wine starts," says Edwards. "The soil and climate are so important."

out well, we want to know why. It all comes out of Brad's philosophy, his hunger for precise information. With him, there's none of that artsy-fartsy stuff. When he'd run an experiment, he'd run a control, too. That used to be unheard of in wineries. And he'd always say, 'If you're standing around with nothing to do, measure something!'"

Today's winemaker, Ted Edwards, has always had a close feeling for the outdoors in general, agriculture in particular. "My father and I raised apples and alfalfa, with a small interest in livestock," says the bearded Edwards, who studied at Davis after finishing high school in Sebastopol. After earning a master's in enology, he worked with Webb and Langbehn, then spent a few years at Rutherford Hill before returning to Freemark Abbey.

"Over the years I have developed a healthy respect for traditional techniques of winemaking," says Edwards, an avid hiker-camper-fisherman-skier (water and snow). "While I believe in traditional methods, such as aging in French oak for Chardonnay and Cabernet, I also believe in the scientific techniques to enhance our controls. Wine will make itself from grapes, but *good* wine is made through a lot of careful guidance and attention to hygiene." *RPH*

Managing partner Chuck Carpy is the driving force behind the Freemark partnership. "Twenty years ago, people came knocking at your door if you had wine to sell," notes Carpy. "Now you have to get out in the market and sell it. The competition is fierce for shelf space, or a place on a restaurant list."

FROG'S LEAP WINERY

The name on the label is Frog's Leap, a take-off on the famous Stag's Leap Wine Cellars. The cork is branded with the word "ribbit." And the motto of the winery is, "Time's fun when you're having flies."

Yet the winery is anything but a joke. In fact, it's one of the most professionally run wineries in the Napa Valley, making a number of exceptional wines without seeking tuxedo service and neon lights for its image. The brand is a joint venture equally owned by John and Julie Williams and Larry Turley. John tells the story of the winery's founding in a most engaging manner:

"I had grown up on a New York dairy farm, and I was at Cornell University studying agriculture," recounts John. "When I was a sophomore I ran out of money, so I applied for a work-study program, where you can earn a little money while you study, and my assignment was to the Taylor Wine Co. in Hammondsport, N.Y. Well, I had never drunk any wine in my life, so I got a

half gallon of Lake Country Pink and that was my introduction to wine.

"But the day I walked through the front door of the Taylor winery, I knew this was it. I got this overwhelming feeling that everything was right. Wine combined my interest in agriculture, tradition, and history — everything about it appealed to me."

Williams graduated from Cornell with a degree in a revised enology/agriculture program, and decided to spend his spring break looking at the wine industry in the Napa Valley.

"I came out on one of those $69 Ameripasses on Greyhound — took five days. I was going to camp out at the [Bothe] state park, but the park was full. Then I saw this abandoned farmhouse across the way, so I pitched my tent over there.

"The next day at seven a.m., this motorcycle roars up, a tire pokes through my tent flap, and this six-foot six-inch guy is standing there and he says, 'What the hell you doing on my property?'

When Frog's Leap started in the early 1980s, fermentation was conducted elsewhere and aging was done indoors at Frog's Leap. In 1985, when the winery was expanded, refrigerated stainless-steel fermentation and blending tanks were added outside, and all production moved here.

There's no million-dollar architecture here at Frog's Leap, a former frog farm. Here, in a utilitarian winery that once was a livery stable, John Williams uses brilliant winemaking to create some of the valley's best wines.

That was Larry. He was a doctor in San Francisco and he had just bought the old house a week before. Well, one thing led to another and we became friends, and he invited me to come back and help him renovate the house." While fixing up the old house, they learned from an old ledger that it had once been a frog farm.

Williams was accepted in the U.C. Davis enology program (one of the top three wine schools in the world) and then got a cellar job at Stag's Leap Wine Cellars. In 1977, he was given some Chardonnay grapes off two vines at Stag's Leap, and he and Turley made five gallons of wine in glass jugs. "We got into it one night before it was even finished fermenting and we came up with our name and motto."

After U.C. Davis, Williams accepted a position as winemaker in New York. Then three years later he moved back west to become winemaker at Spring Mountain Vineyards.

"Meanwhile, Larry kept bugging me to make more home-made wine, and we made a little in 1980. In 1981 he wanted to make even more. I said, 'Larry, go get a license.' Well, he did and then he said, 'You're going to be a 50-50 partner.'

"Come that fall, we needed money to get this thing started, so we both sold our motorcycles and each put $5,000 into it. We crushed the grapes at Spring Mountain, and made 700 cases

of wine. In 1982 we made 1,800 cases, and then 2,600 cases in 1983. By 1985 we were making close to 6,000 cases and the wine would sell in about three weeks. Up to this point I had kind of thought of it as a joke label, with a short life. I had never really thought about it one way or the other as a commercial winery."

By 1988 Williams had left Spring Mountain and Frog's Leap had become a nationwide success. The humorous label grabbed people's attention and the wines were so good people became loyal consumers.

If another brand is needed, Larry and John have a name ready: Clos de Toad. *DB*

Situated three miles north of St. Helena, Frog's Leap has growing on its ranch some of the densest red wine grapes in the valley. Williams styles his wines so they show their fruit and avoid coarseness.

GIRARD WINERY

Girard Winery made a splash in the early 1980s with a string of excellent white wines, followed by success later in the decade with its red wines. The winery won a string of medals at major wine competitions, and displays them in its Silverado Trail tasting room.

By the early 1980s, most of the Napa Valley that could be planted already was; more than 31,000 acres were covered with vines. The cost of planting any more of the remaining, rugged non-residential land was prohibitive.

But in 1982 Steve Girard, with the help of vineyard specialist Tony Mitchell, located a parcel of land that was really untamed, a slice of earth up a draw in the hills west of Yountville. It was for sale so cheaply that he couldn't say "no."

Steve, a former contract negotiator for a San Diego high-tech firm who decided to leave the big city for the agricultural life, was by then a partner in the Girard Winery on the Silverado Trail in Oakville. His winery had already had success with Chardonnay, Sauvignon Blanc, and a stylish, dry Chenin Blanc.

"When I visited it, it was summer and everything was brown, but down at the bottom I saw that ferns were growing everywhere," says Steve. "It was so green, so I went back home and looked in the dictionary under 'green' and I found 'viridian.'"

Girard Winery was founded in the 1970s by Girard's father, Stephen Sr., then chairman of Kaiser Steel, who bought 60 acres of land in the Napa Valley. The first grapes off the 45-acre vineyard were sold and showed up in the wines of Robert Mondavi.

The family decided to enter the winemaking business in 1980, and built a winery right on the Silverado Trail in an oak grove, sitting in the middle of the vineyards. The giant oak tree that sits in the courtyard of the winery gave rise to the use of an oak leaf cluster on the winery's label.

The first wines, made by winemaker Fred Payne from unirrigated vines in rocky, well-drained soil, gave deep flavors. By 1984, Girard was gaining headlines for Payne's second wines, a 1981 Cabernet and a 1981 Chardonnay. (When Fred Payne left in 1988 for Domaine Michel in Sonoma, Steve hired Grgich Hills assistant Mark Smith to make the wines.)

Steve Jr. and his wife, Carol, moved to the valley, permanently leaving their San Diego home, and Steve immediately went on the road to market Girard wines. With California wineries growing rapidly in number, he sensed that competition for shelf space in California would be precious. So he sought out-of-state markets and today the winery sells more than 60 per cent of its almost 20,000-case production outside the state.

The Viridian property (440 acres after the subsequent purchase of adjacent land), now has 40 acres planted. However, no vineyard designation is planned for this amazingly lush property. "I don't want to overcomplicate wine, so we'll just make our Napa Valley and Reserve wines," he says. "But after the 1989 harvest, the Viridian Cabernet looked so good, we feel it will be our Reserve wine." *DB*

Girard knew that if a swath could be cut through trees and dead brush removed, he could create a small but perfect vineyard on the 280-acre untamed parcel. Its location was critical: right behind the famed Napanook vineyard, in a hidden canyon. Napanook was the vineyard that the late John Daniel of Inglenook prized as one of the finest in the valley and the vineyard that today is the heart of Dominus.

Steve and Carol Girard lived in San Diego, where he was a successful negotiator for a high-technology firm. When the Girard Winery was founded, the Girards moved north and began to market wines of high quality.

Local artists have immortalized the work of the Napa Valley grape pickers in a charming bas-relief in stone on a wall of the Girard Winery, which was founded with money made from steel.

GRGICH HILLS CELLAR

In the ever-widening world of wine, it's usually best to shy away from "best" statements. But we can talk about a winemaker who puts science and intuition together in such a way as to create wines that soar and sing, wines that stand, on merit, on an equal footing with whatever muzzy definition we might agree upon as "Among World's Best."

His name is Miljenko "Mike" Grgich. An elfin man, with the most expressive eyebrows in town, he shaped the Chardonnay (for Chateau Montelena) that stunned the French at Paris in 1976. A few years later he fashioned another Chardonnay, this at Grgich Hills Cellar.

This one swept Craig Goldwyn's "Chardonnay Shootout" at Chicago in 1980, besting 220 other Chardonnays from all over the world.

The skills, the science, and the intuition come from time, place, and experience. Grgich was born 67 years ago into an 11-kid Croatian winegrowing family. He crushed his first grape at age two. Or three. He attended Zagreb University, learning, as he puts it, to become a "wine doctor." Later, pressed by politics, he left the turmoil of Yugoslavia for the vinelands of California.

"Even at that time, the Napa Valley was already known all around the world for its

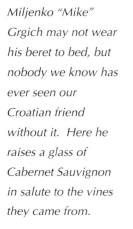

Miljenko "Mike" Grgich may not wear his beret to bed, but nobody we know has ever seen our Croatian friend without it. Here he raises a glass of Cabernet Sauvignon in salute to the vines they came from.

fine, premium wines," remembers Grgich. "My first job was working for Lee Stewart at the old Souverain Cellars [now Burgess]. Lee gave me the indelible impression that devotion and love for wine must exist in order to create fine wines."

Mike spent a short time at The Christian Brothers before joining Andre Tchelistcheff at Beaulieu as a wine chemist. "Andre had brought the French influence to the Napa Valley. He put the accent on the *art* of winemaking. He knew that science wasn't everything." After nine years with Andre, Grgich glided on down the road to Oakville in 1968 to join a

Mike Grgich toiled for years in other cellars — including Robert Mondavi, the original Souverain, and Chateau Montelena — before finally being able to put together his own operation, in partnership with former coffee mogul Austin Hills.

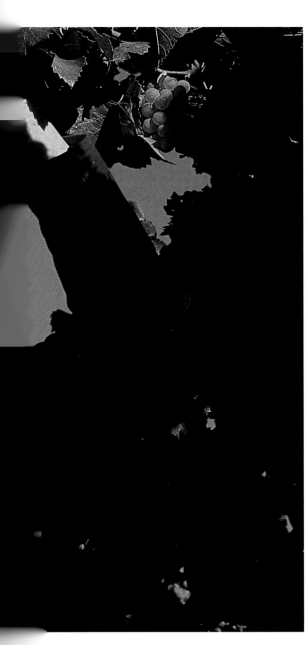

new winery started by an energetic young renegade — Robert Mondavi.

"Where Beaulieu had art, Robert Mondavi was a winery of action!" enthuses Grgich. "Robert is a dynamo, and his winery was busy with so many experiments. There was no better place in America that a young person could learn to make wine. Robert started to import French oak. It was the biggest achievement, to show the importance of different oaks to the maturity and flavor of wine."

With experience, Grgich began to see the value of instinct in winemaking. "For a long time, I was so impressed with our industry's technological achievements," he says soberly. "Then, one day at Mondavi, I tasted a 1967 Zinfandel made by an old Italian. It was a wonderful wine, with wonderful flavors. Yet here was a guy who had no lab, no centrifuge, no nothing! I couldn't believe it. But I began to realize that the less changed a wine is, the better chance it has of becoming a wine that people will like.

"Today, I see myself as a 'wine sitter' rather than as a 'wine doctor.' You have to live with your wines, and learn by observation, by being on the spot. Wines are made in the cellar, and not in the lab. And, if you start them out healthy, they will finish healthy." Indeed, each of his wines has an identity as strong and as individual as their creator. *RPH*

The process of winegrowing begins with the grapes and ends with the glass. Grgich Hills' primary wine varietals are Chardonnay (on the stem) and Cabernet Sauvignon (in the glass).

GROTH VINEYARDS & WINERY

Being the chief financial officer for Atari, the computer company, Dennis Groth was well aware of how much money it takes to establish a winery. He knew how to analyze a spreadsheet. It showed Groth that to start a winery that would make 30,000 cases of wine (his target) and to make that wine entirely from estate-grown grapes (his target), you needed millions of dollars that you didn't need for anything else for seven consecutive years.

Dennis and Judy Groth didn't have a few spare millions, and yet they delved into this business — eyes wide open — in 1981, when they bought a 121-acre vineyard in Oakville, midway between the Silverado Trail and Highway 29. The vineyard had producing vines of Cabernet Sauvignon. That same year they bought 43 acres planted to Sauvignon Blanc and Merlot south of Yountville.

Dennis wasn't trying to cheat the spreadsheet. But he figured that the overall rewards of owning a winery in the 1980s could prove to be great if one used a cautious and sane approach to fiscal management. Besides, he had gotten a number of bonuses at Atari, which had to be re-invested.

In the early years, Groth financed his "winery" by selling his Cabernet to other wineries. But to make the winery pay, not only did you need top-quality grapes, you needed a top winemaker. So he hired Nils Venge as winemaker and general manager.

From the start, Groth made top-quality wine, despite the fact that the spreadsheet said you couldn't have a winery in which to make the wine for the first four years. This put the winemaker to the ultimate test: Venge had to find places to make the wine and store the barrels until about 1985, when the spreadsheet said it was feasible to have a winery building.

"The first year, 1982, I made the wine at Bouchaine," recounts Venge. The first harvest

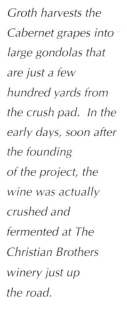

Groth harvests the Cabernet grapes into large gondolas that are just a few hundred yards from the crush pad. In the early days, soon after the founding of the project, the wine was actually crushed and fermented at The Christian Brothers winery just up the road.

Looking out the back door of Groth, one sees first a lovely patio for hospitality functions. Beyond are the estate vineyards. The winery is in the middle of a 40-acre Chardonnay vineyard, with Cabernet vines set back from the building.

produced 7,000 cases of wine. Groth saved money by figuring that he didn't have to buy barrels for the wine until fermentation was completed, in December.

"Then we found we could rent Hopper Creek winery, so we took over the whole facility and brought the barrels in there." That first red wine, the 1982 Cabernet Sauvignon, won many awards and was highly regarded in the marketplace. The winery's rich and herbal Sauvignon Blanc also had wide acceptance.

But that was just the beginning of the traveling road show Groth would put on over the next five years.

In 1983 Groth installed a crush pad for the winery at Oakville, "so I could start making the Cabernet here, but we continued making wine at Bouchaine, and we bottled the wine at Monticello." Then, Groth and the William Hill winery joined forces to store their wine barrels together.

Finally in 1990, the winery at Groth was finished and all operations — fermentation, barrel aging, and bottling — were moved here. Groth is on target for meeting his goals. Today almost all the fruit used in Groth wines is estate-grown, and in 1990 the winery hit a peak of 40,000 cases. It intends to grow no larger. *DB*

The Groth Winery's architectural style, called California Mission by the designer, Napa architect Robert Gianelli, features a bell tower to the left of the entrance and a large courtyard facing the parking area. The building encompasses nearly 20,000 square feet.

HEITZ WINE CELLARS

A family affair, Heitz Wine Cellars is run by all members of the immediate family: founders Joe and Alice; son David (left), the winemaker; son Rollie, the chief financial officer; and daughter Kathleen, director of marketing. David was elected to the St. Helena City Council in 1990.

Heitz Wine Cellars makes a wide line of wines, much of it from its own vineyards, but its worldwide reputation is almost entirely from a single wine that comes from a plot of ground the winery doesn't own. In fact, so famous is Joe Heitz's Martha's Vineyard Cabernet Sauvignon that occasionally it is spoken about without the name of Heitz even being mentioned.

Yet Joe Heitz, a Napa Valley original, is one of the most respected winemakers in California history. Heitz and his wife, Alice, were true pioneers in the making of superior-quality California wine after they founded this small winery in 1961. And they have gone on to establish Heitz Wine Cellars as an innovator.

Heitz came to California just before the end of World War II, through the Air Force, and went

on to earn a master's degree at U.C. Davis in enology. After working for eight years at Beaulieu under Andre Tchelistcheff, Heitz taught viticulture and enology at Fresno State College before deciding to make wine in the Napa Valley.

In 1961 he acquired a small winery that had an attached vineyard with eight acres of Grignolino, a lightly regarded Italian variety. Heitz began making and selling wine, includ-

ing Grignolino, but two of his early successes were actually with wine he bought from others, doing the final blending, fining, filtering, and bottling himself. A magnificent 1962 Pinot Noir gave Heitz his first headlines.

Another wine he aged and blended and then became famous for was his Chablis — always a great bargain as an everyday house white wine. Heitz also produced a marvelous Chardonnay from a small vineyard owned by Zinfandel Associates.

By the mid-1960s, Heitz had a wine he would build his reputation on. It was his "classic" Cabernet Sauvignon from the Martha's Vineyard, then a small parcel of land that had been planted in 1961 by Dr. Bernard Rhodes and his wife, Belle. In 1963, the 12-acre vineyard, not yet bearing fruit, was sold to Tom and Martha May and renamed.

The Martha's Vineyard sits in the middle of the famed Oakville area of the Napa Valley, far west of most of the others there, nestled against the foothills and looking east. The vineyard is in the middle of a mile-square block that gives rise to three of the area's greatest Cabernets — Heitz's, Beaulieu's BV Private Reserve, and Mondavi's Reserve.

The Martha's Vineyard property is unique, however, in that the daily sun exposure is not as long as at some of its neighbors. Being so close to the hills, the sun sets on these vines earlier in the day, lengthening the growing season. This means that harvesting is occasionally delayed later than some others, giving more time on the vine for grape maturity.

The fame of the Martha's Vineyard wines has sparked an international quest by wine collectors for it, and this has driven the price well up into the stratosphere, making it one of the most expensive in California. The Martha's Vineyard wines are big, chewy, and very complex every year upon release, but not so astringent that they can't be enjoyed early in their life, which is one reason they tend to be so appreciated. You don't have to wait half your lifetime to drink them.

The old stone winery at Heitz was originally built by the Anton Rossini family in 1898. It is located on Taplin Road east of the Silverado Trail. The family also operates a separate tasting room located on Highway 29.

With this first vineyard-designated Cabernet in the Napa Valley, Heitz established a trend for naming a particularly great plot of ground on the label and sticking with the same fruit every year. It's a concept parallel to the system in France where wine from a particular estate can come only from grapes growing on contiguous land. It's easier to track a wine this way, to see the way nature changes things and makes the wines stronger in one element some years, stronger in another element other years.

In 1976, Heitz added another Napa Valley vineyard to his stable of vineyard-designates. It was the Bella Oaks Vineyard, the second top vineyard planted by Belle and Barney Rhodes,

noted gourmets who since had become shareholders in the Heitz winery. (Belle is an exceptional cook and educator.) The Bella Oaks wines began a decade after the first Martha's Vineyard wines, so have less of a track record, but they show a trace more grace when they are young. However, they can also be a tad more erratic. When the Bella Oaks and Martha's Vineyard wines were tasted head-to-head in a number of vintages, such as 1980, 1981, and 1985, the Bella Oaks wines were the veritable equal of the Martha's wines, style differences notwithstanding.

One of the last of the Zinfandel Associates Chardonnays Heitz made — the 1973 Lot Z-32

Inside the Heitz barrel-aging cellar is a small office, laboratory, and tasting room that sits, glass enclosed, above the casks. Here Joe and the family, Belle and Barney Rhodes (owners of the Bella Oaks Vineyard), and Tom and Martha May (owners of the Martha's Vineyard) evaluate the new releases each year.

— remains fixed in connoisseurs' memories as a monumental achievement. Soon after that, the Zinfandel Associates vineyard off Zinfandel Lane was struck by Pierce's disease, forcing the removal of the vines and replanting. Heitz then searched for a Chardonnay style that suited him, finally settling on one reminiscent of French Chablis, relatively steely but with a strong, earthy backbone. It was a style the public was unused to, preferring instead the flabbier, more oaky style of wine.

Joe Heitz's unsung star in his firmament is his old faithful Grignolino, which he makes into a red wine as well as a rosé. The two wines are sublime statements about (a) Heitz's

stubbornness and (b) the greatness of the wine. Despite the fact that both wines are hard to sell, Heitz doggedly continues to make them, much to the pleasure of people who understand them. They are excellent as picnic wine or to match with a simple plate of pasta. So good is this wine that Angelo Gaja, the dynamic producer of the most expensive Barbaresco made, imports the Heitz Grignolino to Italy, and says he wished Italy could make a wine this good with its Grignolino grapes.

Joe and Alice are not the sole operators of the Heitz winery. Their three children are involved in the project, too. Kathleen Heitz runs the sales department, Rollie Heitz handles vineyard development, and David Heitz — appointed to the St. Helena City Council in 1990 — is now winemaker. In the late 1980s, Heitz acquired a large parcel of prime Napa Valley vineyard land that was intended to diversify the Heitz line and provide for more hands-on control of the grape growing.

Brusque and direct, Joe Heitz never balks at stating his mind, and has gained a reputation for being rude. But Joe says it's better to be direct with people and let them know where you stand so a discussion can ensue that will enlighten, instead of everyone getting quietly bitter. *DB*

Crusty Joe Heitz has produced great red wine since the early 1960s, but his Cabernet Sauvignons from Martha's Vineyard and from the Bella Oaks Vineyard nearby are among the deepest, most complex wines made in the valley, and sell rapidly despite high prices.

The wooden sign hanging in front of the Heitz tasting room comes from a drawing done by David when he was nine — a stick-man standing near barrels and holding up a glass. Heitz took the drawing to commercial artist Mallette Dean who rendered the picture, and the result has been around unchanged for decades.

THE HESS COLLECTION WINERY

Every aspect of The Hess Collection — from wine to label, from art collection to wine cellar — is imbued with an impeccable sense of taste and style. Here, the barrel cellar is bathed deliciously in low light.

It's really fun to watch somebody do something right, putting together a project that incorporates creative design and function, long-range planning and thinking, and ecologically sound foundations. Donald and Joanna Hess are doing it right in the hills of Mount Veeder. Housed in the old Gier Winery (once operated by The Christian Brothers), halfway up Redwood Road west of Napa, The Hess Collection refers both to wines and art.

"It was Joanna who came up with the term 'collection' for our label," points out Hess, whose successful Swiss mineral water, Valser St. Petersquelle, supports his $26-millon wine venture.

"We had to decide whether to build a museum in Europe or bring Donald's extensive modern art collection here to America," explains Boston-born Joanna. "Bern, where we live in Switzerland, is a conservative society. One does not show off.

"When Christian Brothers offered this huge winery, we wondered what we were going to do with all the space. In Switzerland, everything is too small. This was the first time we had to deal with something that was too big." They use the upper levels of the three-story, stone winery, built by Oakland businessman Theodore Gier in 1903, to house Hess's vibrant collection of modern art.

"I collect few artists, perhaps two dozen, but I like to collect in depth," notes Hess. "Where most galleries only have space for one or two works of any given artist, here I can show the range of an artist's works over decades.

"Art is a love, a passion, and I need to know the person behind the art for as much as ten years before I will collect their work. My father collected Persian rugs, and he always advised me to collect something sensible — meaning, not art! I knew I was hooked when I became captivated by an Alfred Jensen work of little squares. I couldn't sleep and kept pestering its owner until he finally sold it to me."

Great wines offer art in a different format, changing water and sunshine into wine. Hess first began to consider making wine in the Napa Valley after a 1978 trip scouting mineral water spring sites. "At a restaurant I was poured a glass of Chateau Montelena Chardonnay and a glass of 1970 Beaulieu Georges de Latour Cabernet," he recalls. "These were absolutely stunning wines. I was expecting something rather like Algerian wines. Instead, I was blown away."

Hess had inherited a small wine estate when his father died, but sold it because "the wines were poor and the roof leaked." But he later felt guilty about not heeding his father's deathless admonition to "never sell land." After tasting that pair of great California wines, Hess decided to expiate his guilt by founding a Napa Valley wine estate.

"Wine is especially the sort of business that you have to look at in terms of the long run. If you have to report profits every three or four months, you can't justify winemaking. Europeans know that any lasting business takes ten or 15 years to work. We only begin to worry when a business doesn't work after the first generation. I remember reading that it took Chateau Mouton 75 years to become profitable. It'll take us more than a dozen years. But we expected that from the beginning." *RP*

Donald Hess, the art collector, stands before one of his more famous possessions, *Johanna II*, by Swiss artist Franz Gertsch. Hess's more than 100 paintings and sculptures include works by Francis Bacon, Robert Motherwell, Georg Baselitz, Frank Stella, and Magdelena Abakanowicz.

Hess sees the art collection as his "gift to the public." Admission is free. This Underwood typewriter, burning with a gas flame, is the work of Argentine artist Leopoldo Maler. The piece was done in homage to a newspaperman executed by an Argentine death squad.

WILLIAM HILL WINERY

Bill Hill always figured you needed great vineyards to make great wine, so in 1972 he began to look for properties that he could develop to produce great fruit. Steep slopes posed no threat; no matter how hard they were to farm, they made great wine, he felt.

His first discovery was high above Calistoga on Diamond Mountain, a steep, rocky parcel of land that had the well-drained soils that deprive vines of water and lead to intense flavor. It also was cooler than Calistoga, just below. The property had been ignored by some because they felt Calistoga was too warm to grow great Cabernet, and because it couldn't be planted without terraces being cut into the pitched landscape, reducing yield to a couple of tons per acre at most.

Hill, however, saw that the cooling breezes from the Sonoma side of the Mayacamas mountains would lengthen the Cabernet growing season and allow perfect maturity. He knew terracing was feasible. Yield would be small, but flavors intense.

Hill eventually sold the Diamond Mountain property to Sterling Vineyards and began developing other vineyards.

"To understand this odyssey we've been

William Hill sold his winery and a number of related vineyard properties to a British-based international conglomerate in 1990, but he retained a group of vineyards and continued to look for further investments throughout California and in the Pacific Northwest.

on, you have to realize we want to make only a few wines from the noble varieties, and make them the best way we know how, with the hope that we'll be seen as among the best producers in the world," says Hill. "And the most important principal you have to master to make great wine is to realize that the vineyard makes the wine."

Yet Hill admits that he entered the California wine business "with a blank page of knowledge." He learned quickly that funds can be dissipated quickly. "The problem with this business is that the capital and the time to do something like this can be measured in

Rolling hillside vineyards, such as this one on the eastern slopes of the Napa Valley, or steeply tilted vineyards, were Hill's greatest development projects. Hill is now developing vineyard properties in areas as far away as Oregon.

decades unless there is some help, and this was what we needed to proceed."

Hill hit on the idea of limited partnerships, and created nearly two dozen of them to finance various vineyard projects. His properties were sound investments, he points out, and "all other things being equal, investors would like to invest in something romantic, like vineyards and wine."

Hill started his winery in 1974 to produce Chardonnay and Cabernet Sauvignon. In an audacious move, Hill promoted the wines by having expert tasters evaluate them blind against some of the top wines in the world, including First Growth Bordeaux.

Over the years Hill continued buying and planting vineyards, and then selling them to other wineries.

Then in 1990 Hill changed the structure of his firm, selling the Napa operation and much of the vineyard land, and using the funds to develop a portfolio of small wine estates aimed at making great wine from different regions. Hill arranged the deal with Allied Lyons, a British company. The deal was estimated to be worth $72 million.

In 1991, Hill introduced a new label — Van Duzer — which consists of Pinot Noir, Chardonnay, and Reisling made from Oregon grapes. The project was based in Oregon's Eola Hills. *DB*

William Hill specialized in Chardonnay and Cabernet Sauvignon at his Napa Valley winery, but it was the latter variety, most notably a Reserve-designated wine, that gave him the most international recognition.

111

LOUIS HONIG CELLARS

When you're a Napa Valley grape grower whose fruit doesn't sell, or sells for too low a price, one solution is to start making wine yourself. This is one reason the Honig winery exists today.

The venture started in 1962, when Louis Honig, a San Francisco advertising executive, acquired 68 acres of land (part of the original Young Land Grant) from the family of Charles Wagner, owner of Caymus Vineyards. Some 55 acres were planted to Sauvignon Blanc, Cabernet Sauvignon, and Chardonnay. Honig sold grapes to wineries until he died in 1976. His three children,

William, Susan, and Ann, then ran it as absentee owners.

Late in the 1970s, vineyard manager Rick Tracy saw that the ranch wasn't producing high profits. While demand was high for the vineyard's Chardonnay and Cabernet grapes, Sauvignon Blanc wasn't selling as quickly or for as much as it could. Tracy believed in the quality of the grapes and longed to make wine from them. Eventually the Honigs agreed. It was logical that the family make Sauvignon Blanc.

"Also, we started with Sauvignon Blanc because there were a lot of wineries out

The Honig winery, located in the middle of the Napa Valley but off the main roads, has a home that represents, to the Honig family, a respite from the pressures of big-city life. The swimming pool is especially welcome on those brutally hot summer days after long hours in the winery, crushing grapes.

there, and to differentiate ourselves we had to have a specialty," says Michael Honig, William's son. "We felt no one was doing Sauvignon Blanc exclusively; we needed a niche, and that was our niche."

Two hundred cases of 1980-vintage Sauvignon Blanc were released under the HNW name, which combined the last initials of the three partners — (William) Honig, (Ann) Nadel, and (Sue) Weinstein. The label, a modern art design, caught the public eye only as a curiosity. But the wines were fascinating: fairly herbaceous, yet well-liked by consumers who sought a more grassy style of wine.

In the midst of the Honig vineyards, which were planted not far from the Napa River, sits a solitary palm tree — rare in the Napa Valley — that the family was reluctant to move.

Nadel sold her interest in the ranch to her siblings in 1982. The winery name was changed to Louis Honig, and a new, simpler label was designed. Sauvignon Blanc remained their sole wine.

William Honig and his brother-in-law, Daniel Weinstein, were principals in the brand. Honig soon rose to headline status in his "other" career, education, when in 1982 he was elected California's superintendent of public instruction. Yet his name was never attached with any fanfare to the winery.

Rick Tracy left in 1986, replaced by winemaker James Hall. The label was changed again, the family dropping "Louis" from the brand name. And with Hall actively pushing, the owners added Cabernet Sauvignon and Chardonnay to the Sauvignon Blanc.

Hall established a house style for the Cabernet and Chardonnay that accented the richness and deep complexity of the fruit. The new wines were well-received from the start.

In the mid-1980s, Michael Honig and his wife, Elaine, joined the winery to coordinate national sales. With national distribution, and a reputation strengthened after the introduction of the new wines, Honig was producing over 10,000 cases by the end of the '80s. *DB*

After the Honig winery specialized in Sauvignon Blanc for its first wines, winemaker James Hall delved deeply in the late 1980s, and experimented early on with a number of styles and blending techniques.

INGLENOOK NAPA VALLEY

It was just about the time that Thomas Alva Edison finally came up with the first incandescent light bulb at his Menlo Park laboratory. Across the continent, a 35-year-old Finnish sea captain was committing himself to the landlocked existence of a winegrower.

In January of 1979 Inglenook Vineyards celebrated a century of Captain Niebaum's legacy with a grand dinner in the Garden Court of San Francisco's Sheraton-Palace Hotel. The winery introduced its Centennial wine, the Estate Bottled 1974 Napa Valley Cask Cabernet Sauvignon, a huge, powerful wine that might well make the next centennial.

Inglenook's creator was the meticulous Gustave Ferdinand Niebaum. Born in Russian Helsinki in 1842, Niebaum took to the sea as a teen. He had his own command at 21 and, before Lee's surrender at Appomattox, sailed to Russian America — Alaska.

Niebaum saw wonder and opportunity in the virgin territory. He bartered for furs and, when the U.S. acquired Alaska in 1867, he took a $600,000 shipload of furs to San Francisco. He helped form the Alaska Commercial Company, which specialized in the fur trade. In 20 years the company paid more in taxes than the U.S. had paid for "Seward's Folly."

The original cellars of Inglenook are among the most handsome in the world. The stone and wood structure was begun in the spring of 1886 by Hamden W. McIntyre, whom The San Francisco Examiner described as "uncommonly tall" and "a master of civil and mechanical engineering." See for yourself.

After more than a decade of fur trading, Niebaum was ready to retire. It had been his ambition to build a ship to his own exacting specifications and sail the seas at his whim and leisure. There was but one problem: Mrs. Niebaum had not his love for salt air.

The Captain had made several trips to Europe while in the fur business, there acquiring a deep appreciation for the culture of the vine. When his chief aim was forestalled, he channeled his energy and fastidious nature into winegrowing. He carefully selected a 1,000-acre tract that drifted west from Rutherford up the slopes of Mount St. John. This he pur-

Backlit by a leaded-glass window in Captain Niebaum's private tasting room — preserved to the right of the main entryway — is a bottle of Inglenook's Gravion, a blend of Sauvignon Blanc and Semillon that brings together the steely spine of the former and the fleshy mouth-feel of the latter.

chased in 1879 from W. C. Watson, who had given it the name Inglenook (a Scottish term for a cozy fireside corner).

Niebaum took his new task seriously. He read voraciously and had a standing order with a German bookseller to send him every publication on viticulture and enology printed in English, French, Italian, German, or Latin. Niebaum spoke five languages, read several others, and accumulated a library of more than 600 volumes on winegrowing.

Niebaum's monumental care showed in the building he erected and the wines he fashioned therein. The Gothic stone and iron structure, started in 1886, is a model of style and function. The winery was set into the hillside, its three levels providing the necessary gravity-flow pattern for grapes being transformed into wines, which rested finally in German, white oak ovals on the pebbled ground floor.

The Captain was a forceful man who stood six foot two. He wore a flowing beard and was fond of surprise inspection tours, which he conducted wearing white gloves. Since the crushers, presses, tanks, and floors were to be scrubbed with soda and steamed every night, Niebaum expected to have clean gloves at the end of his tours.

He also took great pains to protect his reputation, placing his seal and a wire closure on

The old cellar at Inglenook is one of the most attractive in the Napa Valley. In the main cellar, graveled walkways take you through row upon row of old oak ovals, built by coopers in the last century, and ancient leaded glass adds a festive, artistic touch.

bottled wines in order to prevent counterfeiting. Niebaum had a great sense of humor, too, often telling this anecdote about himself:

Mistaken for a ranch hand by the commandant of the nearby Veterans' Home, Niebaum gave the man a complete tour of the winery, explaining how "the boss" had changed the course of a creek — which had formerly meandered aimlessly across the fields, taking up a great amount of land — confining it to a gently curving route enclosed between concrete and masonry walls. After returning to their point of departure, the commandant gave Niebaum a dollar and asked as an afterthought, "By the way, who's the ass that is doing all this?" Replied the Captain calmly, "A foreigner by the name of Niebaum."

When Niebaum died in 1908, his widow Suzanne entrusted the winery's operations to her niece's husband, John Daniel Sr. Closed at Prohibition, Inglenook reopened at Repeal under the guidance of Carl Bundschu. Mrs.

Niebaum died in 1936, the winery going to John Daniel Jr. and his sister. Wine historian Leon Adams says that John Daniel upheld the Captain's motto of "quality and not quantity" to the point of rarely, except during the war years, turning a profit. From 1935 to 1963 Inglenook wines were skillfully rendered by winemaker George Deuer who, along with Andre Tchelistcheff (across the highway at Beaulieu), defined Rutherford Cabernet Sauvignon for better than a generation.

In 1964 Daniel sold Inglenook to Allied Grape Growers, which, as United Vintners, later became part of Heublein. There are several classes of Inglenook wines today, from top-of-the-line Reunion Cask Cabernet and Estate Bottled wines, produced solely from Napa Valley grapes, to the Navalle wines, which bear a California appellation.

Inglenook's present winemaker, John Richburg, is one serious wine guy. Born in Napa, he worked his first grape harvest at age eight,

married into an old wine family (wife Cheryl is Carlo Forni's niece), farms a small vineyard in the Carneros district, and left the valley only to add to his vinous education.

"When I came to Inglenook in 1972, Heublein was just starting to put some serious money into the winery," recalls Richburg from behind his neatly trimmed beard. "We were able to build a new barrel house and stock it with new, small oak, and also to update our equipment. At the same time, we began to replant some of the historic vineyards."

Perhaps Richburg's most important contribution during his tenure has been the introduction of Gravion — a Bordeaux-type blend of Sauvignon Blanc and Semillon that borrows from the Bordeaux regional name Graves for its new name. "We had been adding increasing amounts of Semillon to our varietal Sauvignon Blanc since 1983," he observes, "and began to feel handcuffed by the 25-percent maximum to retain the varietal designation of Sauvignon Blanc."

So, Richburg and his staff managed to convince the marketing people that a better, more interesting wine — worthy of its own name — could be made by bypassing the 25-percent rule and allowing complete leeway in blending. Allowing, in essence, the wine to determine its own best balance. Novel notion. *RPH*

This bottle of 1906 Inglenook Zinfandel is testimony to the historic prominence of the Napa Valley. Founder Gustave Niebaum was one of the first in the country to bottle wine under his own label, to insure the integrity of his personal reputation.

One of the most intriguing means of viewing Napa Valley vinelands is by balloon, several of which take off from Yountville each morning. The curious thing about sound is that it travels directly upward, so from a balloon hanging in the sky at 500 feet one can hear normal conversations on the ground as clearly as if you were standing beside the conversants.

ROBERT KEENAN WINERY

In the fall of 1974, Robert Keenan purchased 175 acres along the high, heavily forested, northeast slopes of Spring Mountain that had once been a home to grapevines, planted by Peter Conradi shortly after he purchased the land in 1891. Pine and madrona had since reclaimed the land, but the empty stone shell of the winery notched into the hillside in 1904 by Philip Conradi still stood.

There was much work to be done. The bowl below the winery was cleared and Chardonnay and Cabernet Sauvignon vines began life anew. In 1977, the sturdy, native stone structure was transformed into a spa-cious, modern winery. A solid fir gantry in the center of the building holds French oak barrels and supports a sweeping loft-deck tasting room that is connected to the office and lab on the second level. More oak barrels and stain-less-steel fermenters line the inside walls on the ground level, which overlooks pond, vine-yard, and forest below.

The same year, 51 tons — mostly Char-donnay — were crushed under the direction of winemaker Joe Cafaro. A quiet fellow who has since left to found his own winery, Cafaro tends to hide behind his tinted, horn-rimmed glasses. He also likes sparring with the wind,

The warm wood of this loft reception area, at the apex of Keenan's turn-of-the-century cellar, makes for a cozy, comfortable tasting area. The stone structure was first built in 1904, and completely renovated in 1977.

formerly in airplanes, more recently as captain of small sailboats.

Just as he works with the wind as a sailor, Cafaro likes to work with nature as a wine-maker. "I want to get the best possible grapes and do as little as possible to spoil what nature has produced," he has always said. "In practice, this principle is a bit difficult to follow. Balances must be struck between modern technology and traditional practices. Modern technology can, at times, lead to a revolving door, producing more problems that require more technology. On the other hand, traditional winemaking has pretty much let nature

A rubber bung sits atop an oak barrel so that more wine can be added, replacing that lost to evaporation. Barrels have to be topped at least once a month during the cold months, more often in spring and summer.

go its merry way. I prefer to assist nature at the proper time, both in the winery and in the vineyard."

Owner Bob Keenan, who flew dauntless dive-bombers in the Navy at the end of World War II, had been in the insurance business in San Francisco during the more than 30 years since his graduation from Stanford University. Now retired to the winery, he still dabbles in real estate, fly-fishes on the Feather River, and plays a mean game of tennis.

"I was the number-one player at Stanford one year," he says, pausing for the punch line. "There were only two of us." Still, he has good ground strokes, volleys well, and can run almost anything down in the back court. "Used to run a lot," he says, by way of explanation.

Though Keenan started out to focus on Cabernet and Chardonnay, Merlot has come to nearly define the winery almost by accident. "We had made a little Merlot from Rene di Rosa's famed Winery Lake Vineyards [today owned by Seagram/Sterling] in '78 and '79," recalls Bob. "We hadn't planned on making any beyond that, but then the medals started pouring in. The wines kept getting high ratings and winning competitions. So I went back to him, kind of sheepishly, and asked him if he'd take me back, if he'd sell us some Merlot again. Rene's a great friend, and he said, 'Yeh, okay.'" *RPH*

Tiny berries of Cabernet Sauvignon are pushed by a stainless-steel screw toward the crusher-stemmer, which knocks the berries off the stems and through a perforated screen toward a must line that will pump berries and juice into a fermentation tank. The stems will be returned to the vineyard and disked into the ground for nitrogen replenishment.

HANNS KORNELL CHAMPAGNE

Greatness in the demanding business of winemaking often prompts writers to describe the successful with terms like "indomitable spirit" and "severe hardships" and "lean years." But the rigors of winemaking can't compare to the arduous life of Hanns Kornell, who brought the *méthode champenoise* system of making sparkling wine to the Napa Valley.

Kornell, the third generation of a Rhine Valley winemaking family, grew up in the trade of German sparkling wine, or sekt. Being Jewish, he was imprisoned in 1938 in the Dachau concentration camp. His parents also were arrested. Inexplicably, Hanns was freed, but was ordered to leave Germany. He emigrated to England, never to see his parents again.

He saved the money he earned there and in 1940 bought passage to the United States. But the ship was torpedoed by a German submarine. Hanns was rescued and landed penniless in New York. He hitchhiked to California and began working at odd winery jobs, from washing dishes to cellar work, and rose to champagne master.

In 1952, Kornell finally made his own wine, in a small rented cellar. The wine was entirely handmade — bottled, riddled, disgorged, and labeled by Hanns by night. He sold the wine by

The French méthode champenoise used in Champagne was brought to the Napa Valley when Hanns Kornell came to the area after a hazardous journey from his native Germany. The method produces amazingly fine bubbles that are persistent and tingly.

day. By 1958, Hanns had saved enough money to acquire a winery of his own. Kornell wanted the historic Larkmead cellar south of Calistoga because it resembled the wine cellars of Germany.

Kornell believed in using the Riesling grape, so common in the sekt of Germany. He crushed no grapes himself, instead buying wine on the open market and fermenting it in the bottle. This was fine at first, but soon the public began to see that Kornell wines lacked uniformity. Also, by 1980, the public found the Riesling aroma in Hanns' wines less appealing than Chardonnay and Pinot Noir, traditionally used for French

Hanns Kornell made the wine, but his wife, Marylouise, ran the winery as president. She is a descendant of the respected Rossini family, who were among the first winemakers in the Napa Valley and built what is today called Burgess Cellars.

Champagne. Kornell's sales suffered. From a peak of 80,000 cases in 1981, the winery fell to 50,000 cases in 1988.

"What dad was doing was not wrong, not bad," says his daughter, Paula. "The wine he made was fine when he was the only one making *méthode champenoise.*"

Kornell's top wine was actually delightful for those consumers who understood it, and many did. Called Sehr Trocken, which in German means "very dry," it was created to go with food. Though made from Riesling, its aroma was less flowery than steely and the balance was fine. The other wines in the line, however, were a tad too sweet for the growing numbers of connoisseurs who sought drier sparkling wines.

By 1982, Kornell's family persuaded him that it was time to become more traditional. They had the expertise to make that judgment. His wife, Marylouise, had grown up in the Rossini family, Napa Valley pioneer winemakers. Daughter Paula knew the marketplace. Son Peter, trained in enology, assumed the role of winemaker. A press was installed in 1986 and grapes were purchased for the first time.

The result in 1990 was a new direction for the Kornell wines, a line including a Blanc de Blancs (from Napa Chardonnay), a Blanc de Noirs (from Sonoma Pinot Noir), and a Brut, which is a blend of Pinot Noir and Pinot Blanc — as well as the Sehr Trocken. *DB*

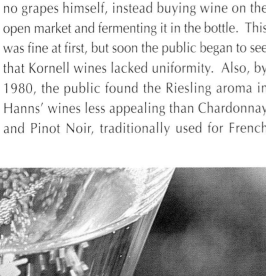

The Hanns Kornell logo, here etched into a glass plate, is derived from a biblical reference to the discovery of a massive cluster of grapes so large it had to be carried by two men on a pole.

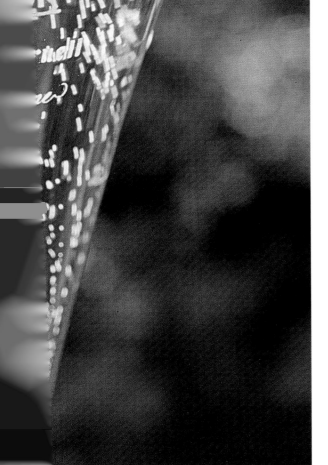

CHARLES KRUG WINERY

This old cellar stands as a living monument to founder Charles Krug, a prime mover at the wine industry's birth in California. Krug led by example, and trained many of the state's finest early winemakers.

During the last century, Charles Krug was the bell cow of Napa Valley's fledgling wine industry. Almost single-handedly he led wine from cottage commerce to major industry.

Born Karl Krug in 1825 in Trendelburg, Prussia (now Germany), Charles emigrated at age 22 to teach in August Glasser's Free Thinkers School in Philadelphia. But in the year Marx and Engels were finishing *The Communist Manifesto* (1848) he went home to participate in a vain attempt to overthrow a reactionary parliament.

Krug returned to the United States to take a job as editor of *Staats Zeitung*, the first German newspaper published on the Pacific Coast. In 1854, he quit to farm a government claim at Crystal Springs (San Mateo County), then went to San Francisco to work at the U.S. Mint with Agoston Haraszthy, a man who would prove important in his life. (Haraszthy was later accused of embezzlement, but Krug had walked a straight path.)

In 1858, he purchased a plot in Sonoma from Haraszthy and planted 20 acres to vines. That fall he made 1,200 gallons of wine for John Patchett of Napa, using a small cider press borrowed from Haraszthy. It was the first wine

pressed in the Napa Valley by means other than Indian feet. (Twenty years later that historic press would be presented to Krug by the liquidating Buena Vista Vineyard Company. Today it stands proudly in the Charles Krug retail room.)

In December of 1860, Krug married Caroline Bale, the daughter of settler Edward Turner Bale and grandniece of General Mariano Vallejo. Caroline's dowry included a 540-acre ranch in St. Helena. The following spring Krug planted 20 acres to vines, built his first cellar, and produced his own first wine.

Krug flourished. His winery was a model of neatness and order and his generosity leg-

The old carriage house is a historic landmark at Krug. Once used as a production area, it now houses the elder Peter Mondavi's library of wines, and is also used for barrel storage.

endary. Said wine historian H.F. Stoll, "He encouraged every newcomer to set out vines and helped them generously with his own time and money to get results. He was liberal to a fault." Several great winemakers of the day served their apprenticeships in the cellars of Charles Krug, including Jacob Beringer, Carl Wente, J.C. Weinberger, and Clarence J. Wetmore (brother of Cresta Blanca founder, Charles A. Wetmore).

Said Frona Eunice Wait, a prominent 19th century wine historian, Krug was "a man whose name has been associated with every venture for the promotion of the industry throughout the state, from its inception to the present, giving a lifetime and a fortune to the work." Despite his efficient and orderly ways, Krug was to be defeated by the root louse (phylloxera) that decimated European and California vineyards alike. When Krug died in 1892, two of his daughters were running the winery and the estate was sadly in debt.

In 1894 Linda and Lolita Krug turned over operations of the winery to cousin Bismark Bruck. Bruck produced wine until Prohibition and also produced red grape juice that retailed for $4.50 per case of 12 quarts.

At Repeal, James K. Moffitt (the paper merchant, banker, and patron of education who was Krug's creditor) leased the vineyards and cellars to Louis Stralla. A decade later Moffitt found the

This is Krug's grape-receiving area, out behind the main plant. What looks complicated is made simple by extensive computerization, developed by Peter Mondavi Jr. to better manage the thousands of tons of grapes crushed each harvest season.

man he judged capable of carrying on the Krug tradition. In 1943 he sold the entire ranch to Cesare Mondavi, a calm, serious businessman.

Mondavi, a native of Italy, came to work the iron mines of Minnesota in 1906. He went home to claim Rosa Grassi for his bride, then returned to Minnesota, where all four of his children were born. In 1922 Cesare moved his family to Lodi, California, there shipping grapes to his winemaking friends in Minnesota. At Repeal, he opened a winery in Acampo (near Lodi) and began to produce wine himself.

Satisfied that both sons were interested in wine, Cesare acquired the Sunny St. Helena Winery in 1937 to produce table wines. Six years later he purchased Charles Krug for $75,000.

Son Robert became general manager, Peter, the winemaker. Early on, winery and vineyard restoration occupied much of the Mondavis' time and money. When Cesare died in 1959, Rosa stepped in to head the company until her death in 1976, when Peter Sr. took the helm. He had assumed management of Charles Krug in 1965, after a family dispute that caused Robert to start his own winery in 1966.

Peter Mondavi has always loved the production side of winery management. A Stanford graduate, he later spent a semester at U.C. Berkeley researching cold fermentation techniques under Dr. William Vere Cruess, the world-renowned food scientist. He later applied the fruits of that research to the famed Krug Chenin Blanc.

Thousands of oak barrels are needed to impart just a hint of oak spiciness, as well as aging characteristics, to the Charles Krug wines, from Chardonnay to the Vintage Selection Cabernet Sauvignons.

Charles Krug Chenin Blanc made its debut in 1954 and became an instant hit, moderately sweet and aromatically flowery in the nose, the easiest-drinking summer-sipper since Coca Cola. Writer Bob Thompson once pegged Krug's Chenin perfectly, calling it "the hammock wine." Indeed, large numbers of the baby boomer generation cut their wine-drinking teeth on Krug Chenin Blancs. And today Krug grows a sizeable percentage of all the Chenin Blanc in the Napa Valley.

"Our winemaking philosophy has always been to let the grapes speak for themselves, to bring out the best character of each grape in our varietal wines," says Peter. Peter's sons, Marc and Pete Jr., are extending their father's philosophy. The curly-haired, bearded Marc

These glass-lined milk tanks are used to ferment and store white wines. The Charles Krug Chenin Blancs owe their success to cold fermentation techniques developed at the winery by Peter Mondavi Sr.

has gradually taken over most of the sales responsibilities, and also manages the family's extensive vineyard holdings. Pete Jr., who majored in mechanical engineering at Stanford, is more interested in the financial and production sides, seeing to the needs of the physical plant with his computer skills.

You can see the sons following the father in Krug's oldest tradition, the Vintage Selection Cabernet Sauvignons — Krug's reserve Cabernets, made only in the best vintages since 1944 — which remain an expression of Cabernet Sauvignon and nothing but Cabernet Sauvignon, the current trend toward "Meritage" Bordeaux blends notwithstanding.

"We're not looking for Bordeaux character in our Vintage Selection Cabernets," says Pete Jr. "We want our Cabernets to taste like Cabernet. My grandfather got into the wine business after selling fresh grapes — table grapes, for eating — and he always loved the way that grapes tasted. So do we." RPH

Tasting is encouraged at the Charles Krug Winery. The basket press that the founder used to make his first wine in 1858 is on display in the tasting room, where everything from Chenin Blanc to the famed Krug Vintage Selection Cabernet can be sampled.

LA JOTA WINERY

The Napa Valley's greatest claim to fame is the worldwide success of Cabernet Sauvignon and Chardonnay. But a few producers favor Rhone varieties.

Indeed, some of the Rhone varieties (Syrah, Grenache, Petite Sirah) do quite well in this warmish climate. And now La Jota is making its mark with the Viognier grape. When they bought the La Jota Winery on Howell Mountain in 1974, 76 years after its founding, Bill and Joan Smith didn't know that Viognier would make La Jota a cult winery with collectors.

"But it did exactly that," says Bill. "It brought us notoriety, something people talk about." The fact is, not much of this wine has ever been tasted, and that's because the Viognier variety is extremely difficult to farm. In 1986 La Jota could make only 25 cases; in 1987, just 90 cases; in 1988, 25 cases, but in 1989, a bumper crop of 350 cases. In 1990, production dropped again, to 75 cases.

So small is the production of this variety that one year Smith joined forces with Pete Minor of Ritchie Creek Winery to sell their

Bill and Joan Smith's La Jota Winery makes excellent, deeply concentrated Cabernet Sauvignons, but the barrel-aged Viognier, made from a rare Rhone grape variety, has become a hit with wine connoisseurs, even though only a tiny quantity of it is made each year. The wine is very appealing, but perhaps its scarcity is what has made it so popular.

Viogniers jointly in a four-pack, two bottles of each brand.

"We try to make it like the French do," says Smith, an oil and gas lease specialist. "We went to the Rhone Valley (in 1987) and talked to a dozen producers, and learned how they like to make the wine. And we make it that way, too."

Smith puts the wine through full malolactic fermentation, attaining creaminess that others don't aim for. He also ages the wine in French oak barrels for additional richness.

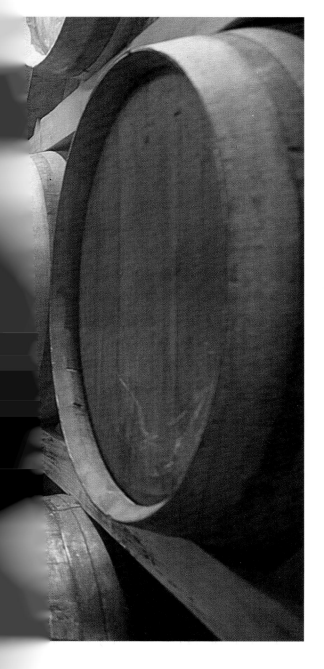

La Jota is located high on Howell Mountain, where the winery once grew grapes for, and produced, an excellent Zinfandel. However, those vines were later converted to Cabernet Franc, and the winery hopes one day to make a wine solely from that grape variety.

Because of their love for the Rhone wines, the Smiths also import them. Under the name Rhone Wine Imports, they bring in four different Condrieus and a line of reds including St. Joseph, Cornas, Gigondas, and Cote Rotie.

Founded as a winery in 1982, La Jota is located 1,800 feet above the valley floor. When the Smiths bought it, the land was barren, except for a few trees. The ancient building on the property, with 26-inch-thick walls made from locally quarried rock, was perfect for restoration and use as the new La Jota. La Jota now has a total of 28 acres of vines: Merlot, Cabernet Franc, Cabernet Sauvignon, and Viognier. There also is a small planting of the white Rhone variety Marsanne, just for fun.

In its the early days, La Jota made one of the most stylish Zinfandels in the state, but those vines were eventually budded over to Cabernet Franc. Smith intends to make a varietal wine from that grape annually.

The soil here is essentially volcanic ash with a considerable amount of iron. This so-called tuffa shows a chalky white and has excellent drainage, which makes for dark, dense, powerful Cabernet Sauvignons. La Jota's Cabernet is packed with black cherry and spice, and complex from the blending of Merlot and Cabernet Franc. It is made in the tradition of Caymus, spending the first months of its life in used French oak barrels, then a time in new barrels before bottling. *DB*

LONG VINEYARDS

Robert B. Long Sr., a property manager and real estate investor, bought this Pritchard Hill property in 1965 as a summer home. The following two years saw just over l5 acres of Chardonnay and Johannisberg Riesling planted there by Long's son, Bob, and Bob's then-wife, Zelma Long. For ten years the grapes were sold.

Zelma, who turned an education in nutrition into a career in winemaking at Robert Mondavi, is president and CEO at Simi Winery, in Healdsburg — and a very active consulting owner of Long. "She's here at least once a week during the crush and we talk all the time on the phone, so she has a great deal of input into style and everything," says Bob.

Between Zelma's inspiration and expertise and Bob's dedication, the sweet Rieslings and barrel-fermented Chardonnays of Long Vineyards have won widespread critical acclaim. The initial Chardonnay (1977), was made at Trefethen. Their own facility was ready for the 1978 crush, when the first Riesling was made in the mold of a German Mosel.

The following year a Cabernet Sauvignon was added. It was egg-white fined with eggs from Long's own Rhode Island Reds, "before they expired at the hands — feet? — of coyotes

At Long Vineyards, high up Pritchard Hill, steeply terraced hillside vines look north toward Lake Hennessey. Most of the 16 acres are planted to Chardonnay, but three acres remain planted to a long-time favorite of Bob Long's -- White Reisling.

and other predators," explains Bob. A barrel-fermented Sauvignon Blanc, enhanced with 20 percent Chardonnay, is also produced.

Still, it's Chardonnay that defines Long Vineyards (and accounts for almost two-thirds of production). Long leans toward Old World techniques with his Chardonnays, meaning he takes the fruit from a single vineyard, then ferments the wine without benefit of stainless-steel tanks, but rather in small oaken barrels, half of which are new each year.

"Two events influenced me to return to the Burgundian tradition," says Long. "First, a visit to my mother's family in Northern Italy; second,

a 1970s visit to Germany and Burgundy. Those visits revealed the cultural reasons for winemaking and grape growing on a very small scale. My Italian relatives all grew or had available small quantities of grapes, which they processed in a spare room or basement, along with olive oil, fruit and vegetable preserves, vinegar, and sun-dried tomatoes.

"Some of their red wines were of remarkable quality and demonstrated that size and technology are not necessarily the most important aspect of winemaking. In both Burgundy and Germany we saw that great quality can be produced from exceedingly small quantities of grapes. It is not unusual for wines to be made from a few dozen or hundred vines — perhaps three to four barrels' worth. All this, plus the small-wine-lot experiments Zelma Long, my partner, did at Robert Mondavi, convinced me that it was technically feasible and desirable to make small quantities of very good, commercial quality wine. Indeed, the small winegrower is the guardian of the cultural tradition of Chardonnay."

Long is quick to give equal and ample credit to a pair of long-time Long Vineyards employees, Sandi Belcher ("she's the real winemaker here — she threatens to fire me every once in awhile") and viticulturist Lorenzo Padilla ("he takes the caring, careful approach of a gardener in our almost 18 acres of vineyard"). *RPH*

The vinelands of the Napa Valley amount to less than one percent of the surface committed to wine grapes in the state of California. Yet the Napa Valley has one-third of the Golden State's wineries!

MARKHAM VINEYARDS

Often, objects in plain sight are the most difficult to find. Markham Vineyards, founded by Rocky Mountain ad man H. Bruce Markham, has graced the corner of Highway 29 and Deer Park — just north of the very visible Charles Krug, Beringer, and The Christian Brothers' Greystone Cellar — since 1978. Yet it is completely hidden.

"It's true, we'd never done much to promote ourselves," admits red-bearded, curly-haired President Bryan Del Bondio. "Our founding owner preferred to crunch numbers on his computer. And I'm not much for spending too much time away from my family. But we do have a winemaker who is good at personal appearances. He speaks French and German, and is very energetic. So we're going to promote him and let him tell our story."

"He" is Bob Foley. Foley grew up on the eastern side of San Francisco Bay, where his father, a rocket scientist, made home wines. For more than a dozen years Foley has been quietly crafting wines from Markham's three vineyard sites, improving each vintage.

Markham's northernmost ranch is north of Calistoga, on the slope of Mount St. Helena. This vineyard of nearly 70 acres was originally planted to Cabernet Sauvignon, Napa Gamay, and Muscat Canelli. Cabernet grows quite well in this area, so that variety has been kept. Markham also makes a delightful Muscat Blanc, so the Muscat stayed as well, but the Napa Gamay was wisely plucked from the ground in favor of Merlot.

"Merlot has become an important varietal for us," notes Del Bondio. "Our '87 was rated second by the Vintners Club in San Francisco, against some pretty good competition."

The Yountville vineyard lies about midway between warm Calistoga and the cooler climes of the Carneros (at the northern reach of San Francisco Bay, there called San Pablo Bay). This 100-acre planting is on the Yountville bench and was once owned by the van Loben Sels (who

A two-year, $10 million cellar renovation replaced ancient redwood tanks with gleaming stainless-steel fermenters, viewed here from the catwalk that cellar rats scramble through — like sailors through rigging on tall ships — during crush.

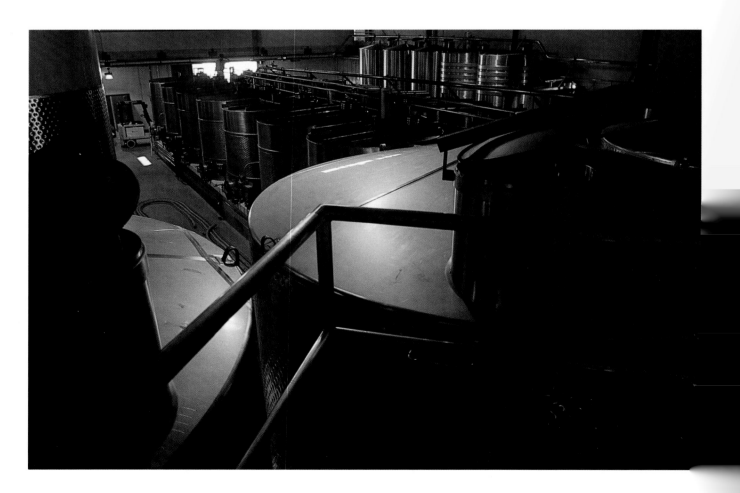

The winery building Markham occupies was originally erected by a Bordelais vintner in the 1870s. "1876 is carved into a stone on the front of the building," says general manager Bryan Del Bondio, "but wine historian William Heintz thinks 1873 is the actual date. It's been here awhile, in any case."

had Oakville Vineyards in the '70s). Acquired in 1977, it was first planted to Cabernet Sauvignon, White Riesling, and Muscat de Frontignan. The latter two varieties have since been pulled in favor of Merlot and Cabernet Franc.

"Cabernet Franc adds a great deal to our Cabernet Sauvignon," asserts Napa Valley native Del Bondio, whose father has been with Inglenook more than four decades. "We're using 12 to 15 percent of Franc in our Cabernet Sauvignon, and are seriously considering going to a proprietary name so we'll have greater leeway in blending."

At the southern end of the Napa Valley proper (north of the town of Napa) is Markham's Napa Ranch, just west of the Red Hen Restaurant (a landmark on Highway 29). Also acquired in '77, it was initially given over to Chardonnay, Gamay Beaujolais, and French Colombard. Since then, the last two have been discarded in favor of Sauvignon Blanc.

As the vineyards have been reconstituted, the winery is now undergoing reconstruction, having been purchased in 1987 by Japan's Mercian Corp. "Mercian is the largest wine company in Japan," says Del Bondio. "They've produced domestic wines there for more than a century, mostly from the Koshu grape, which is not like anything we know." *RPH*

A hollow glass tube called a wine thief is used to draw wine samples from a barrel. The samples are sent to the laboratory for analysis: a chemical checkup as well as "sensory evaluation" — i.e., tasting. Rotten job, winemaking.

LOUIS M. MARTINI WINERY

With the exception of Zinfandel, California wine has almost always been created in the image of the great wines of France, notably Cabernet Sauvignon and Chardonnay. Yet the ethnic influence on the creation of a wine industry in California was overwhelmingly Italian. That story is no better depicted than in the three generations that operate the Louis M. Martini Winery — one of the true forces of fine wine in the Napa Valley.

Founder Louis Michael Martini was one of the first to test such now-famous regions as Carneros and Sonoma County and one of the first to plant vast mountain vineyards. His winemaking was at the cutting edge of the technology of the times. At his death in 1974, at age 87, he left the industry with a legacy it will never be able to repay.

It all started in 1900 when Italian-born Louis M. arrived in San Francisco at the age of 13 to assist his father in the fish business. He wanted to make wine, and sold his first attempts door-to-door in the city's Italian area. When this proved an utter failure, the young Louis was sent back to Alba in the Piedmont region of Italy to learn winemaking. On his return, he started working as a winemaker.

When Prohibition went into effect in 1920,

The Louis M. Martini Winery tasting room on Highway 29, just south of St. Helena, is one of the most hospitable in the valley. Here visitors can often sample not only new wines, but occasionally re-released older selections. Moreover, when it's available, the rare and famed Moscato Amabile can be bought here.

many wine operations died, but Louis established a winery at Kingsburg in the San Joaquin Valley to make Forbidden Fruit, a grape concentrate for home winemaking, which wasn't outlawed. In 1932, anticipating the end of Prohibition, Martini used two small "ghost wineries" in the Napa Valley. By 1934, just months after Prohibition was repealed by the 21st amendment to the Constitution, Martini was prepared.

Within four years he had founded his Napa Valley winery south of St. Helena, and begun acquiring vineyard land in both Sonoma and Napa counties. Like the other major forces in

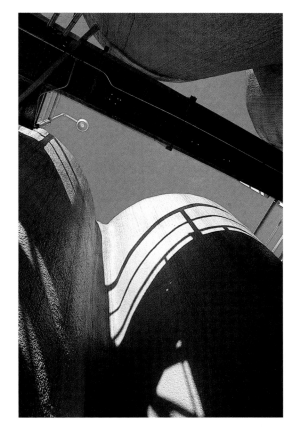

Some of the wine storage tanks at the Louis M. Martini Winery are outdoors, but the rest are inside the large winery. Some of the interior tanks are in a "cold room," where the temperature is kept near freezing so the special dessert wine Moscato Ambile can ferment slowly, for years, taking on amazingly delicate bubbles while it retains the Muscat fruit.

the valley at the time (Inglenook, Beaulieu, Charles Krug, and Beringer), Martini made non-vintage blends (the bulk of sales) as well as vintage-dated varietal wines. All of these wineries made wines that aged well, vintage or not, but Martini's surprised the "experts." His wines were considered to be lighter and less rich when young, but usually aged better than others.

Blending was one of the secrets of the Martini "formula." Whereas Beaulieu and Inglenook emphasized the 100 percent nature of their varietal wines, Martini was eager to make the best wine he could and often would make additions of other varieties to improve the final product. A case in point was Martini Barbera, made from the respected Italian variety. At a time when it was permissible to make a varietal wine from 51 percent of the grape named on the label (the rest could be anything else), Martini's Barbera, arguably the best in California, was seldom more than 58 percent of that variety. Older bottles of Martini Barbera from the 1950s and 1960s still are amazing for their quality.

The legendary Martini Moscato Amabile is another one of California's greatest achievements. This sweet, slightly sparkling, Muscat-based wine has very little alcohol (usually under seven percent) and is so fragile that it is sold only at the winery and must be stored refrigerated — otherwise it might re-ferment.

The far-flung Martini vineyards are a testament to the founder, the late Louis Michael Martini, who pioneered in such regions as the Carneros, the top of the Mayacamas Mountain ridge, and Sonoma County's Russian River.

In 1959, the elder Martini gave the wine-making chores to his son Louis Peter, who had graduated from the University of California at Berkeley in the class of 1940 — a famed "vintage" for winemakers. Louis Peter was one of the first in the Napa Valley to experiment with different clones of grape varieties. He continued the tradition of quality his father had established at Martini, making some of the best wines the winery had yet made. In the late 1970s, he turned the reins over to his son, Michael.

The founder of the winery was a fast-talking, intense man with great enthusiasm and a notorious driving style: fast, with only a passing regard for the laws of the road. Louis P. is more conservative — a tall, broad-shouldered man with a warm grin and a calm nature. Mike, like his grandfather, is a jocular fellow who doesn't mind saying what's on his mind. He readily admits, for instance, that he wasn't as good a student as he should have been at Fresno State and U.C. Davis.

Through the decade of the 1980s, the Martini wines went through a series of changes, partly due to Mike's enthusiasm to try new styles of winemaking and partly due to the lack of exceptional grapes. The Napa Valley became overrun with new wineries run by wealthy people who didn't balk at paying higher prices for grapes. Martini did, so some of Martini's grape sources changed periodically.

During that period, the Martini winery wasn't static. Louis P. and his wife, Elizabeth, were the models of Napa Valley professionalism, promoting the valley's wine with the grace and wit the family has always displayed. Meanwhile, under the guidance of Mike's sister, Carolyn Martini Cox, who runs the whole show as chief executive, and their other siblings, Patty and Peter, who work in the company in other capacities, Martini continued to experiment.

Over the last few years, the family pared down its line of wines from dozens to a handful and changed its concept of style. Having once

specialized in red wines, the winery made major strides in its white wines late in the 1980s. As a result of technical improvements in winemaking, all Martini wines have become more distinctive.

But Cabernet Sauvignon remains the heart of the winery's list. Words usually used to describe the wines are "delicate fruit" and "balance." Over the years, some collectors have knocked Martini Cabernets because they lacked as much obvious fruit or as rich a concentration of flavors as other Cabernets. Yet true wine lovers say that despite this "failure," all of Martini's red wines age better than most of the red wines in the world. It's always amazing to taste an older Martini wine that originally sold for $1.59 and see, 20 years later, how it knocks off some of the greatest and most expensive wines from the most prestigious houses in Europe.

Over the years Louis P. Martini has been reticent to praise his winemaker son openly. However, a breakthrough did come one day early in 1990. Michael and his father were hosting a national sales meeting. After going through the wines, Louis unexpectedly rose and said to the assembled salesforce: "These are the best wines you've ever had the opportunity to sell." *DB*

The second- and third-generation principals of the Louis M. Martini Winery: Louis Peter Martini, left, son of the founder, and his children, Mike, the winemaker, and Carolyn, chief executive.

The Louis M. Martini Winery owns marvelous vineyards, but many of them are in other counties because the late founder of the winery was a visionary who saw the great potential of mountain Sonoma grapes as well as Russian River grapes. Martini also has planted test vineyards in largely untested Lake County.

MAYACAMAS VINEYARDS

D ue to a fork in the range, the Mayaca-mas Mountains actually form both boundaries of the Napa Valley. The word itself comes from the Nappa tribe, and means "standing place." Indeed, cougars and bobcats are still heard and seen along the ridges and canyons of the range.

The stone winery building that houses the present Mayacamas winery was built in 1889 by John Henry Fisher, a sword engraver from Stuttgart. Fisher was a pickle canner in San Francisco when he founded the winery, which he named after himself. He produced bulk red and white table wines from Zinfandel and "Sweetwater" grapes and built a small distillery. His cannery was wiped out by the 1906 quake and his assets assigned to Owens-Illinois in lieu of his unpaid glass bill. The Pickle Canyon property had many owners before coming to Jack and Mary Taylor in 1941.

The Taylors were amateurs possessed of great enthusiasm and endurance. Rabbits, deer, and birds of all description robbed them of vines and crops many times before they were able to successfully re-establish the vineyards and winery, renamed Mayacamas. Through grit and determination they carved broad terraces out of the rocky, stubborn hillsides of the extinct volcano.

A scraggly cluster of Chardonnay hangs from a vine at Mayacamas. The Chardonnay at the winery is the famed Wente clone, which the later Ernest Wente (viticulturist) damned for its low crop yields and the later Herman Wente (Ernest's brother, the winemaker) praised for its exquisite wines. They were both right.

The Taylors turned the distillery into a cozy little home, incorporated the winery, and built a wine list of 17 different wines. In 1968 they sold the business to a partnership headed by Bob and Elinor "Nonie" Travers. A former investment banker who likes to fly, Bob cut the number of wines produced. Most of his production is now devoted to the rich, long-lived wines made from the 32 acres of Chardonnay and 12 acres of Cabernet Sauvignon grown at the winery.

While Chardonnay and Cabernet define Mayacamas, like any craftsman Bob tries his hand at other wines. A high-alcohol, late-harvested Zinfandel has long been a standby. "It's

The old stone cellar at Mayacamas Vineyards, built in 1889 by John Henry Fisher, a sword engraver from Stuttgart, Germany. Mayacamas established the lead for mountain-grown wines dense with fruit and made for the long haul.

good as an aperitif, with walnuts; we enjoy it after the dinner entrée with salad and cheeses, and it's especially good with chocolate-covered almonds." In 1977, after a European trip, he produced both red and rosé from Pinot Noir. "A trip to Burgundy is always an inspiration," he says brightly.

Bordeaux provided the push for experimental lots of botrytised Semillon and Sauvignon Blanc: "I like a higher level of Sauvignon Blanc in the blend than the French do. Our wine will probably be at least 30 to 40 percent Sauvignon Blanc, perhaps more." Rich in body, and lush with honey and fig fruit, this botrytised beauty has been made, off and on, in rare vintages.

A folksy, homespun newsletter, started by Mary Taylor in November of 1949, has introduced wines to the Mayacamas faithful semi-regularly for over 40 years. In the first epistle, Mary chronicled the difficulties she and Jack had in planting Chardonnay: "Our first planting was destroyed by deer, the second by rabbits, the third by grasshoppers, and the fourth by a particularly voracious type of small blue jay, but we confidently look forward to having our first crop in 1950 and will make our first white wine from it." In 1953 Mary estimated that her frost-damaged crop cost her about ten cents a grape — which meant that the wine, in order to turn a profit, would have to have been sold at better than $1,000 a case! *RPH*

When we say "handcrafted wine," it's not a throwaway line. Vines are tended by hand, often harvested by hand, and it's very important to go through harvested grapes by hand to pick out MOG -- material other than grapes. That can be rocks, twigs, and even live critters.

MERLION WINERY

Merlion Winery's winemaker John McKay (left), President George Vierra, and George's wife, Bobby, operate their premium winery out of the city of Napa. Merlion specializes in wines that are more delicate than many producers in the Napa Valley make.

Merlion Winery owner George Vierra admits that the wines he makes may not be well understood by the average wine consumer. But he's driven to make wine in a style he likes.

"I strongly disagree with most winemakers as to what a balanced wine is," says the outspoken Vierra, once on the winemaking team for the Robert Mondavi Winery. "Napa Valley wines are usually way too low in acidity."

His style isn't traditional. For instance, he was one of the first winemakers here to bring in 130-gallon puncheons for aging wine. Most other wineries use 55-gallon barrels.

"I felt the wines we were making, in many cases, could be too intensely woody, but with puncheons, the greater volume of liquid to surface area means you can have a lot less wood in the wine for the same amount of aging time."

Vierra also was the first in the Napa Valley to experiment with long contact of the juice on the lees of the wine — the dead yeast cells — after the fermentation is complete. This *sur lie* process, used widely in France, requires great care so the wine doesn't pick up foul aromas.

All Merlion white wines are aged on the lees. One of them, called Sauvrier, which is half Semillon and half Sauvignon Blanc, is austere when it comes to market, but ages beautifully. Likewise, the all-Semillon wine Chevrier is so austere when released it takes about four years before the wine starts tasting like it was meant to taste, lush and complete.

"Yes, I know, this goes against all the marketing techniques in America because a lot of people look down their noses at aged white wine. But that's what we do."

Merlion also makes a stylish Cabernet

George Vierra is one of the most politically active men in the valley; he has fought bureaucracy at the state and local levels. It was his petition that led to the adoption of the 500-milliliter bottle for wine. He also has worked with designers to develop a better style of wine glass, one that helps improve the aroma of wine when swirled.

Sauvignon. Again it's made the Vierra way. In the early days, under his Vichon label, his Cabernets were truly rough and tannic due to a long aging regime called extended maceration in which the juice was kept on the grape skins for a long period of time after fermentation.

"We still do extended maceration, à la Bordeaux, and we know that with some vineyards you have to be very careful, or you get too much tannin." Vierra now uses only hillside grapes for his red wines, and the efforts of the latter 1980s were better structured than the earlier ones from Vichon.

Merlion is really the reincarnation of Vichon, the winery Vierra built in 1980. Vichon dissolved when Vierra and his partners had a falling out. Vierra turned Vichon over to the Mondavi family in March 1985 and by mid-April had developed a new partnership of seven investors. With a $1 million bankroll, Merlion was born.

However, $1 million doesn't get you a winery building, so Vierra made an agreement with the Napa Valley Cooperative Winery. He was made a winemaking and marketing consultant to its brands and given a corner of the co-op to make his wines.

Vierra has worked with glassware companies to design special glassware to improve the aroma of fine wine. He also is active politically, fighting excise taxation and petitioning the federal government to get interstate approval for use of the half-liter bottle for wine. *DB*

The Merlion style of wine is crisper than many others in the Napa Valley, so the white wines are usually not very approachable when they are released. However, they become rich and expansive with a few years in the bottle.

MERRYVALE

Merryvale is the new coat of paint on the old Sunny St. Helena Winery. The first Napa Valley winery built at Repeal, it was bought in 1937 by Cesare Mondavi to serve as his family's foothold in the Napa Valley. He sold it in 1943, when he and sons Peter and Robert bought the old Charles Krug facility on the north side of town. In the '60s Sunny St. Helena was owned cooperatively by two dozen growers; in the '70s it served The Christian Brothers as extra storage space.

In 1986 the spacious, stolid structure was purchased by partners in the Pacific Union Company, a San Francisco real estate development company (Opera Plaza in San Francisco, Gateway at the Napa Airport). Partners Bill Harlan, John Montgomery, and the late Peter Stocker had first come to the Napa Valley in 1979, when they purchased Meadowood Country Club and turned it into a world class resort complete with its own wine school run by John Thoreen. But that was only a prelude to a deeper foray into winedom.

Desiring to make Meadowood a meeting place for wine people, they hired Robin Lail, whose father (the late John Daniel Jr.) once owned Inglenook. Later, Robin's husband, architect Jon Lail, also joined the partnership.

There's nothing like a backlit barrel cellar as backdrop for an elegant dining experience. The folks at Merryvale have refurbished the old Sunny St. Helena Winery with subtlety and style.

They then bought the old winery a stone's throw from Meadowood, rechristened it, gutted its 22,000-square-foot interior, and installed modern winemaking equipment, but preserved the feel of the ivy-covered building's 1930s architecture. A large fountain stands guard at the entrance and *bocce* ball is played on the front lawn.

Their first wines, produced at Rombauer in 1983, came out under the Merryvale label. The next wines bore the Sunny St. Helena label, and include a range of popularly priced offerings, from a barrel-fermented Chenin Blanc to the easy-quaffing blush, "Picnic."

Merryvale's wines span a wide range -- from a Reserve Chardonnay and Meritage blended red to a barrel-fermented Chenin Blanc and an easygoing blush, Picnic.

Merryvale's winemaker is Bob Levy, who grew up around movie studio lots MGM and Desilu in Culver City. After high school, he started out in premed at U.C. Davis. "The prerequisites for enology and premed were pretty much the same, and everybody took Vit 3, the introductory course on wine," says Levy with a chuckle. "By my sophomore year I had switched to fermentation science."

One of the more interesting lessons of winemaking is that what you've learned at school doesn't carry much weight in the real world. "At Davis, they separate winemaking from grape growing, and they teach you to make technically correct wines," explains Levy. "In the real world, you have to quickly break down that wall between you and the vineyard, and you also learn that 'correct' wines are rarely interesting wines.

"Thus, your source of grapes is the first and most important aspect of making quality, interesting wines. Second, you have to get your butt out into the vineyards to personally see what's going on, to get an overall view of all the vineyards, to see how maturity is progressing. In 1989, for example, flavor maturity was well ahead of sugar maturity. That's the first time I'd ever experienced that, but if I hadn't been out in the vineyard all the time I might have missed that and made some bad decisions." *RPH*

While this fountain adds a formal touch to the winery's entryway, a bocce ball court turns the mood festive. A warm, comfortable, casual tasting area, set between the two main cellars, invites lingering conversation.

ROBERT MONDAVI WINERY

Though Robert Mondavi turned over day-to-day operations of his winery to sons Michael and Tim in 1991, he's still winedom's version of Frank Sinatra: Chairman of the Board. His vision and energy stand behind the success of every winery in the Napa Valley.

Architecturally, the Robert Mondavi Winery evokes the Spanish colonialism of early California. The mission-like complex has a low profile, accentuated by the graceful curve of its central arch and its companion tower. Long, covered corridors and Spanish tile floors complete the effect.

But more importantly, the winery is symbolic of a spirit, a spirit that embodies vitality, strength, and enthusiasm. Those were necessary characteristics for a man who, at the age of 53, set out in 1966 to build the first new winery of any size in the Napa Valley since the end of Prohibition.

Thus, the Robert Mondavi Winery is a touchstone for the Napa Valley, and its founder an inspiration to those who work with him. You see, 95 percent of all the wineries in today's

Napa Valley were built after Robert Mondavi's!

Robert Mondavi was one of four children born to Cesare and Rosa Mondavi in Virginia, Minnesota. While Robert and his brother, Peter, were still at Stanford University, Cesare made a move that put a down payment on their future: he bought a Napa Valley winery. Though dessert wines were then king, Cesare knew that table wines were the future.

Robert joined his father at the old Sunny St. Helena Winery in 1937. Six years later the family sold their Acampo Winery and the Sunny St. Helena Winery so as to acquire the forlorn Charles Krug Winery. Even then Robert had an inquisitive mind that thrilled at daring new concepts. At Krug in 1954 he helped introduce a varietal Chenin Blanc with some residual sugar. A dozen years later he was among the first American producers to recognize the value of European oak.

That his investigative inclinations and powerful promotional excursions were often stifled at Krug caused wrenching family friction — to the point of fisticuffs — enough that Robert felt compelled to erect his own launch pad.

It is a tribute to Robert that his three children embrace his enthusiasm. Michael, the oldest, came to learn the business from the ground up, dragging hoses and cleaning fermentation tanks. He eventually became responsible for production, then sales and marketing, and is now joint managing director.

Daughter Marcia Mondavi Borger, who calls New York home, is in charge of Eastern marketing, sales, and educational efforts. Tim, a 1974 graduate of U.C. Davis, is in charge of wine production and oversees all vineyard operations as the other joint managing director.

The winery itself is replete with innovative equipment. In 1969 Robert brought the first horizontal rotating tanks to the United States. Rotated three times a day, the tanks allowed maximum skin extraction during fermentation, which added depth to the already fine Mondavi Cabernets.

In the early days, the Robert Mondavi Winery set new standards for Napa Valley Cabernet Sauvignon, going first to maximum ripeness and extraction, later pulling back in an effort to retain roundness and elegance. Mondavi also rescued Sauvignon Blanc as a varietal wine by taking the French term for smoke, "*fumée*," and using that as a jumping-off point for his ever-after-famed Fumé Blanc.

The full moon descends behind the Spanish archway and tower at the Robert Mondavi Winery. The local Indians called Sonoma Valley, over the hill, "Valley of the Moons," as the moon seemed to rise several times each night as it darted behind a succession of mountain peaks.

The Mondavis' experimental focus has made for dramatic improvements in Pinot Noir, but not all of it translates immediately into production. Tim and his crew have been working with sparkling wines for more than a decade. "We're still playing with it," he laughs, "but it's not our main project. We drink it all, and we enjoy it, but our priorities are our Reserve and varietal programs, Opus, and our 'Table' wines. Also, we added 500 acres in the Carneros in 1988, and that's taken a bit of our time."

Mondavi also owns the former Filice Winery at Acampo (San Joaquin Valley), where the Robert Mondavi Table Wines — now varietals — are produced and oak aged. In the old days, the red was referred to as "Bob Red" and the white, quite naturally, as "Bob White."

In 1979 Bob formed a unique partnership with Baron Philippe de Rothschild (of Château Mouton-Rothschild) of Bordeaux to create a new wine, one that melded French experience and California fruit. The result, Opus One, has been one of the priciest, most praised of American red wines. A decade after the partnership was formed, ground was broken on Opus One's own winery, half-buried in an earthen berm.

In 1985 the Mondavis purchased nearby Vichon Winery, just up the Oakville Grade. Vichon, while making distinctive Cabernets and Merlots, is best known for its masterful

The Harvest Room is usually filled with tables and chairs for one of the constant food-and-wine explorations held by the Mondavis to gain a better understanding of the place of wine in American culture. No one has done more than the Mondavis to bring wine into the American consciousness.

marriage of Sauvignon Blanc and Semillon, called "Chevrignon." Later Byron, a superb Santa Barbara Pinot Noir producer, was added.

Though much attention is paid to things scientific in the winery, aesthetics are hardly neglected. The Mondavi personnel offer thorough tours and educational tastings in the several small tasting rooms of the south wing. The Vineyard Room houses gourmet cooking classes and art exhibits throughout the year and the grassed, immaculate courtyard is the site of the celebrated Summer Jazz Concerts, featuring such stars as Ray Charles, Chuck Mangione, and perennial favorites, the Preservation Hall Jazz Band.

The arts are very big at the Robert Mondavi Winery. The Harvest Room is awash with paintings at all times of the year; music festivals are held in the central courtyard through the summer; and sculptures such as this are on display throughout the facility.

Perhaps the most significant aspect of the Mondavi operation has been its ability to put forth remarkable quality from a winery that is by no means small. Much of that is a matter of attitude. Says Tim, "The fact that we have a large winery means that we can literally play with different, experimental concepts. We can try almost anything." Adds Marcia, "We've been fortunate enough to be able to grow without any loss of control, which has given us a wide range of choices. Thus, our style is the result of our choice."

Though his kids now run the winery, Robert nears his 80th birthday at full gallop. For he is on a mission to bring the facts about wine and health to an American public that little understands wine.

"Wine has been part of the human experience since civilization began," he says with fervor. "It is the natural beverage for every celebration: births, graduations, engagements, weddings, anniversaries, promotions, family gatherings, meetings with friends, and toasts between governments.

"Our industry has not done its job in educating about wine and most of us are apparently content. We have launched a mission to tell people about wine's rightful place in our society." *RPH*

Attention to vineyards is a key to the success of Mondavi. One of the family's finest vineyards, To Kalon at Oakville, was originally planted in the 1870s by Hamilton Walker Crabb, Napa Valley's first research viticulturist. Crabb chose the name "To Kalon" from the Greek. It means "the highest beauty," but he told visitors it stood for "the boss vineyard."

MONTICELLO CELLARS

I f Thomas Jefferson had done nothing more than draft the Declaration of Independence, his reputation would nonetheless live forever. But his wisdom was far-ranging. He founded the University of Virginia, put a damper on slave imports, acquired Louisiana (and more) while President, and devoted a great deal of time and effort to agriculture. A lover of fine wine, he opposed taxing wine, suggesting that "no nation is drunken where wine is cheap."

Jefferson would be proud of the vinous enterprise Jay Corley started in 1970, when the one-time linguist turned his talents from investments to grapes. "Jay got some of the best advice available — from Beaulieu's Andre Tchelistcheff and Freemark's Chuck Carpy — and took the lead in using metal grape stakes, closer vine plantings, and planting bench-grafted vines," notes Monticello's youthful executive director and winemaker, Alan Phillips. "And, being of Burgundian bent, he planted most of his 125 acres to Chardonnay and Pinot Noir."

Corley sold his grapes initially, but began to notice a pattern: the wineries he was selling to — Domaine Chandon, Burgess, Shafer, and others — were making superb wines from his grapes. By 1980 he had decided to open a

If you suspect that this structure bears a strong resemblance to the back side of a nickel . . . well, you're right. Founder Jay Corley, a Jeffersonian enthusiast whose family had once farmed in Virginia, wanted to honor the Declaration of Independence author, who himself had been one of America's first viniculturists and wine lovers.

winery whose wines would be designed for the table. (So committed was he to this then-new notion, Corley hired culinary director Richard Alexei before he even had a winemaker tabbed. The visitors' center is modeled after the famed Jefferson Virginia home, Monticello.)

The original plan was to focus on white wines, but Cabernet Sauvignon soon snuck aboard. "It's one of our most popular wines now," admits Phillips with a grin. "Since Jay doesn't grow any Cabernet here — it's too cool — we use fruit from our own State Lane Vineyard plus buy from eight others all over the Napa Valley."

While the winery's formal dining room looks to have been taken directly out of Jefferson's Monticello home, the kitchen is state-of-the-art. Indeed, Corley hired his original culinary director even before hiring winemaker Alan Phillips.

Monticello has developed a fine reputation for subtle, supple Chardonnays. "We started out making exactly the wine we wanted," notes Phillips, who was working at Rutherford Hill when Monticello's first wines were custom-crushed there. "We aimed for a table wine, a lighter style than most, with less oakiness. Others were aiming at that big, ripe, oaky style. In fact, we didn't really want to make a Reserve Chardonnay, with that 'bigger is better' connotation. We felt that we were already making the wine we set out to make."

But the marketplace had different ideas, so Phillips made a separate wine in 1982 designated "Barrel Fermented," changed the following vintage to "Reserve." Phillips is not reluctant to admit that his preference still lies with Jefferson Ranch's "regular" Chardonnay. "That's the style I like. The wine is my fingerprint, and I hate to see what we perceive of as our best wine looked at as if it were a lesser wine, just because it's not labeled Reserve."

Curiously, when it comes to Monticello's sparkling wine — called Domaine Montreaux — Phillips takes the opposite tack, expressing a marked preference for the robust, creamy styles of Krug and Bollinger. He also makes an apricot-succulent, Sauternes-like, botrytised Semillon when conditions allow, bottled as "Chateau M.," and, despite a vow to the contrary, a Pinot Noir. *RPH*

Demptos is one of the better coopers who supply winemakers the world over with quality white oak barrels. Headquartered in Bordeaux, Demptos opened a cooperage in the Napa Valley to better serve the growing needs of the California wine industry.

MONT ST. JOHN CELLARS

The grand experiment called Prohibition might have wiped out the Napa Valley as a great winemaking region, but a number of winery operations persisted by making sacramental and medicinal wine, and by selling grapes to home winemakers.

During the 13 years of Prohibition, it was legal for the head of a household to make a small amount of wine at home for personal use. And it was on those grounds that Andrea Bartolucci founded his Mont St. John Cellars in Oakville in 1922 — just two years after Prohibition began and long before anyone was talking about its repeal.

"My grandfather bought a piece of property with an existing winery on it and he grew grapes and sold the fruit in the Bay Area for home winemaking purposes," says Andrea "Buck" Bartolucci, who today owns and operates Mont St. John Cellars in the Carneros region of the Napa Valley.

In 1933, upon Repeal, Andrea and his oldest son, Louis, began making wine under the name Madonna Winery.

"That first year," says Louis's son, Buck, "we refurbished the winery and made 5,000 gallons of wine, which my dad told me was sold to Petri Wine Co. for ten cents a gallon."

Mont St. John's mission-style winery building and tasting room sits on the junction of Highway 12/121 and Old Sonoma Road, west of the city of Napa. Buck Bartolucci's winery was one of the early properties to tap the resources of the cool Carneros in the 1960s as the California wine industry finally awoke from its post-Prohibition slumber.

The Madonna Winery name was used through the early 1940s, largely for wine sold in bulk. Then the name was changed to Mont St. John Cellars.

Andrea retired in the late 1940s, selling the property to his three sons. Louis operated the winery by himself and eventually his two younger brothers, Henry and Bruno, joined him. The family continued to make wine under its original bond, most of it sold in bulk. And during the latter 1960s, a lot of Mont St. John wine was going to Rod Strong at Sonoma Vineyards. "We had a lot of vineyards that were planted to single varieties, which was rare back then," says Buck.

By 1970 the Bartoluccis had the home winery, with a capacity of 500,000 gallons, and they had 300 acres of land in three separate parcels. Over the next few years the family sold all its holdings to Heublein because the face of the wine market was changing.

"We were making mostly fortified wines then, which had been popular earlier, but which by the 1970s were becoming a more and more difficult business," says Buck. "My dad knew we needed to have premium vineyards and that we needed to be doing premium wines. So we backed out of that end of the business, but all along we were positioning ourselves to come back."

The sale of Mont. St. John dispersed the brothers. Bruno's family stayed in the heart of the Napa Valley to grow grapes; Henry's family moved to Lake County to grow grapes; and Louis and his son moved south to the Carneros.

"We had bought grapes for many years so we knew the high quality of the Carneros fruit," says Buck. He bought 160 acres of land in the Carneros, planting 140 acres by 1976. Then Louis, now semi-retired, bought a four-and-an-half-acre plot and together they planned the winery. It was completed in 1978 and opened to the public in '81. The classic grape varieties of the Carneros — Pinot Noir and Chardonnay — are the winery's main thrust today. *DB*

The gently rolling hills of the Carneros, where Mont St. John has its vineyards, offer winegrowers soils that are not so fertile they generate vegetative growth, and yet not so undernourished that the vines struggle to give tiny crops. It's a region yet to be fully explored.

MUMM NAPA VALLEY

Of the numerous French Champagne houses that have invested in California, perhaps none did it with as much care as Mumm Napa Valley.

A joint venture between G.H. Mumm et Cie of Reims, France, and The Seagram Classics Wine Co., Mumm Napa Valley was founded not only to make a consistently styled, non-vintage wine, but also to explore the top end of the sparkling wine game by locating the greatest vineyards and then vintage-dating them so the consumer can see what the difference in vintages permits. Moreover, the winery intended to make a vintage-dated Reserve wine when appropriate, as well as a Blanc de Noirs. Other experimentation was considered, too.

The venture started out in 1985, working out of a building at Sterling Vineyards. And the first wines, made by Jim Gifford under the direction of French-trained Guy Devaux, were a stunning example of depth and richness, with a faint toasty quality rounding out the appeal.

But the best was yet to come. The winery hired Greg Fowler, who had been sparkling winemaker for Schramsberg, arguably the top producer of sparkling wine in California for two decades at that point. Fowler brought with him an understanding of California fruit that Devaux liked, and Devaux had a wealth of French aging techniques that Fowler liked. The synthesis worked like a charm.

The first vintage-dated wine, the 1985 Reserve, was excellent, but the 1986 Winery Lake was even better.

Then came 1987 Winery Lake Cuvee. A blend of 60 percent Pinot Noir and 40 percent Chardonnay, it was more elegant, with more finesse, and not quite as obvious a wine as was the '86.

"This just proves that even with sparkling wine, the vintage makes a big difference," says Fowler.

Mumm Napa Valley also produced, when weather conditions permitted, a Vintage

Many champagne producers in California charge visitors a small fee for a glass of their wines. Mumm Napa has constructed an airy patio with umbrella-shaded tables at which guests can sip the Cuvee Napa. On cool days, sips may be had inside the tasting room.

Getting the sediment out of the bottle after the second fermentation is one of the reasons that wines made by the méthode champenoise *are so* expensive. The sediment is a cloud of dead yeast cells that must be moved to the neck of the bottle and then removed carefully so none stays behind with the wine.

Reserve sparkling wine that was more elegant than the other wines in the line. Mumm thus became the only winery in the state to make a vintage-dated reserve only in special years.

The winery's other wine, a delightfully rich Blanc de Noirs, was widely praised.

Along the way, Devaux and Fowler experimented with a near-commercial lot of sparkling wine from Oregon grapes. (The wine was never marketed as a Mumm product, even though it was excellent.)

In 1988, Devaux and Fowler began to blend into some of their wines a small amount of Pinot Gris — a grape variety that Devaux discovered was planted widely in the past in the Champagne district in France. The variety was liked by winemakers in Champagne, so the story goes, but it was discarded by growers because of their difficulty with it in the vineyards.

When the non-vintage Mumm Cuvee Napa was released in late 1990, the wine was significantly better than any of the past non-vintage wines, a true connoisseur's delight. It was believed to be the first in California to contain a percentage of Pinot Gris. Thus the revival of an old, traditional variety that once was popular in Champagne added a new chapter to California sparkling winemaking history. *DB*

Mumm Napa Valley is one of the most modern sparkling wine facilities in the world. The great number of tanks gives winemaker Greg Fowler plenty of flexibility in assembling his blends for the four wines he produces here.

NEWTON VINEYARD

When winegrowers use the word "terraced" to refer to vineyards, they are speaking about steeply tilted, hillside land that has had flat cuts made into it, literally terraces, that each hold one row of vines.

This, clearly, is an expensive way to grow grapes. For one thing, you can plant fewer vines per acre, so the amount of wine you get from terraced land is usually less than what you'd get from a valley-floor vineyard. Moreover, the land has to be cut and then irrigation equipment hauled up a hill. And tending such vines is more costly because so little of the work can be done mechanically. Tractors can fall down steep slopes.

Yet Newton Vineyards in the hills above St. Helena has literally staked its future on the terraced hillside. In a manner more reminiscent of Chianti than of the Napa Valley, British-born businessman Peter Newton and his wife, Dr. Su Hua Newton, have developed from raw, woodland-covered land a unique and most improbable estate. Reached by driving up steep, winding roads from St. Helena, the Newton winery sits 800 feet above the valley floor. This winery isn't one large building, however, but four separate entities that are level with the first layer of

Newton Vineyard above St. Helena is a joint project of businessman Peter Newton and his wife, Su Hua, who did many of the paintings on the walls of the tastefully decorated winery and ancillary buildings.

vines. The vineyards then wind their way up hills and through ravines around a wide arc circling the 560-acre ranch.

The Newtons acquired this place following the sale of Sterling Vineyards, which Newton had founded with two partners in 1964. Sterling's first winemaker, Ric Forman, remained with Newton when he founded his new property.

At first, word was that the winery would be named after Forman. He had been a raw, untested, and unknown — but brilliant — technician and artist when Newton tapped him to be Sterling's winemaker. However, by the time

Newton designed much of the exterior of the winery, including a garden that literally sits atop the barrel-aging caves adjacent to the fermenting cellar. The Chinese theme is carried out throughout the grounds.

Forman joined the new Newton property, he was a world-recognized winemaking star.

Still, the Newtons were the driving spirits behind this property, not to mention the financial power behind it. Peter designed the interiors of the buildings as well as much of the landscaping, and Su Hua, an educator and painter, designed the exteriors and did many of the paintings that adorn the walls in the spacious rooms of the winery's offices. The Newton home, surrounded by an exotic garden, completes the visual picture. The Newtons named their property after themselves.

After a brief period Forman left and the Newtons hired as their winemaker John Kongsgaard, who grew up in the area and still marvels at the ways in which Newton has turned the raw property from untamed wilderness to terraced hillside vineyard.

Kongsgaard covers this outcropping of Spring Mountain in a four-wheel-drive vehicle that has to make such steep ascents at times that passengers looking out the front windshield can't see anything but the sky.

The rocky terrain encompasses numerous soil types. The two basic types are Franciscan, which is ancient ocean-bottom soil typical of the Sierra foothills, and white volcanic ash. But from the pagoda sitting atop one portion of the winery, one can see several different shades of brown dirt, from russet to a dusty gray.

The gateway to the Newton property stands on a long driveway off Madrona Street in St. Helena. The winding private drive takes visitors onto the property, then they still must climb more hilly terrain to reach the top where the offices and winery are located.

Such a variety of soils means that planting one grape type in each would be a danger. In any vintage, a variety could be wiped out in one spot, leaving the winemaker with no blending possibilities, and leading to rather one-dimensional wines.

To avoid that possibility, the Newtons decided to plant the four Bordeaux red varieties in all the different soil types, with all the various exposures possible. This gives them a wide choice of different elements when making the final blend of the wines. The Newton Cabernets were somewhat erratic at the start, due in part to young vines and bizarre vintages, but have taken on a more complex charm, notably from 1984 onward. One reason may be Kongsgaard's better understanding of the various elements from which he has to choose.

He uses four of the traditional Bordeaux grape varieties for his wines — Cabernet Sauvignon, Cabernet Franc, Merlot, and Petit Verdot — giving complexity from the differences each variety yields. Because the drainage is excellent, Kongsgaard can get some of the mountain-grown flavors so typical up here on Spring Mountain. But he attempts to keep that aspect of the fruit modest, preferring instead the more traditional cherry and herbal notes. He also shoots for an early drinkability by careful blending and fining. Newton's Merlot, especially since the spectacular 1984, has been one of California's outstanding wines of the variety, offering an amazing depth of flavor and yet an early drink-

The first building visible at Newton is the entrance to the lower barrel-aging cave, which leads to the upper barrel cellar. The winery, with its unusually shaped tanks, is located well above the underground cellars.

ability, so unlike the classic wines of Pomerol and St. Emilion. Newton's rich, complex Chardonnays and deeply scented Cabernets now team with the Merlot to give the property some of the finest wines in the Napa Valley.

When the winery wanted to expand production, there was no place to add on to the octagonal building that houses the main fermentation room, so Newton had to design non-standard, non-round tanks. A German firm was able to supply trapezoidal, square, and pie-shaped tanks, fitting them in jigsaw-puzzle fashion. That boosted capacity from 16,000 to nearly 36,000 gallons — equivalent to about 15,000 cases of wine.

To improve the quality of the wines, Kongsgaard adopted a unique vine-training

Jon Kongsgaard handles much of the tractor work on the steeply sloped, terraced vineyards that Peter and Su Hua Newton carved into the Spring Mountain hillsides. Newton Vineyard goes halfway up the mountain and makes deeply complex wines from the fruit.

system in the vineyards in which two layers of grapes are grown on alternating vines. One vine is trained to deposit its clusters along a low-lying wire; the next vine is trained up higher, so its fruit appears on an upper wire. This permits the sun's rays to reach all the fruit, maximizing the photosynthesis capabilities of the vine without developing an excessive canopy of leaves, which creates shading and slows down maturity.

Kongsgaard, who previously worked at the big Christian Brothers, small Stony Hill, and world-renowned Stag's Leap wineries in the Napa Valley, has developed his own unique style for the wines here. But Newton's mountain terraces provide him with the raw materials to achieve what few in the valley even dream about. *DB*

Newton Vineyard, with its terraced vineyards on steeply sloped land, is one of the industry's most dramatic properties and one that has already made a major impact on the premium wine field with a string of top wines.

NICHELINI WINERY

Aside from its claim of being the oldest winery in the county still operated by the same family, the nice thing about Nichelini is that it's away from the crush of Napa Valley proper. Eleven miles east of Rutherford, on Highway 128, the sturdy lime-green frame house sits perched atop a stone cellar.

With its accompanying wooden cellar, this is the old-fashioned, roadside winery of the Nichelini clan. Literally roadside, for there is barely room to park between the red, rust-coated hopper and highway blacktop.

The winery was built in 1890 by Anton Nichelini, a native of Switzerland who had studied winemaking in France. In 1884 he homesteaded in Lower Chiles Valley, later building the winery from native stone, bonded with sand and lime. He could not afford cement.

Anton and Caterina Nichelini raised 12 children in the frame house above the winery. He planted a vineyard and sold his wines to the miners who mined magnesite nearby. When other wineries closed for Prohibition in 1919, Anton did not understand why he could not

Two rows of oak barrels rest near the tasting area, where picnic tables look out over a pocket valley and an orchard of ancient walnut trees. The winery is now in the hands of founder Anton's grandchildren.

continue to earn an honest living. Only after a six-month jail term (as a trusty) did he cease making wine.

Anton's son William took over after the dreadful failure of Prohibition. A sales rep for Beaulieu Vineyard, William Nichelini lived in Oakland and journeyed north on weekends to make wine and tend the vineyards.

In 1947, when the price of grapes dropped precipitously to $35 a ton, William pulled his son Jim out of high school to run the winery full-time. "In the old days, the old-time Italian

The winery at Nichelini is situated under the old frame house, built by Anton Nichelini in 1890. An old-fashioned basket press, with a huge log fulcrum, stands guard in front of the native-stone cellar.

bachelors would come up here and we would fill their jugs and barrels," Jim once told me. "We would sell it any way we could then. We were lucky if we could get rid of it."

Jim produced wines mainly from grapes he and his cousin, Joe, grew a quarter-mile north-west of the winery. Loyal customers clamored for specialties Chenin Blanc and Sauvignon Vert, which sold for $2.35 a bottle in 1978.

Jim was especially known for entertaining weekend winery visitors on his accordian, out on the open-air terrace "tasting room," as well as for driving his Model "T" every year since 1948 in the Napa County Fair. Jim Nichelini died suddenly in April 1985.

Since Jim's own children weren't interested in running the small winery, four of Anton's other grandchildren gathered to buy them out. In July 1990 Greg Boeger, the son of Anton's youngest daughter, took over as winemaker. (If the name Boeger rings a bell, it's because Greg and his wife, Susan, have operated the successful Boeger Winery in Placerville, in the Sierra Foothills, since 1973.) Grandson Joe Nicheli-ni, a stockbroker by day, manages the hundred-plus-acre vineyard and his wife, Carol, serves as office manager; Toni "Cookie" Nichelini-Irwin, Jim's sister, handles public relations and helps in the tasting room; and IBM exec Dick Wainright helps Greg in the cellar and handles all maintenance problems, along with Toni's husband, Don. *RPH*

ROBERT PECOTA WINERY

R ob Pecota. Are we talking the salesman as artist? Or is it the artist as salesman? It's hard to tell sometimes, but suffice it to say that the lean, handball-playing Pecota is perhaps the most artful salesman of them all. Ask him why a winery his size has distribution in only a handful of states.

"A lot of wineries our size would be shotgunning their product into as many states as possible," he admits, "but I want to keep the chain between myself and the ultimate consumer short."

"I work directly with distributors in California, New York, Colorado, Massachusetts, Michigan, Minnesota, North Carolina, Georgia, and a few other states." Minnesota is illustrative.

"I like to do business in places where I enjoy being, where I enjoy the people," he explains. "Nobody likes to go to Minnesota, yet it's an incredibly beautiful state. These are very conservative people, yet you can do business there on a handshake. If you're in a state with less than 100 cases a month, you're going to get lost in the shuffle."

The key to Pecota's identification in a fragmented marketplace is his commitment to promoting local artists, using an original piece of

Rob Pecota planted his vineyard on the low, flat land at the northermost end of the Napa Valley, at the foot of 4,343-foot Mount St. Helena (named for a Russian princess a century and a half ago).

art on each vintage's label. "For the winery, it has worked out exactly as I had hoped," says Pecota with satisfaction. "It has gotten to the point where our customers cannot remember the vintage so much as they remember the piece of art. One guy called to say how much he enjoyed one of our Sauvignon Blancs. I asked him which vintage, but all he could remember were the poppies on the label. 'Oh,' I said, 'the '79!' Others talk about 'The tiger bottling' ('83, and my personal favorite) or 'The duck bottling' ('84)."

His concern when he released the first vintages was that the change in art each year

The Pecota home sits next to the winery, and the swimming pool often interrupts the journey from one to the other. Early on, Pecota made Petite Sirah and French Colombard, but Cabernet and Chardonnay are today's staples.

might cause confusion among consumers. He needn't have worried. Dedicated consumers now anticipate the release of his Nouveau Beaujolais each November to get the first look at that vintage's new artist. "We've kept the script typeface constant on each label, so only the art changes each year," says Pecota as we sit in his winery office. It is practically an art gallery, with the original art works of each label framed and hung on the neutral, white walls.

Pecota's wines run the gamut from the rich, buttery Canepa Chardonnay through the lean, supple Sauvignon Blanc, the firm Kara's Vineyard Cabernet Sauvignon, to the aromatic, silky-sweet Muscato di Andrea dessert wine (the latter pair named for Pecota daughters).

Rob is not above promoting the wines of other wineries as a sales technique. "Look, every bottle of good wine sold helps all of us," he says earnestly. "Part of the reason I talk about other wineries is to gain credibility. I'm also the severest critic of my own wines. It's almost a shocking approach to wine marketing, and things are pretty tight today, but ours is a sharing business and I see nothing to be lost by giving credit where credit is earned." Such was the attitude expressed by Pecota's "Dedication Series" bottling of his 1981 Sauvignon Blanc, whose label lauded the pioneering work of Robert Mondavi in bringing the variety to center stage. *RPH*

Small stainless-steel fermenters are crowded into the limited space of this still-small winery. If one daughter gets a Muscat named for her, it's only fair that daughter Kara have a Cabernet named for her, too.

PEJU PROVINCE

The story of the last two decades of the 20th century in the Napa Valley is one of concern for the agricultural lifestyle that is the valley itself, a lifestyle and a business temperament that account directly for the valley's worldwide acclaim as one of the greatest winemaking regions.

Beginning in the mid-1980s, the Napa Valley was rife with disputes between growers and winemakers, between no-growth advocates and those favoring progressive development, between Wine Train foes and champions, and — one of the most basic — between the city slickers and the country folks. Board of super-visors' meetings were more rancorous than a Liverpool/Everton soccer match. During this period one winery represented the valley's socio-political tone better than any.

Peju Province was a dream of Tony Peju, whose self-described "mid-life crisis" prompted him to leave his nursery business near Los Angeles and move north. After a long search, in 1982 he found a 30-acre parcel and a house in Rutherford. Then began the tedious and costly struggle to get permits to build a winery and to raise the cash to finance it.

The first public outcry over this winery arose because Tony had his first two crops

The attractive entrance to the Peju Province winery in Rutherford was built well before construction of the winery got under way. Then Tony Peju ran into opposition to his project. But he persisted, and eventually the winery was built and resistance faded.

crushed elsewhere. He wanted to sell his wine from his own tasting room, a few feet from where the grapes grew. But when he applied for a temporary tasting-room license, the furor over too many tourists was at fever pitch. And Tony took the brunt of no-growthers' wrath.

"It is customary for wineries to custom-crush their first vintage at another winery," Tony says. But the fact that his tasting room also sold T-shirts and other memorabilia smacked of too much commercialism to some of Tony's neighbors. They charged his was little more than a gift shop calling itself a "winery."

"We went to the county and said, 'It just

Wind machines like this one in Rutherford are used to circulate the air when temperatures drop. Another technique is the use of overhead sprinklers to cover the grapes with a blanket of ice, which protects the vine from even colder temperatures.

doesn't make sense.' State law says I am allowed to sell the wine I grow, but they [the county] said I can't sell the wine I make if it's made elsewhere. But nowhere in the definition of a winery does it say you have to crush the grapes on the premises."

Then the question of just what a winery really was came into play. Some said a winery was a place where grapes were crushed, and under that definition, Peju Province wasn't a winery. A court ruled Tony was right: in 1986 he got his temporary tasting-room permit as well as a permit to build a winery.

That didn't end it though. The winery was partially constructed in 1987, when the county sought to have Peju post a sign declaring he had "no public tours or tasting." Tony again raised legal battle: lots of other wineries without tours or tastings were also without signs. Again the court ruled in Peju's favor. By 1990, most of Peju's problems were over. Financing was obtained, the winery built, and in 1991 it opened to the first visitors as a real, certified winery.

On his 26 acres of grapes, Peju grows Cabernet Sauvignon and Chardonnay. His Cabernet gave him his first acclaim. The 1986 Cabernet from Peju won a double-gold medal at the San Francisco Fair wine competition, a prestigious event with stingy judges. By 1990, case production was 5,500 cases and included two Chardonnays. *DB*

Tony Peju spent his first years in the Napa Valley fighting political and legal battles so he could build his winery and make wine from his own grapes. By 1989, Peju was able to concentrate on winemaking and his first wines won medals at major wine competitions.

ROBERT PEPI WINERY

Robert Pepi Winery was founded by a San Francisco fur dresser with the goal of simply growing grapes. But since the first release in 1981, the wine (made essentially from Sauvignon Blanc and Semillon) has been excellent and the Pepi winery now anticipates that red wine, especially the Italian Sangiovese, is the wine Robert Pepi will build its future on.

A number of wine-country families started out merely to grow grapes as a way of creating a stronger family bond. And it's true that farming does sometimes seem therapeutic.

The city dweller looks to the malleability of the earth to remind him what life is about — seed to harvest, working with the hands to create a living product that has soul and heart.

And for some reason, grape-growing often is seen as the perfect project to inspire the imagination. Perhaps it's biblical — water into wine. Or possibly it's that growing grapes and raising a family are such parallel activities that one gives insight into the other.

Robert Pepi, a fur dresser in San Francisco in the mid-1960s, looked to farming in search of his past. "The vineyards were something dad bought to get back to the family's farming roots," says his son, Bob Pepi, now winemaker for Robert Pepi Winery. "Dad had spent a lot of time in Santa Rosa when he was growing up. The family heritage was Italian peasant farmers, and he thought we'd do that weekends and summers."

The 70-acre ranch on the east side of Highway 29 was bought in 1966, and the family farmed part-time. Bob had no immediate interest in making wine, but he did receive his zoology degree from Pomona College in Southern California. Though it offers no formal program in winemaking, a number of winemakers do graduate from Pomona.

With that mystical connection, Bob decided in the late 1970s to move to the winery and make wine under the family name, from the family grapes. In 1981, the Robert Pepi Winery was born. Chardonnay, Sauvignon Blanc,

and Cabernet were produced. Bob also liked the so-called "orphan" varieties, such as Semillon.

However, the Pepi family heritage was Tuscan, and it was that background that prompted the family to plant the Sangiovese-Grosso variety that is so rare in the Napa Valley.

"All my relatives are from around Florence, so we thought, why not grow a variety from where my folks were from? We planted the vineyard in 1983, and we make the wine more like a Chianti than Brunello, with delicate fruit," says Bob.

Not satisfied with the quality of his Sauvignon Blanc vineyards, Bob developed a new vine-training system called the two-heart canopy. The head of the vine is split and gradually, over five years, trained into two canopies. "This gives the grapes greater sunlight and better aeration," Bob explains. Not only is the quality of the grape improved, but he gets 12 tons per acre of fruit, about double the normal weight.

Pepi's vineyards include 25 acres of Sauvignon Blanc, about seven acres each of Chardonnay and Sangiovese-Grosso, and five acres each of Semillon and Cabernet.

By 1990 case production at Pepi reached about 20,000 cases a year. The Sangiovese project, which started out with just 240 cases in 1988, jumped to more than 1,000 cases in 1990 and eventually will top out at about 2,000 cases. *DB*

Robert Pepi's Sauvignon Blancs from an experimental trellising system aroused academic interest in the Napa Valley in the late 1980s. The winery also experimented with a Sangiovese, the grape variety from Tuscany, Italy. Pepi's first release of it in 1991 gave wine lovers their first real opportunity to see what this Chianti grape variety could do in the famed Napa Valley.

JOSEPH PHELPS VINEYARDS

The old Spring Valley Schoolhouse provides the first impression. Dark green, neatly trimmed in white and topped by a belfry, it marks the turnoff from the Silverado Trail onto Taplin Road. A short distance brings one to the strikingly bold gateway, built with century-old, railroad bridge timbers. The horizontal trelliswork, a theme that is carried through in a winery breezeway, is supported by massive beams.

The integrity and charm of the physical plant is to the credit of owner/founder Joseph Phelps, the board chairman of Colorado's Hensel Phelps Construction Company. In Cali-

fornia to fashion the two Souverain wineries in 1972, he purchased the 670-acre Connolly Hereford Ranch on Taplin Road. The following year vineyard and winery development commenced when he was joined by Walter Schug, a graduate of one of the top winemaking schools in the world, Geisenheim, in Germany.

Schug fully demonstrated his winemaking brilliance with several vintages and varieties of superb dry and sweet Johannisberg Rieslings. In 1977 he added a golden, honey-thick Late Harvest Gewurztraminer and later an equally lovely Late Harvest Scheurebe. In conjunction with Phelps's interest, he also began exploring

This gateway entrance to Joseph Phelps Vineyard was fashioned from century-old railroad-bridge timbers. The horizontal trellis-work theme is continued in the breezeway between two wings of the winery.

the California variations on French Syrah, the Rhone variety at the heart of the great Hermitage and Côte Rotie wines.

"We feel that Syrah will ultimately be at least the equivalent of Zinfandel in importance in California," says Phelps. "This is red wine country. Someday, Syrah may even rank with Cabernet and Pinot Noir as a classic variety."

Craig Williams, who succeeded Schug, is very excited about the possibilities of Rhone-style wines. "California's climate, with its marine influence, gives us the cool nights necessary to retain acid in red wine varieties. What's fascinating about Rhone-style wines is

the range of flavor dynamics, the variety of fruitiness. That's what wine is all about."

The folks at Phelps are so taken with the Rhone concept that they have introduced a whole series of Rhone wines, bottled under the Vin du Mistral label. (The mistral is the powerful northern wind that blows cold and dry into southern France and the Rhône Valley.)

Williams is the son of a Rockwell aerospace engineer, and the love of research had a way of rubbing off. Williams was studying biology at Long Beach State when a U.C. Davis professor was presented as a guest lecturer. "I skipped the rest of my classes to have lunch with Dr. Ralph Kunkee, and soon transferred to Davis, where I studied with Tim Mondavi, Eric Wente, Allison Green (Firestone) and Tom Rinaldi (Duckhorn)."

After he graduated in 1975, he spent two harvests at a central valley winery before joining Phelps in December 1976. He worked in the lab a couple of years, was in charge of cellar operations for a time, and then was promoted to head winemaker prior to the 1983 crush, when founding winemaker Walter Schug slid full time into the Pinot Noir-based winery he had started for himself a few years earlier.

Where Schug was known especially for his late harvest Rieslings, Williams gave that theme his own personal twist in 1977 with a wine labeled Early Harvest White Riesling.

Wine, as the sages have said for centuries, is merely water mixed with sunshine.
The Burgundians add their own twist of wisdom to the forum, noting that the first duty of a wine is to be red. These fulfill that dictum. The water is there only to prevent dehydration.

Vines grown on the flat, valley floor tend to produce larger crops of fruit, which in turn produce wines of lesser intensity. This apparently flat area, however, is on a raised "bench," and thus blends the greater intensity of hillside fruit with the greater ease of cultivation that comes to flatland vinelands.

"This wine is an attempt to make a Riesling that can be consumed earlier," offers Williams. "It took us a few of years to decide which vineyard was most suitable for this 'Early Harvest' wine. We finally settled on a warm spot at the winery ranch, which allows us to pick earlier, at low pH and high acidity." Curiously, such wines handle up to a decade of age quite well.

Though winemakers are often compared to medieval alchemists who were thought to have been able to change baser metals into gold, Williams clearly understands, despite academic lessons, that much of what goes into wine quality happens before he gets his hands on the grapes.

"When I was in school, we were taught that soil just holds the roots up for the vine.

Vineyard site selection was irrelevant, unless you had high boron content or some other chemical imbalance," recalls the wavy-haired winemaker.

In the mid-'80s Williams joined with winemakers from seven other wineries — Jordan, Beringer, Simi, Domaine Chandon, Sterling, Mondavi, and The Christian Brothers — to form a research group dedicated to finding ways of improving wine quality at the vineyard level.

"Yes, there are still things we can learn in the winery," says Williams. "And much of what we're learning seems to take us full circle back to traditional methods, except that now we have a better idea of why those methods were and are successful."

German oak ovals fill one long wall in the hospitality room, while a piano dominates one corner. If you look closely at the shelf atop the left wall, you'll see scores of empty wine bottles, sampled through the years at Phelps. To know good wines, one must taste all the great wines of the world. They certainly do at Phelps.

Along with fine Chardonnays, especially a rich, ripe wine made from Angelo Sangiacomo's Carneros vineyard, Phelps also makes some extraordinary, long-lived Cabernets. Phelps's "Insignia" designation was first used to mark the finest wine of the vintage. In 1974 it was a Napa Valley Cabernet, in 1975 the Merlot from John Stanton's Oakville vineyard (including 15% Cabernet), and the following year it was Milt Eisele's Cabernet Sauvignon. From 1977 on, however, "Insignia" identifies a proprietary blend of Cabernet, Cabernet Franc, and Merlot, a wine made in the Bordeaux mold.

Above the wines, though, is a sense of family far beyond that bandied about in press releases and brochures. When founding wine-

Colorado construction magnate Joseph Phelps has created a true sense of family at his winery.

maker Schug expressed an interest in starting his own winery, Joe Phelps set up a five-year financial plan to help him make the transition smoothly. Bruce Neyers, head of marketing, has his own label for Cabernet and a barrel-fermented Chardonnay, again partly financed by Phelps. And Joe has so organized the corporate ownership of his winery that, at his death, those who are operating it can buy it.

"Employee ownership is a dynamic, productive way to run a business," says Phelps quietly and simply. "If you surround yourself with achievers, and provide them with opportunities for growth — without regard for your own ego, or fear of competition — they'll succeed. The alternative is mediocrity." Not a word ever associated with the Phelps phenomenon. Ever. *RPH*

This portion of Spring Valley, east of St. Helena, was a cattle ranch when Joe Phelps bought the property in 1972.

PINE RIDGE WINERY

Pine Ridge has vineyards at the winery and at several other locations in the Napa Valley. Each place has a different soil type, soil texture, drainage, slope, water, and sun exposure; each is best suited to particular grape varieties. Chardonnay does best in cooler loci, while Cabernet requires a warmer spot.

A striking ridge of pine juts up just north of Stag's Leap Wine Cellars on the west side of the Silverado Trail. In its winter shadow, former U.S. Ski Team member Gary Andrus built a basic winery around the remaining wall of a winery built in 1902 by Luigi Domenicani. Today Andrus and winemaker Stacy Clark work in expanded facilities that include 6,548 square feet of caves capable of holding more than 800 oak barrels.

Clark grew up south of San Francisco, and was sold on science by a high school teacher who made science real to his students. "Mr. Holm's classroom was covered with biological artifacts — he'd leave out old sandwiches so we could watch molds grow."

She drew cartoons for the newspaper while taking her degree in fermentation science, signing on at Pine Ridge directly out of U.C. Davis in 1983. "Winemaking is an art and a science where you can really get your hands dirty," Clark says with glee. "Yet it's a mind-blowing mental challenge, too."

Pine Ridge's initial success was based on a flinty apple and sweet grass Chenin Blanc and a green olive, cedary, soft, and elegant Cabernet Sauvignon that unmistakably proclaimed its Rutherford origins. Now Chardonnay is a close rival to cash cow Chenin Blanc in volume, followed by several regionally designated Cabernets and a fine, fleshy Merlot.

But it's the Cabernet that gets Gary's vinous juices flowing. "Every day as I taste the lots of wine resting in barrels, I am reminded of the mystery of Cabernet," proclaims Andrus. "In my many tasting groups, whether we are tasting old wines or new, French or Californian, the mystery of Cabernet remains hidden.

Here, red wine juice (called "must") is being separated from the solids (skin, pulp, seeds) by a hydraulic press. The fresh juice, which is quite tasty, is nearly one-quarter sugar. Fermentation will convert that to carbon dioxide and alcohol.

"The question is this: why do the tastes of Cabernet wines from grapes grown in different vineyards differ so much? Wines made from other grape varieties grown in different vineyards also show subtle taste differences, but I am convinced that no other wine shows as much variability due to the vineyard as does Cabernet Sauvignon."

Because Andrus and Clark employ the same winemaking style with each lot, what differences remain must be attributed to the grape source. "Stacy Clark and I make Cabernets from Rutherford, Diamond Mountain, Howell Mountain, and Stags Leap District, and each one is consistently different from year to year. Cinnamon and eucalyptus dominate in wines from Diamond Mountain vines; green olives, cassis, and dusty flavors are the hallmarks of the Stags Leap District.

"In addition to these tastes, think about the range of green bean and broccoli flavors of Monterey Cabernets, the spinach and coffee flavors of the Alexander Valley, and the Bing cherry flavors of Mendocino County Cabernet Sauvignons. French and Chilean wines exhibit many of the same flavors."

The why of it may remain a mystery but Andrus remains intrigued by the differences. "Blending Cabernets from different areas does not necessarily make a better wine, but it does make a wine that is more diffuse. Other mesoclimates exist, and many fine, distinctive wines are made from them." *RPH*

Winemaker Stacy Clark tastes a sample directly from the fermenting tank. It is vital to monitor wines constantly throughout their lives, literally tasting grape juice while grapes are on the vine, the must during fermentation, and the wines themselves as they age in barrel and bottle.

RAYMOND VINEYARD & CELLAR

Balance is the word one thinks of when tasting wine from Raymond Vineyard & Cellar, off Zinfandel Lane in the heart of the valley. Walter Raymond, winemaker for this family-founded winery, has a delicate hand, and never tries to beat the tar out of the grape to extract more than the grape would yield naturally.

For this reason, Raymond rarely gets the skyrocket recognition it truly deserves for its Cabernet Sauvignon and Chardonnay. Wine critics seem to prefer the darkest, densest, stormiest Cabernets and the oakiest, butteriest, most intensely flavored Chardonnays.

Walt and his brother, Roy Raymond Jr., rankle a bit when they fail to get the acclaim of others. Yet connoisseurs know the value of the Raymond wines, especially when they open those with a few years of bottle age and realize that the greatness is in the very delicacy that the brothers seek. "We could make a darker wine, but would it be a better wine?" asks Walt.

The Raymond winery was founded in 1974, but wine's been in the family for much longer. Roy Raymond Sr. came up to the Napa Valley from San Francisco the year Prohibition ended (1933) just to work the harvest at the Beringer vineyards. There he met Mary Jane

The modest ranch-style Raymond winery building and tasting room are not far from heavily traveled Highway 29, but they are located off Zinfandel Lane, and set well back from the road.

Beringer, the owner's daughter, married her, and never returned to the big city. Eventually Roy and Mary Jane Raymond took over Beringer.

In 1970, Beringer was sold to Nestle Inc. The following year the Raymonds planted the 80-acre vineyard that would become the focal point of their family winery. However, over the years the Raymonds' winemaking outgrew their vineyard. By 1990, Raymond was buying from more than 40 Napa Valley growers.

Roy Jr., the viticulturalist and marketing manager, has acknowledged openly over the years that the cost of production of certain

Founded by the family that operated the Beringer winery after that winery was sold to Nestle, Raymond Vineyard & Cellar made a wide range of wines, but later specialized in the top three varietals in the valley: Cabernet Sauvignon, Chardonnay, and Sauvignon Blanc.

wines hasn't risen appreciably, so prices for the wines shouldn't rise much, either. Thus Raymond wines have been kept reasonable in price. But he has also said that a winery's image is tied directly to the price it charges for its best products, so the price of their Private Reserve wines rose to just over $20 a bottle in the late 1980s. Even though the Raymonds thought this a move fraught with peril, consumers saw the price as no more than justified for the excellent wines. Moreover, most of the Raymonds' competitors were charging $30 to $50 a bottle for wine of the same — or sometimes lesser — quality.

Through the 1980s, Raymond went along increasing production quietly, based on the industry knowledge that its wines represented good value. By 1990 it was making more than 140,000 cases of wine and selling it all readily.

In 1989, the family chose to sell most of their winery to Kirin Brewing, the Japanese giant. However, they retained a share of the winery and stock options as well. Most of the Japanese forays into this industry have been lock, stock, and barrel deals, but Kirin saw in the Raymonds a valuable asset.

So a deal was struck in which the Raymonds' compensation is partly tied to the quality of the wine. It's a deal that ensures great, consistent, Raymond-style wine for a long time. *DB*

Winemaker Walter Raymond uses gentle methods to make his wines and the results often produce supple qualities and accessibility when the wines are young, yet they evolve in a graceful manner.

RITCHIE CREEK VINEYARDS

In 1965, Napa Valley had fewer than a dozen wineries. It was unspoiled, with wild brush and trees covering the hillsides, and unpaved trails meandering off into the undergrowth. Vineyards were interspersed among other crops, including walnuts, prunes, and hay.

Pete Minor was a dentist in Sonoma County then. He was 31 and a lover of fine wine. "We started out drinking [Louis] Martini wines, then some other Zinfandels, and then we discovered BV, Inglenook, and Krug. That's about all the wineries there were in the Napa Valley at the time."

Fascinated by the business, Pete bought a 50-acre parcel of land — mostly brush and timber — on Spring Mountain, at about the 2,000-foot level, just up from St. Helena. He began to clear the land and plant vines in 1967.

His first wines were good and his winemaking improved progressively, so, following the excellent 1974 harvest, Pete bonded his property as Ritchie Creek Winery and began to market the wines. Their style is similar in some respects to that of neighboring Smith-Madrone Winery. The Cabernet Sauvignon is fairly concentrated and rich, but with a spiciness and an occasional herbal note that Minor's neighbors

One of the earlier wineries founded in the Napa Valley's second revolution in the 1970s, Ritchie Creek is situated on a ridge that offers a dramatic view of the sunset over the lush vegetation.

don't get. It sometimes has a lean, Bordeaux-like finish.

Pete planted an old clone of Cabernet, obtained from the Mondavi family when they all toiled together at the Charles Krug Winery. The clone came from the vineyard that usually produced the Krug Special Selection Cabernet Sauvignon.

One reason for the relative austerity of the Ritchie Creek Cabernet is that the vineyard here faces north, which means it's cooler than the south-facing vines of his neighbors that get afternoon sun. "Because we're north-facing, we get slower ripening and nice high acids."

Pete Minor, a former dentist from nearby Santa Rosa, produces a small quantity of high quality wines from his shallow, mountainous soils, including a wine from the rare Rhone variety, Viognier. It is a cult item with wine lovers.

Also, soils here are rocky and thin, leading to a "tighter" wine.

Today, Minor operates the vineyard and winery with his wife, Maggie, and with "two little kids and four older kids."

In the last few years, it has become one of the few wineries making wine from the Rhone white grape Viognier. Minor's vineyard now includes four acres of Cabernet Sauvignon, three of Chardonnay, and one of the rare Viognier grape.

It is the Viognier that has brought Ritchie Creek all its recent acclaim. Minor makes it conventionally, crushing the grapes and fermenting them cool, to capture as much of the floral quality of the variety as possible. "The real joy of the wine is the smell of those flowers, and I try to hang on to that as much as possible."

Minor adds, "On top of this ridge it's usually pretty cold for Viognier, and I didn't plant it for commercial purposes. I really did not anticipate all this interest in the Rhone varieties." He makes about 120 cases a year; and marketing it is no problem because of the recent demand for such wines by Rhone lovers.

Production of the winery has never varied. Pete makes about 1,200 cases of wine a year. Asked what his method of production entails, the modest man says, "We pick it, stomp it, and put it in barrels." *DB*

Harvesting grapes on the mountain isn't a picnic, especially since the vines yield small crops, and the clusters of grapes aren't as full of fruit as vines in other areas. This does, however, give depth to Ritchie Creek's Cabernets.

ROMBAUER VINEYARDS

Rombauer Vineyards has a poster showing a pair of glistening bottles in a straw-filled, wooden box. The caption reads, "From Out Of The Blue." If the bottles look like rockets about to take off, it is fitting, for Koerner Rombauer has a love of flying that knows no bounds. On a round, white, tasting-room table stands a two-foot model of the Braniff DC-8 Rombauer used to fly to South America.

"I still love to fly," the stocky, solid Rombauer says with boyish enthusiasm. "Flying is a dimension of freedom, of free thinking. A few years ago we got a pressurized twin, an Aerostar, that has a 220-knot cruise." Koerner

and Joan Rombauer can now hightail it to sales meetings, marketing trips — and friends' fishing cabins — at more than 250 miles an hour!

There's also the implication from the poster that Rombauer Vineyards isn't very well known. There's more than a kernel of truth to that notion as well. For, thus far, the largest part of the wines made at Rombauer do not carry the royal blue trim-and-capsule color that identifies Rombauer wines.

You see, Rombauer has always been a "community winery." Though it has increased production of its own label steadily to what is now more than 10,000 cases a year, the facility

Koerner Rombauer uses oak as a cook uses spices to subtly change wine flavors. That's not terribly surprising since his great-aunt, Irma Rombauer, co-authored The Joy of Cooking.

puts out 75,000 cases each year. The difference? Custom crushing, making wine for labels without wineries. And some pretty distinguished folks have made wine at Rombauer, from the John Daniel Society (Dominus) and Sam Sebastiani (Viansa), to Merryvale.

Rombauer, fiftyish, was born and raised in Escondido, California, on a citrus ranch. At San Diego State, he was "sort of a business major." In the Air Guard he learned to fly. As that passion kindled, he applied for and earned a position with Braniff, flying out of Dallas. At first he flew to the Orient; later, he flew South American routes from the West Coast.

Airplanes and automobiles are Koerner's "toys." "Had to put 'em all down as collateral for our winery loan," he recalls. In addition to his airplane and a '59 Mercedes 300SL, Koerner owns this 1947 Mercury. He still dreams of owning a P-51 Mustang, World War II's hottest fighter aircraft.

Owning a winery can bring you down to earth with a jarring ka-thump. "When we first applied for our loan, I had to put all my Braniff toys down as collateral," Rombauer recalls with a morose, twisted grin. "My airplane. The '47 Mercury. The '59 Mercedes 300SL. Aggh."

Though many do, Koerner did not start his own winery out of ignorance. He had originally come to the Napa Valley in 1972. In 1977 he and Joan became general partners in Conn Creek Winery, then ready to expand.

In 1980 the Rombauers sold their interest in Conn Creek to a French group and began designing their own winery. Half-buried in an oak-studded knoll north of St. Helena, just off the Silverado Trail, Rombauer Vineyards opened for business in 1982.

Current winemaker is Greg Graham, who grew up in a farming family in Ohio, making wines as an amateur from the likes of Catawba, Niagra, and Concord. The soft-spoken Graham looks primarily to good grape locations for his Cabernets and the Rombauer Le Meilleur Du Chai ("best of the cellar").

"Hillside fruit gives us Cabernet ripeness and that cherry/berry fruit component," explains Graham. "We get our Merlot and Cabernet Franc from valley floor sites, which adds the herbaceous element that is desirable for further complexity." *RPH*

ROMBAUER
VINEYARDS

1985
LE MEILLEUR DU CHAI
Napa Valley
RED WINE

Le Meilleur de Chai means "the best of the cellar." As a proprietary wine, it gives Rombauer and his winemaker a free hand in blending Cabernet Sauvignon, Cabernet Franc, and Merlot to come up with a wine that represents the epitome of each vintage.

ROUND HILL WINERY

The Round Hill label was introduced as a *négociant* label in 1976 by wine retailer Ernie Van Asperen. "We bought 'distressed wines,'" explains Ernie. "They weren't bad wines. It was just that there was a surplus of grapes and a few wineries were having marketing problems. With more than 80 retail stores, I was able to bottle them under my own label and resell them inexpensively. It was great for the consumer."

When Van Asperen decided it was time to make a little wine as well, he enlisted the cherubic, ebullient Charles Abela — a former marine mechanic — to oversee operations. In 1977 Abela leased an old winery building behind The Arbor complex on Lodi Lane and began refitting it.

That structure, crammed with steel tanks and French oak, was inaugurated with a crush of 216 tons in 1978. Abela's thick, strong hands gesture as he talks about that little winery. "I got into this to slide into retirement," he says with a laugh. "I figured about three days a week, and then I would have plenty of time for hunting and fishing. As it happened, I've never worked so hard in my life. But I've always felt good about it."

With wines selling at reasonable prices and tasting good to boot, demand quickly outstripped supply. The little winery on Lodi Lane was soon bursting at the seams. By 1987, production had jumped from 40,000 cases to more than 200,000. It was time to move. So, Round Hill slid south along the Silverado Trail into a wholly new facility, built at the corner of Rutherford Cross Road and Highway 128, at the foot of Auberge du Soleil's slope, with neighbors Rutherford Hill, Conn Creek, Caymus, ZD, and Domaine Mumm.

Round Hill has four product lines. The Round Hill label covers three: the successful "House" wines; a group of varietal wines from Napa Valley fruit; and a Napa Reserve Chardonnay, Merlot, and Cabernet. The Rutherford Ranch brand is the high-priced spread, limited

The ample elbow room at Round Hill's new winery is a far cry from the cramped "sailor's" quarters at their former facility on Lodi Lane. The old winery encompassed just 5,000 square feet; the new has 27,000 square feet of floor space. "We don't have to pitchfork grapes into our crushers anymore," notes partner Virginia Van Asperen.

to small lots of Napa Valley Chardonnay, Cabernet Sauvignon, and Merlot.

"Our Rutherford Ranch wines get different cellar treatment," notes Ernie, "usually more time in small oak, or perhaps in newer oak, and are thus richer, more distinctive wines. They're also a little bit more expensive, but that's to be expected when you're starting with the best grapes and giving them kid-glove treatment in the cellar."

Mark Swain has been making wine at Round Hill since 1983 and had 11 years in the business before that, at Mont St. John and Charles Krug. "He's extremely intelligent, is a talented blender, and just has a great feel for wine," notes Virginia, Ernie's wife and partner. Swain also has the benefit of input from general manager Phil Baxter, formerly head winemaker at Rutherford Hill and Domaine Michel.

If Round Hill made its initial impression and sales gains based on word of mouth and exceptional pricing policies, the winery has captured a good deal of national attention through a series of ad cartoons designed by William Hamilton (*The Now Society*). A favorite has a wine shop owner apologizing to a patron, "I am devastated with embarrassment. All the Gold Medal Round Hill Cabernet was bought up by our employees." *RPH*

Where small oak barrels lend a sharper spiciness to wines aged therein, larger oak uprights — with much less wood-surface-to-wine ratio — give a much more subtle seasoning to wines that require less influence from the oak itself.

RUTHERFORD HILL WINERY

Rutherford Hill, in one sense, is the logical outgrowth of Freemark Abbey. As new vineyards came into production, the partners had to decide between increasing production or building a second winery.

Wisely, the latter choice was made. Fortunately, the old Souverain of Rutherford winery, owned by Pillsbury Mills, became available at the time. Plans for a new winery (expensive) were gladly scrapped for the purchase of the thoroughly modern, albeit large, used winery (not quite so expensive). It was an exceptional opportunity, for the big, barn-like, concrete structure, sheathed in cedar, had been outfitted with automated crushing and fermenting equipment, a sterile bottling room, and a barrel cellar stuffed with all sizes of American and European oak upright tanks.

The Freemark Abbey partnership purchased the facility in 1976 and renamed it Rutherford Hill Winery. Though several wines are produced, Rutherford Hill's standard-bearers are Merlot, Chardonnay, and Cabernet Sauvignon. To contrast winery styles, the

An elaborate trelliswork frames the entrance to Rutherford Hill's barrel-aging caves, which extend a half mile into the cliff behind the winery. It is the most extensive wine-cave system in America.

Chardonnay is aged in Allier, Nevers, and Limousin oak at Rutherford Hill (they're aged in Nevers at Freemark). The Rutherford Hill Cabernets are blended with much less Merlot than Freemark's. Rutherford Hill also produces a spicy, perfumed Gewurztraminer, a particular favorite of managing partner Bill Jaeger.

In a way, it's a return for winemaker Jerry Luper, who was wine master at Freemark Abbey for six years in the early '70s, working with many of the same owners and creating Napa Valley's first botrytised Johannisberg Riesling —

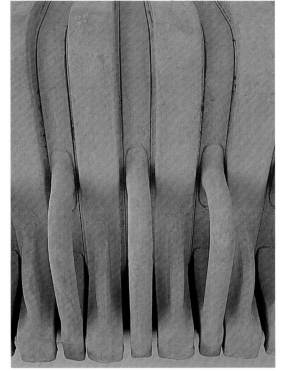

the famed 1973 Edelwein. Modesto-born Luper's first wine job was at age 18, with Gallo. "That was quite an education," he says in wonder. "I started out taking samples and washing glassware, then became an assistant to the 'blender.' Gallo was a graduate school in wine, because we were constantly tasting, comparing, and analyzing wines from all over the world. Thus, I tend to be very open-minded in tasting and criticism."

An Army stint and a flair for languages took Luper to Germany. He returned to finish his formal schooling at Fresno State, then worked the 1969 crush at Louis Martini. "That's where I learned that winemaking is more than a mere exercise in chemistry," says Luper. "Though great wines begin in the vineyard, they are really made in the cellar. Which means living with your wines. 'Raising wines' is a term I use. I think that my insistence on precise timing of cellar operations contributes more to my reputation as a winemaker than anything else. Sometimes the difference between good and great can be a matter of minutes."

One thing that pleased Jerry was Rutherford Hill's increasing attention to Merlot. "I really walked into a very positive situation. We had very good sources for grapes, equipment was state-of-the-art, the production staff was motivated and skilled and enthusiastic about making good wine, and the ownership was dedicated to quality." *RPH*

RUTHERFORD VINTNERS

M any wineries have opened in the Napa Valley, failed to achieve any recognition, and closed. Often these wineries have made good wine, but for various reasons they didn't succeed. Rutherford Vintners, as quiet as any, *has* succeeded, and the main reasons are consistency and the ability to sell a major portion of its product directly to the consumer from the cozy tasting room off Highway 29.

Bernard and Evelyn Skoda's modest Rutherford Vintners property is an anomaly among the grand properties around them. It sits unassumingly on the west side of the road under a bank of stately eucalyptus trees. The advertising budget here is zero, so few newcomers to the valley know of the place. But familiar faces know that the hospitality is warm under the red tile roof, and the wines are good. So the tasting room is often alive with friendly faces.

Despite the cachet of being a Napa Valley winery that makes Cabernet Sauvignon from the esteemed Rutherford soil, Rutherford Vintners was never meant to be a "statement winery." The Skodas opened it in 1976 intending only to make tasty, consistent wines and to sell them at reasonable prices. And they have achieved amazing consistency, most notably with Caber-

net Sauvignon. This pays homage to Louis Michael Martini, founder of the famed winery across the road, and to his son, Louis Peter.

Skoda worked at the Martini winery for 15 years as a manager, until 1976 when he could afford to open his own winery. This was during an era when much experimentation was going on in the Napa Valley wine industry to refine techniques for growing grapes and making fine wine. And Skoda was with the Martinis, two of the greatest pioneers of experimentation — to see all the trials.

One result is that Skoda now believes in taking good quality fruit and allowing it the appro-

The age of a grapevine may be guessed by the thickness of its trunk, and at Bernard Skoda's Rutherford Vintners, the Cabernet Sauvignon grapevines' trunks are thick, indicating the decades-old age of the vineyard.

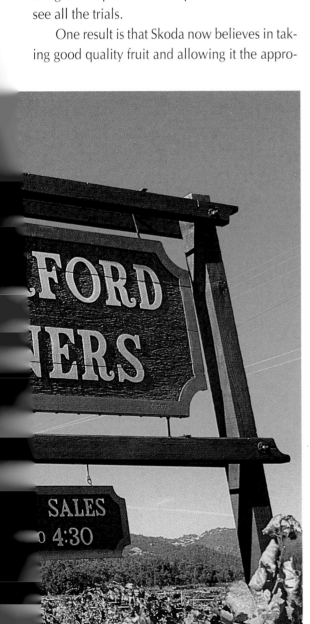

priate time to age in older oak casks and new barrels. Using only new small barrels tends to infuse wine with an overly oaky taste and smell, Skoda says. He feels the oak flavor in a wine dominates the fruit and makes the wine less a product of the grapes than of the tree.

This aging regime for Rutherford Vintners wines is evident in the style of Cabernet Sauvignon. Even in Skoda's Special Reserve Cabernet Sauvignon, the oak is handled discreetly, as little more than a grace note to flesh out the aroma. By the time you begin sipping the wine, you taste more the fruit and its natural slow oxidation rather than any wood.

Moreover, Skoda believes in varying the kind of oak in his barrels, using oak from France, Yugoslavia, the United States, and Germany. He likes to age the wine in varying sizes of barrels, including large and medium tanks that allow the wine to mature more slowly without excessive oxidation.

The other wines that have been made here — Chardonnay, Pinot Noir, Sauvignon Blanc, and Merlot — also display charm and Skoda's mild hand. All show a traditional style with one exception: Johannisberg Riesling. Where the Alsatians traditionally make Rieslings bone-dry, Skoda chooses to make a wine with a trace of residual sugar and *Botrytis cinerea* — a curious choice, because Skoda was born in Alsace. *DB*

Making red wine in a small winery can be hazardous to your hands. Not a few winemakers at harvest time find their hands stained for the duration. It's possible to remove the color, with acids, but that's not the most pleasant feeling, so many winemakers simply let the color wear off over time.

ST. ANDREW'S WINERY

St. Andrew's was founded by a man who split his year between Lucerne, Switzerland and the Napa Valley (through the growing season and crush). Imre Vizkelety — Hungarian-born, once a sheepskin tanner out of England — was the grape grower who founded the venture, based in an olive-drab, sheet-metal structure on the Silverado Trail, just north of Napa. His 63-acre vineyard, which fans out south and west toward the Napa River from the strictly-basics winery, is entirely Chardonnay, the largest part of which was originally sold to Domaine Chandon for sparkling wine.

The St. Andrew's label, named after Vizkelety's youngest child, is devoted to Chardonnay. The first vintage, in 1980, produced a wine that was fleshy with fruit, with an underlying sweet clove character. At that time, the winemaking was handled by Chuck Ortman, the commercial artist turned brilliant, itinerant, consulting winemaker who, like a magician, later turned his own label (Meridian) into a winery (previously called Estrella River).

A small deck on the winery's second story looks out toward Napa and St. Andrew's estate vineyard of Chardonnay. "We get a buttery, citrus-like fruit, with a green-olive earthiness, from this vineyard," says winemaker Daryl Eklund.

In April 1988, St. Andrew's was purchased by another winery — Clos Du Val. "We wanted to grow, but we didn't want Clos Du Val to grow any further," says Clos Du Val president Bernard Portet. "St. Andrew's was perfect for us, because its Chardonnays are quite different and distinct from our own. It has an earthy characteristic that seems to come directly from the vineyard.

"St. Andrew's is run separately from Clos Du Val, under winemaker Daryl Eklund, but its wines will be marketed by our distributing company."

Chardonnay is the focal point at St. Andrew's. "Our estate-bottled Chardonnay is entirely barrel fermented, then sits on the lees for six to eight months," notes Eklund. "Our regular Chardonnay is fermented in steel tanks, then barrel aged."

Daryl Eklund, who is responsible for both vineyard and winemaking, earned his spurs working at nearby Trefethen Vineyards and at Conn Creek Winery. Born in Mendocino County in 1953 and raised in Humboldt County, the stocky, solid Eklund studied international relations at U.C. Davis before turning to bacteriology, then wine. "I really got burned-out in the lab, and wanted something a little more practical," says Eklund. "Dr. Michael Lewis, who taught beer brewing, turned me toward fermentation science. He was quite a character — brilliant — with that Welsh wit, and such style. He was a great teacher, too."

Eklund came to St. Andrew's in May 1989, and clearly enjoys honing in on Chardonnay. "We make two Chardonnays here," he says. "We have our Estate Bottled Chardonnay, labeled 'St. Andrew's Vineyard' because it comes only from our vineyard. This wine is entirely barrel fermented, then sits on the lees for six to eight months, and then in bottle for a year. Our second Chardonnay, labeled 'St. Andrew's Winery,' is fermented in stainless-steel tanks, and then barrel aged."

Until 1988, St. Andrew's made a little Sauvignon Blanc (which is Ortman's favorite varietal) and the odd Cabernet. But since the purchase by Clos du Val, Chardonnay has been the key. *RPH*

ST. CLEMENT VINEYARDS

Winemaking isn't a recent phenomenon in the Napa Valley. In fact, the area was booming in the 1860s and early 1870s. Wineries sprouted; vine acreage by 1891 exceeded 18,000. It was into this busy culture that San Francisco glass merchant Fritz Rosenbaum leaped when he bought the property we now call St. Clement. Rosenbaum constructed an attractive Victorian home in 1878, made wine in the small stone cellar underneath, and sold it under the name Johanaberg Vineyards.

The property was bought by Mike Robbins in the late 1960s and renamed Spring Moun-

tain. In 1975 Robbins sold it to Dr. William Casey and his wife, Alexandra. Casey rechristened the facility St. Clement, after the patron saint of mariners and the small Chesapeake Bay island where the Casey family owned property.

Casey brought in Charles Ortman, one of California's new-wave winemakers. He loved wine that developed bouquet in the bottle, and set the style for St. Clement: delicate, refined, yet flavorful. The wines showed little early on, but their charm was evident with just a few years in the bottle. One of the early Ortman wines, the '75-'76 Cabernet of St. Clement

St. Clement, founded by a San Francisco merchant, was renovated first by Mike Robbins, who called it Spring Mountain, and then sold to Dr. Bill Casey. But the facility wasn't opened to the public until Sapporo USA acquired the property and renovated it further in the late 1980s.

blended from wines made in those years, is still prized.

Casey constructed a modern winery of native stone in the hillside behind the mansion in 1979. The next year he gave the head winemaking job to Dennis Johns, who had assisted Ortman for a year. With Ortman continuing as consultant, the wines remained consistently elegant. The winery prospered through this period even though it owned just one acre of Cabernet Sauvignon, buying the rest of its fruit from growers around the valley.

In a deal valued at more than $5 million, Sapporo Ltd. USA, the American division of the

For years, during the tenure of the Casey family, St. Clement owned virtually no vineyards of its own. Only later, under Sapporo, were vineyards purchased, giving winemaker Dennis Johns a more consistent source of fruit.

Japanese brewing company, acquired St. Clement in 1987. Sapporo added new French oak barrels and acquired a 20-acre Carneros vineyard, planted by Abbott Williams to Chardonnay and Pinot Noir. That year, St. Clement made its first vineyard-designated Chardonnay wine, called Abbott's Vineyard.

While St. Clement's Cabernet Sauvignon comes from fruit grown in many different areas, the Sauvignon Blanc comes almost entirely from a ranch in Pope Valley, regarded as a wonderful location for the variety. Johns ferments Sauvignon Blanc in stainless-steel tanks and then ages it in older oak barrels. The style is more like Graves, with a lemon-lime twist. Johns says his style of wine is aimed at the middle of the market, halfway between lean and unctuously overdone.

"When we went through the yuppification period, people asked themselves, 'What can I get that will impress the boss?' Well, that ended and eventually you come back to the style of wine we make. It's easy to make big sloppy wines, but I fell in love with this business because of the history of it, and I'm not out there chasing the consumer."

Sapporo has also made the Victorian Rosenbaum home a visitors' center, open to the public (by reservation) for the first time in more than a century. *DB*

Throughout the 1980s the red wines at St. Clement were a miracle of blending skill as Dennis Johns — despite having ever-changing grape sources — blended to a house style that was consistent from year to year and avoided the pitfall of variations of the vintages.

SAINTSBURY

In 1970 a winemaker would have been thought loony if he had sunk any money into the soil of the cold Carneros region, near San Pablo Bay. Too cold, said the experts. Not enough water or rain, said the experts.

Today, however, the Carneros region is known as an area perfect for growing top-quality grapes to make Chardonnay, Pinot Noir, and sparkling wine. The climate and soils are particularly suited for the fickle Burgundian varieties: the soil is well-drained and the weather is cool — almost too cool. The moist marine air that blows in off the bay brings with it a fog that seems, in spring and early summer, to be so persistent that there's almost not enough sunlight to grow mushrooms, let alone grapes for fine wine.

Yet the region's wind-whipped climate and

Saintsbury's winery was not built to look like the Taj Mahal, but a typical, functional California barn. The roomy facility is the birthplace of some of the state's best and most consistent Pinot Noirs.

makes some of the best Burgundian-style wines in California.

The winery is named in honor of Professor George Saintsbury, the English man of letters who is best known to wine lovers as the author of one of the classic works of wine literature, *Notes on a Cellar-Book.*

The idea behind Saintsbury is simply to make Pinot Noir and Chardonnay in a way that takes great advantage of the long, cool Carneros growing season, meaning that grapes stay on the vine longer and produce flavors that should be fully ripe, yet the grape sugars will not be so high that the resulting wine will be too alcoholic. This method, reason Ward and Graves, should duplicate closely the style of wine of Burgundy as well as can be expected in California.

The partners first met while studying winemaking at the University of California at Davis in 1977, and discovered that both were fanatical about wines from Burgundy. They saw the potential in the Carneros region, and after brief stints at other wineries, they began talking about doing a joint project, focusing on their favorite wines. So in 1981, using a leased facility, they began making wine from Carneros grapes. By 1983, construction had begun on their own property.

That year, while they were planting their 13-acre vineyard adjacent to the winery, they heard of a vine-training system that appears to solve a lot of problems for cold growing regions. Called the Open Lyre system, it calls for the vine to be split into two growing cordons, and then the canes (the arms of the vine) are trained off the cordons up onto catch-wires that hold the foliage in place.

Instead of having a thick canopy of leaves late in the growing season, which would shield the grapes from the sun, the Open Lyre system holds the leaves up into a fan and permits the sun to ripen the grapes more evenly. Moreover, the leaves still act as a sun shield in late afternoons, preventing the grapes from getting excessive sun, which would cause sunburn.

close-by bay also mean that the vineyards rarely experience frost. It never gets so cold that the plants die. A drive through the Carneros region shows that there are few wind machines or smudge pots, equipment that other regions use extensively to protect the vines during spring's cold snaps.

It is here that Saintsbury, operated by winemakers Richard Ward and David Graves,

Dick Ward and David Graves at Saintsbury know that ripening Pinot Noir grapes in the cool Carneros is not easy. They have planted their estate vineyard entirely with the pruning method known as the Open Lyre, in which the vine is trained into twin catch wires in a V or lyre shape, to make ripening a bit more predictable.

Ward and Graves adopted this system for their vineyard, and when the first wines resulting from this growing regime began to appear on the market in the late 1980s, the public was wowed by their quality.

Ward and Graves make wine from just the two Burgundian varieties, and they do so stylishly. The Chardonnay is fermented and aged in barrels coopered in Burgundy. The wine is put through a complete malolactic fermentation to convert the stronger malic acid (which smells more like apples) into the weaker lactic acid (which can add a buttery note to a wine). This technique broadens the wine on the palate and gives it a more lush, dense mouth-feel.

However, the aromas Saintsbury gets from the grapes of the region are so amazingly rich in floral qualities that in most vintages the Chardonnay offers superb tropical fruit characteristics with a trace of lemon or lime and a richness and butteriness that implies Burgundy. There are two Chardonnays here, a "regular" bottling and a reserve, and both offer broad, rich flavors with crispness in the finish.

The Pinot Noir is made in three different styles — two red and a pink. The wine the partners have called Garnet is a fresh, lightly styled wine that Graves and Ward describe as having cherry and raspberry fruit. The lighter structure of the wine, with lower tannins and earlier bot-

The partners in Saintsbury believe that the high acidity and low pH found in grapes grown in the Carneros region mandate the softening of the Chardonnay through the procedure called malolactic fermentation.

tling, makes it a perfect wine for summer sipping (served at cool cellar temperature) or to match with lighter foods in a restaurant.

Saintsbury's more substantial wine, the one that has gained the winery worldwide acclaim, is designated Carneros Pinot Noir. It is a more classic wine with fairly dense, complex fruit and a black cherry and cinnamon-clove component that competes successfully with the lighter wines of Burgundy, notably those from the Beaune region.

To make that point, Ward and Graves issued a T-shirt adorned with a stylized American flag and the Springsteenian phrase, "Beaune in the USA."

In addition to a traditional red Pinot Noir, Ward and Graves also make from that variety a wine like a French vin gris. Theirs is a pinkish wine that they have chosen to call, in their own audacious manner, Vincent Vin Gris.

The partners' third wine in the line is a great bargain. Saintsbury uses its Pinot Noir juice and makes the wine into a rosé, but it's a most serious wine, with a color more salmon than pink. It is a wine styled like the *vin gris* of France, where the black grapes give just a trace of color to an otherwise "white" wine.

Pinot Noir is the grape that provides the backbone for most of the classic Champagnes and when that wine is made as a rosé, as this one is, the result shows the evidence of the fruit of the grape a bit more strongly than in sparkling wine. Ward and Graves have styled their Vin Gris along the lines of wines of the Rhone, totally dry and aged in oak barrels.

Moreover, the juice goes through a complete malolactic fermentation, adding that buttery component. The fruit of the wine is faintly cherrylike, and the finish is broad and rich, more like Chardonnay than anything else. The humor of Ward and Graves is also broad and rich. The partners gave the wine the proprietary name Vincent Vin Gris, and a label that sports a local artist's illustration done in the style of Vincent Van Gogh. *DB*

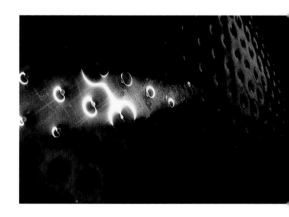

The stainless-steel tanks at many wineries these days have two layers, including an exterior shell welded to the interior one. Through the walls of the tank flowsa coolant that keeps the wine inside at a constant temperature.

ST. SUPÉRY VINEYARDS & WINERY

New wineries often start slowly, building reputation as they go. But there's nothing bashful about St. Supéry's splashy, yet graceful, entrance into Napa Valley's crowded winegrowing pool. People of experience and reputation have been recruited to execute the dream; full attention has been given to vineyard development; a good-sized model winery has been built; and an information-laden and useful visitors' center has been created to ease consumers into the newness of it all.

Though it's the Skalli family — based in Paris — who put up the francs, the pivotal person in St. Supéry's quick recognition and

acceptance is CEO Michaela Rodeno, the long-time PR/marketing presence at Domaine Chandon. Rodeno's innovative thinking and winning personality have given St. Supéry (pronounced "soop'-ery") instant credibility in an increasingly competitive marketplace.

And though the winery is new, there is more than a bit of history that comes with it. "The winery is situated a half-mile south of Rutherford, right in the middle of the Rutherford bench, a great Cabernet Sauvignon growing region," begins Rodeno. "That's the reason we removed the Chardonnay vines that were planted here, converting the 35 acres

A giant oak shades the Atkinson House, built in the 1880s and restored by the owners of St. Supéry as a living museum of the era. The demonstration vineyard shows the different trellising methods employed.

surrounding the winery to Cabernet Sauvignon. "The property was first purchased in 1881 by Joseph and Louis Atkinson, whose original home next to the winery has been restored as a living museum of the period. The Atkinsons lost the property after phylloxera devastated the vineyards they had planted, and in 1904 it was bought from the bank by French winemaker Edward St. Supéry, who had been living in Oakville. Since the Skallis had no interest in naming the winery after themselves, they decided to honor St. Supéry, a winemaking pioneer with Franco-American roots akin to their own."

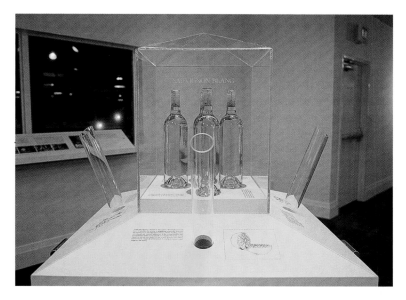

St. Supéry offers a self-guided tour, brilliantly conceived by Oakland Museum designer Gordon Ashby and the winery's own Lily Thomas.
This station invites visitors to smell the primary aroma components of Sauvignon Blanc.

The Skalli family had originally come to the Napa Valley as visitors in 1974, when they were taken by the enthusiasm of one Margrit Biever (now married to Robert Mondavi). As the family had long been involved in food and wine in their native France, their first move was to acquire land for vineyards. Their first parcel, over the hill in Pope Valley, was purchased in 1982. Vineyard planting began immediately at the 1,530-acre ranch, called Dollarhide. In 1986 they added the Atkinson property in Rutherford and began winery construction.

Removed from the Napa Valley proper by the eastern ridges of the Mayacamas Range, Pope Valley has had few wines in the market to demonstrate its character. "Pope Valley grapes have distinctive characteristics," notes winemaker Bob Broman. "Pope Valley fruit is delicate yet complex, with layers of flavors coming together in a very subtle way.

"That said, we may not always keep our Pope Valley fruit separate from our Rutherford grapes. What we're looking for is the 'complete wine.' No one type of flavor should be overpowering."

As a founding member of the Society of Blancs (SOBs), St. Supéry hopes to keep Sauvignon Blanc on a par with Cabernet and Chardonnay. For those of us who recognize Sauvignon Blanc's ability to sustain extensive bottle age well, it's a pleasing stance. *RPH*

St. Supéry's tasting room is surrounded by interactive exhibits that cleverly and clearly explain the metamorphosis of sun and water as they work their way through the vine to become wine.

V. SATTUI WINERY

The incredible success of the V. Sattui Winery is one of those improbable stories often used as an example of how someone with a dream but no money can achieve a goal through hard work.

Daryl Sattui acknowledges that he worked hard to create a winery to make great wine and he "lived like a pauper for 11 years." And he confesses that even he is amazed at his own success. In hindsight, he admits that what he faced in 1973 was a next-to-impossible task, yet he also notes that back then, he didn't know how impossible things really were. Naiveté was a blessing.

"I was so stupid, I didn't know the experts were saying you needed a million bucks to start a winery," says Daryl.

The V. Sattui Winery started in 1885 when Vittorio Sattui opened a winery in San Francisco's Mission District. But Prohibition put the venture into hibernation for a half-century until his great-grandson, Daryl, revived the idea. Daryl Sattui had graduated from college and toured Europe for two years before moving to the Napa Valley. To support himself, he washed barrels at The Christian Brothers, worked as a tour guide at Beaulieu, and sold wine at a San Francisco retail shop.

The V. Sattui Winery was founded in San Francisco by Daryl Sattui's great-grandfather, Vittorio, who made and blended wines sold out of his San Francisco store. The operation was closed during Prohibition, but Daryl revived the family winery in the Napa Valley in the early 1970s.

To open V. Sattui winery in the Napa Valley, he cajoled friends into investing $52,500 to build a small winery and salesroom. His enthusiasm was so infectious that a local real estate agent bought a four-acre parcel of land on the east side of Highway 29 near St. Helena and leased it to Daryl with an option to buy.

Sattui, who had invested just $5,000 of his own money, thus faced the prospect of paying back investors and covering overhead out of a tasting room — no guaranteed income. So to save money he lived out of his Volkswagen bus.

Back then, the Napa Valley was still to be discovered as a wine mecca, but tourists liked

In homage to his great-grandfather, Daryl built the V. Sattui Winery from old stone with an old-fashioned porch, to look as if it had been here before the turn of the century. It has become a must-see Napa Valley tour stop.

the idea of free tastes of the local product. In the 18 miles between Yountville and Calistoga, they could sample wine at two dozen wineries. Yet getting a bite to eat was difficult.

Sattui saw a chance to develop a premium winery through lunch meat, sourdough bread, cheese, prepared salads, and — the main attraction — picnic tables out on his lawn. This was the perfect spot for an inexpensive lunch, served with a bottle of Sattui wine poured into plastic wine "glasses." Travelers from San Francisco would hit Sattui before they reached St. Helena, so Sattui drew a big noontime crowd. "The first year we sold more food than wine," recalls Daryl.

Sattui made wine from the day he was bonded in 1975. While that wine aged, he bought wine in bulk from neighbors and bottled it under his own label. Sattui once sold magnums of 1973 and 1974 Napa Valley Cabernet Sauvignon for $9. Years later he revealed he had bought it in bulk from the Robert Mondavi Winery, and hauled it back to V. Sattui in his VW bus.

There were some Sattui barrels on the property, but the place looked half empty. To have the ambience of a winery, Sattui needed wine casks. "I couldn't afford any barrels, but Al Brounstein [owner of the now-famed Diamond Creek Vineyards in Calistoga] had barrels, and he didn't have any place to store them. So I told him he could store the barrels in my winery."

Sattui worked hard those early years, and saved money any way he could. He couldn't afford a place to live and often slept on an air mattress on the floor of the winery, occasionally showering in the morning under a winery faucet. He recycled cardboard boxes to save money. And after his first year in business, Sattui actually showed a small profit, a virtual impossibility in this cash-intensive business.

The V. Sattui Winery of San Francisco was resurrected in the Napa Valley by Daryl Sattui, who realized a dream through hard work and a concept: direct sales to the consumer through a tasting room.

By 1980, Sattui had become so successful with his small winery that he hired a winemaker: Rick Rosenbrand, the son of Theo Rosenbrand, who had been winemaker at Beaulieu (under Andre Tchelistcheff), and later at Sterling Vineyards. Daryl's own wines were excellent, but Rosenbrand and Sattui made a fine team.

Interestingly, Rosenbrand and his father were little alike. Shorter Theo wore suits and a trim haircut. Tall, lanky Rick had long hair and in summers rarely wore a shirt. The ex-star basketball player at St. Helena High School became, however, as talented as his father at recognizing great wine.

By the mid-1980s, Sattui wines were winning gold medals at major competitions. His Cabernet Sauvignon, Zinfandel, Riesling, and dessert wines were excellent. The success permitted Sattui to greatly expand his winery. The new structure is made of old stone and it looks 100 years old. The winery has a partially underground wine cellar for slow maturing of the wines, and the size of the tasting room has been doubled. Now the ambience is real, not partially borrowed.

The lean living and dedication to quality products, both wine and food, paid off. By 1991 the winery was approaching $5.5 million a year in gross sales, and every bottle sold went out the door of the winery; virtually nothing was sold in stores or restaurants. This resulted

in a higher profit margin than probably anyone in the Napa Valley. Sattui once said that he sold 11 bottles for every one he poured in the tasting room, meaning his "cost of sales" was less than ten percent.

The success of the V. Sattui Winery is a tribute to Daryl's vision and hard work, but had he attempted to start a winery the same way in 1989 or 1990, opposition might have been as fierce as it was against the Peju Province winery down the road. Back in the 1970s, however, nobody quibbled over what a winery was. In fact, local wineries liked Sattui. One winemaker, who used to work at the Louis M. Martini Winery, said years later, "We'd send people down there to have a picnic with a bottle of Martini wine. We all thought it was a great idea — having a place with tables, cheeses, bread. . . ."

Fifteen years later, though, the valley became sensitive to the words "tourism" and "development." Local activists wanted to halt any operation from starting unless it made all its own wine. It is evident that had that mentality existed in the mid-1970s, Sattui might never have gotten permits to open his winery.

Today, however, the V. Sattui winery that began essentially as a cheese shop is one of the top wine producers in the Napa Valley. *DB*

In the days before Prohibition, most of the wine sold in the Napa Valley was generic, and sipping wine and other potables on the premises of a winery was not an uncommon practice. Here Daryl Sattui's grandfather, Mario, hosts a group of friends.

Vittorio Sattui (second from left) with his sons Romeo (left) and Mario (right) with a cellar worker. The winery was located on 23rd and Bryant streets in San Francisco's Mission District. Vittorio lived to be 94 and instilled the spirit of the business in Daryl.

One of the concepts that gave Sattui his springboard to success was the addition of picnic tables on his front lawn, the perfect place for tourists to the valley to enjoy the local fresh produce: cheeses, sourdough breads, and, of course, a bottle of V. Sattui wine.

SCHRAMSBERG VINEYARDS

Jack and Jamie Davies, who in the 1960s bought an ancient house filled with bats, have become the symbols of modern winemaking in the Napa Valley. Today the elegant caves and modern offices mark the facility, and Schramsberg's sparkling wine is seen around the world as an example of California's pioneer spirit.

In 1964 Jack Davies was a successful executive with a major corporation in Southern California, as well as a collector and lover of fine wine. His wife, Jamie, had grown up in Southern California and had friends there.

It was at a time before there was any boom in the Napa Valley, even before the vestiges of Prohibition had been shaken loose. Moving north was considered insane for a successful business executive. But the Davies were hooked on the idea; they wanted that wine-country lifestyle.

The Napa Valley, however, was daunting. The places they saw were run-down and in need of tender care. Jack and Jamie finally were shown the old Schramsberg property, founded by Jacob Schram in 1862 and praised in Robert Louis Stevenson's little book, *Silvera-*

do Squatters. Thus the place had a sense of history about it, not to mention rats in the walls and bats in the belfry. They bought it and began to dream.

Jack and Jamie were committed to wine, but to what kind? After a good deal of discussion with friends Eleanor and Fred McRae of Stony Hill, Joe Heitz, and Andre Tchelistcheff, the Davies decided that sparkling wine would

be their goal. Few were doing it, they reasoned, and there might be a degree of interest in a top-quality product.

But things are never easy in the wine business. Jack had no money for most of the accoutrements of the trade, such luxuries as a winemaker, for instance. The result was that Jack wound up calling all around the valley asking for advice. There is a grand image of Jack holding a phone between shoulder and cheek as he fiddled with a filter, led step-by-step by Warren Winiarski across the valley.

Getting enough Chardonnay to make the wine was also a problem, since very little of that grape was available. A friend suggested that Jack buy Riesling and then trade it for Chardonnay. Jack approached young Robert Mondavi, across the road at the Charles Krug Winery, and proposed the idea. Mondavi agreed.

"Then I heard that there had been a little altercation at Krug and that Bob wasn't there any more," recounts Jack, referring to the famous feud that split the Mondavi family, forcing Bob out at Charles Krug and putting his brother, Peter, in charge.

"So I went over there and I said to Peter, 'You know about my deal with Bob?' And Peter said he didn't know about the agreement to swap Chardonnay for Reisling. 'But if Bob said he'd do that, I will, too,' and he did," says Davis. It was neighborliness like that that made the Napa Valley what it was in the 1960s.

With directness, faith, and, above all, hard work, things moved apace for the Davies. Schramsberg soon became a respected though tiny sparkling wine brand. But Jack, a politically active businessman, couldn't remain the calm, laid-back winemaker. Just a few years after the 1965 founding of the winery, an idea was proposed that would protect the Napa Valley from encroachment by real estate specula tors. It was a controversial notion: formation o an "agricultural preserve" that would limit hov a landowner could divide up his property an sell it. Though some in the valley opposed th concept, Jack and Jamie were staunch suppor

Schramsberg is located well off the Napa Valley floor, up Peterson Road, along a one-lane road and through a green glen. Jack Davies says he doesn't relish busloads of tourists. In fact, Davies shudders when he considers the possibility "of a flashing, neon hand pointing the way up here."

ers and played an active role in getting the agricultural preserve approved.

Through all this turmoil, Schramsberg has done an incredible job of improving the quality of its sparkling wines through innovation of technique and maintenance of production standards, even when the best grapes were not available. Jack limits himself to Napa Valley grapes, which occasionally are scarce because of the demand from other wineries for grapes for their table wines. Though he annually tests the grapes of other regions to see what they can offer, Napa still remains the name on the label and Schramsberg pays top dollar to get the best grapes.

The rewards have been obvious. Schramsberg's sparkling wines have been served in the White House; President Richard Nixon took some to China; menus from major affairs of state dot the winery's walls these days.

During the first seven years Davies made the wine with his consultant Dmitri Tchelistcheff, Andre's son. Schramsberg's first full-time winemaker was Harold Osborne, followed by Greg Fowler, and then Alan Tenscher. In the early 1970s, some of the wines were inconsistent. In the 1980s, quality soared. And by the time of the winery's 25th anniversary, Schramsberg was planning yet another innovation: a unique bottle shape made from a

The caves at Schramsberg, dug over 100 years ago by Chinese laborers, have recently been enlarged and are used to age the young wine en tirage for years — until the wines take on a complexity that can be gained only through time.

specially designed mold for the winery's top wines.

It was not an isolated idea. In the past, Jack and Jamie imported a top-quality Cognac from France, then became investors with Rémy Martin in a California brandy. (That partnership ended in 1987.) Another business idea was the sophisticated joint marketing arrangement Jack and Jamie worked out with Trefethen Vineyards. The concept was well ahead of its time.

Yet another business venture — an investment in a major Portuguese sparkling wine house to make wine jointly — seemed the most adventuresome, but was typically far-sighted. Jack and Jamie announced the venture in 1989

Schramsberg makes one of the most elegant sparkling wines in the country; it has been served at state dinners and is rated as one of the most sublime products from year to year. The Davies family also has a major investment in a Portuguese sparkling wine venture.

but said the first wines from the project might not be released for a decade. To run the international division of the expanding company, in 1990 Jack hired Tucker Catlin, director of vineyard operations for Sterling and one of the top minds in the wine business. It was a coup that surprised many.

In the end, Schramsberg remains the quintessential example of second-era entrepreneurial spirit. The post-Prohibition rebirth of the Napa Valley was accomplished fitfully by hard-working and dedicated people, principled and committed to quality wine, to their neighbors, to the valley, and to its soil. The third wave of growth, sparked more by money than by romance, has benefited us too, but not with the same emotional drive that brought us Schramsberg.

One day recently, inside the caves under the old winery, Jack and Jamie spoke of the good times they had raising their three sons in that earth. That project was at least as important to them as the wine, probably more so. It was the valley that gave them this opportunity, they said, and they intended to repay the valley in kind.

But their neighbors say that repayment is unnecessary. They all say the world of wine is indebted to people like the Davies for their vision and style. *DB*

Schramsberg was originally the home of Jacob Schram, a barber who elevated his wine hobby into a business and became a Napa Valley pioneer. In the period after the Civil War, Schram used Chinese laborers to hew out of his mountain a network of caves for the aging of the wine.

SEQUOIA GROVE VINEYARDS

Though the winery makes an elegant Chardonnay, it is the estate Cabernet that has become such a prized item at Sequoia Grove. The wine is made from grapes grown on the Allen ranch just east of Highway 29, in a location that the Allens feel is a prototype of the famed Rutherford Bench — an area whose bounderies have yet to be fully defined.

Immediately after a harvest is concluded, the crews at all wineries are exhausted from 18-hour days with no breaks except for a sandwich on the run. This amount of work would drive John L. Lewis to drink, yet the harvest is the most critical time of the year.

It's the time when the most important decisions must be made, when a winemaker must determine the fate of a vintage based on instant decision-making. It's at this time of the year, when the troops are looking forward to an at-ease, that many winemakers ask them to do one more critical step — transfer to barrels the red wine that has just completed fermentation.

Sequoia Grove Vineyards, which has made a name for itself with its excellent, deeply scented, and opaque Cabernet Sauvignons, uses a technique for its Cabernet that makes more sense. Jim Allen, the co-owner of this Ruther-

ford-area winery with his brother, Steve, is a student of European winemaking techniques, and he decided years ago that transferring Cabernet to the barrel immediately after the harvest is simply too wearing on the crew. Not to mention unnecessary in terms of wine quality.

Jim says that with a production of about 10,000 cases of Cabernet, Sequoia Grove would need 400 barrels in which to put the wine, requiring the staff, right after harvest, to haul a hose around to 400 different barrels and fill them to the bung.

Instead, after the fermentation of the Cabernet is complete, Sequoia Grove keeps the wine sitting in upright wooden tanks for six months. It gives Sequoia Grove's cellar crew an early out from the harvest, and Jim Allen points out that it also helps get some of the wine's natural maturation out of the way in

This Model-T parked among the redwoods, near buildings originally built in the 1860s, reminds visitors that Sequoia Grove Vineyards respects both the old and the new.

neutral oak tanks before the wine is placed, six months later, into barrels that will add some flavor. By then it's spring and the winery is calm. The wine is then aged for an additional 12 to 14 months in small oak barrels, for complexity and oak aroma.

No one is certain whether this is the main reason for the success of the Sequoia Grove Cabernets, but the winery with the low-key image won a flock of medals through the 1980s, and established a style for its estate-bottled wine that reflects the Rutherford soil in which the grapes grow.

Jim first had contact with wine when, as a philosophy student at the University of Innsbruck in Austria, he noticed that different villages made different wines from the same grape variety. For years, traveling around Europe as a United Nations translator, Allen questioned how grapevines reacted in different soils and climates. When he returned to the U.S. to teach philosophy in New Mexico, he planted grapes there, but found his homemade wine was best with grapes flown in from the Napa Valley.

In 1980, Jim and his wife, Barbara, moved to the Napa Valley and asked Steve to tend the vineyards. Soon after, the brothers acquired a vineyard in the Carneros region, which they eventually swapped to a joint venture headed by the Champagne house, Taittinger, for the development of Domaine Carneros. The Allens own a small portion of the joint venture in exchange for their contribution of the land. *DB*

The towering redwood trees that dwarf the Sequoia Grove tasting room and the winery behind it also hide the place from the view of passing cars. Inside the tasting facility, visitors can sip excellent Chardonnay and Cabernet Sauvignon, and see the many gold medals the wines have earned over the years.

SHAFER VINEYARDS

S hafer Vineyards was never intended to be a job placement service for John Shafer's son, Doug, but the result of perseverance on the part of the scion has given the father one of the best winemakers in the Napa Valley.

The Shafers moved here from Illinois where John had been an executive with a textbook company. The 209-acre property in the heart of the Stags Leap region was bought in 1972 as part of John's move into a second career. On the ranch were 30 acres of grapes; the Shafers later added another 20 acres.

By 1978, Shafer was prepared to make wine under his own label, and his first releases, including a stunning 1978 Cabernet, were excellent efforts. The Chardonnay was lean and delicate, and the Merlot soft and generous. But the Cabernet was a true prototype of the famed Stags Leap region, offering deep, cherry-like fruit and chocolatey undertones. In 1979, Shafer had a winery constructed.

Doug, meanwhile, had earned a degree in education, as well as a teaching credential, and was happily teaching school in Arizona. But he also went to U.C. Davis to learn winemaking. One day, two years after he began teaching, on a

John Shafer made a courageous decision when he handed the winemaking job to his son, Doug. But the move has turned out brilliantly. Shafer's red wines especially have been widely received, winning medals at major wine competitions and selling rapidly.

visit home to the family farm, Doug told his father he'd like to be a winemaker. Dad was surprised.

"We had hired Nikko Schoch as our winemaker," recalls John, "and when Doug said he wanted to pursue winemaking, I told him there were two things working against that. I told him, 'We have no job for you, and you don't know enough.'"

But Doug Shafer was determined, so he quit teaching and took a position as an assistant winemaker to Randy Mason at Lakespring, across the valley. In 1983, Schoch left Shafer, so Doug came back to speak with his father about taking over.

The Stags Leap region in the southeastern part of the Napa Valley is one of the country's best for Cabernet Sauvignon. But because of the region's hilly and rocky nature, much of the land has yet to be planted, and may never be.

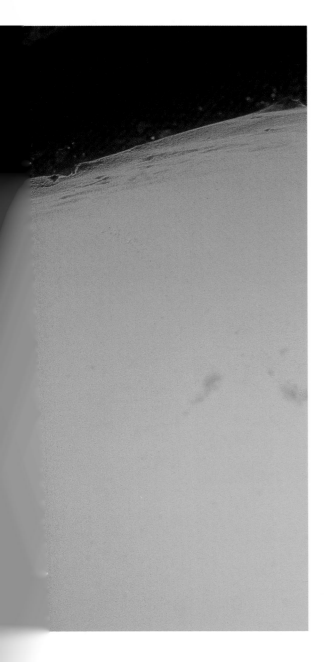

"We had some long conversations," says John. "I told Doug that he wasn't that experienced, and I told him there was too much at stake here. We had the choice of either hiring someone with experience or bringing Doug in and surrounding him with consultant help and nursing ourselves along. Well, we chose the latter.

"Also, Doug had the greatest of all motivations — he had a stake in the winery," says John. "It was never part of my game plan to have the children in the winery. If they wanted to do it, they had to beg for it."

The result, however, was the serendipitous discovery that Doug has a true talent. With the aid of consultants Chuck Ortman and Tony Soter, his Cabernets have been complex wines with a richness typical of the Stags Leap area, but without coarseness. The Hillside Select Cabernet now sells for above $30 a bottle and is ranked as one of the best red wines in California.

Moreover, Shafer's Merlot is among the best in the state, and the winery's Chardonnay, not as rich and buttery as some, remains a wonderfully scented and flavored wine with a delicate structure.

The Shafer operation is a true family affair. John is the president and Doug makes the wine — about 15,000 cases per year. Daughter Libby (who is married to Sinskey winemaker Joe Cafaro) and John's wife, Bett, handle public relations and hospitality. *DB*

Forty-pound lug boxes like these are quickly filled by experienced pickers, whose hands sing underneath the vine as they quickly separate ripe clusters from vine shoots with razor sharp knives. Spend a day picking grapes and your appreciation for a bottle of wine will increase manyfold.

CHARLES F. SHAW VINEYARD

"I want to be the 'light red guy' of the Napa Valley." So says Charles F. Shaw Jr., the West Pointer whose fondness for Cru Beaujolais provides the philosophic grounding for his north valley wine estate. "With my Estate Bottled Gamay, it's that aromatic, spicy flavor and soft texture of the more feminine Beaujolais — the Fleuries, the Brouillys — that I'm after. I don't want that fruit-salad character of the nouveau wines — except, of course, in my Nouveau!"

Shaw caught the wine bug doing graduate business work at Stanford, on a major project involving the analysis of several nearby wineries. Working with Bank of the Southwest when oil was discovered in the North Sea, he was transferred to Paris, where he developed a fondness for Beaujolais. By 1974 he had purchased a parcel near Lake Hennessey, moving four years later to the edge of the Napa River, just north of the old Bale Mill.

The old farmhouse and stables-cum-winery are restored in New England hues. Shaw has always liked to spend part of each summer on Nantucket Island ("You can't beat the striped bass fishing"). The gazebo which appears on the Shaw label today has its own history. It was built in the summer of 1981 for MGM, which

Chuck Shaw's home, a restored farmhouse, has a decidedly New England feel. Seated comfortably on the broad porch, you almost expect to look out and see the sand dunes of Martha's Vineyard and swells of the Atlantic beyond.

filmed "Yes, Giorgio," starring Luciano Pavarotti, at Shaw's estate.

Shaw originally intended to produce only Fleurie-type Beaujolais. "Well, we started making the Sauvignon Blanc when Ric Forman was here," Shaw laughs lamely. "Ric had made such great Sauvignon Blancs at Sterling and Newton that it only seemed right to do it here." And then there's Chardonnay. Which could be said to fall within the framework of Shaw's Burgundian model. Or not.

But the focus of Shaw remains the light reds, an idea that has taken hold nationally. So, it shouldn't be that much of a surprise that nearly

The gazebo sits behind the house. The focal point of the winery's label, it was built in the summer of 1981 for MGM's filming of Yes, Giorgio at the estate, called Domaine Elucia. The movie, not a major hit, starred opera star Luciano Pavarotti.

three-quarters of Shaw's 50,000-case production is given over to three Gamay Beaujolais wines, light, red wines that feature fruit over muscle, soft over hard. The "Nouveau" leads the way ("we don't release it on any particular day, don't put it on the Concorde, nor have I kissed Miss France . . . yet"), followed by the regular Gamay Beaujolais (akin to a French "Villages") and a much smaller release of Estate Bottled Gamay Beaujolais (equivalent to a Cru Beaujolais).

In the converted stone stable, Shaw employs carbonic maceration — whole berry fermentation —to extract maximum spiciness and fruit, followed by aging in large French cooperage to "calm the wine down and remove its petulance."

"The whole idea of carbonic maceration red wines, where the fermentation of whole berries imparts loads of fresh fruit to the wine, is taking off now," contends Shaw. "Consumers are slowly gaining confidence in their ability to determine their own tastes, and as they do they're looking for a transition wine from White Zinfandel to dry reds.

"Well, we've got the perfect wine for them! It's no secret, we're all laying for the blush guys. Carbonic maceration reds are the next logical step for someone looking for a lower-tannin, easier-drinking red. We're here to hold the hand of the consumer and take him over that big step from the blush wines to the bigger, dry reds." *RPH*

The Charles F. Shaw Vineyard & Winery uses open-topped, stainless-steel fermenting tanks for its light Gamay wines. The fruit is put in whole so that many berries ferment internally, making for a fresher, fruitier wine. The technique is called "carbonic maceration."

SILVERADO VINEYARDS

When, in 1981, it became clear to the residents of the Napa Valley that the rumor was correct, they began to buzz about it in coffee shops and supermarkets: the Disneys were coming.

At that point, more than two million people visited the Napa Valley annually, lining two-lane Highway 29 from Yountville to Calistoga with smog-makers, casting refuse on the road, clogging the limited bathroom facilities, and in general making life unlivable for the residents of the once-peaceful valley.

When it was formally announced that the widow of the cartoon, motion picture, and amusement park magnate, Walt Disney, was indeed buying property and would open a winery, the mere thought of a giant helium-filled Mickey Mouse flying over the parapet had locals gasping for breath.

What then took place, to the naked eye, was nothing. The Silverado Vineyards winery building was constructed, not on heavily traveled Highway 29, but on the lightly traveled Silverado Trail. Yes, it was erected on a hill, but it was invisible from the road. Moreover, the entrance was unmarked, save for a small, elegant sign. The wines of Silverado are pretty much the only story to tell about this 185-acre property. It has

Winemaker Jack Stuart, who made striking Cabernet Sauvignons at Durney Vineyards in Carmel Valley, is a master at getting wonderful extraction from his grapes without any of the harshness associated with the variety. Silverado Cabernets, from the first day, have shown grace and the ability to age.

little historical heritage other than that created by the family. And the family — Lillian Disney; her daughter, Diane Disney Miller; and Diane's husband, Ron — are quiet people who rarely grant interviews, who rarely are seen at public functions, and who have adopted an almost anti-Disneyland image about their affairs.

"The family made a deliberate choice not to use the Disney name as a promotional element," says Jack Stuart, the winemaker, whose Cabernet Sauvignon, Sauvignon Blanc, Chardonnay, and Merlot are not bold, but delicate, with a grace that speaks legions about the way the family chose to enter the wine business.

Silverado's Chardonnay is made in a leaner style than many of those in the Napa Valley. Stuart's Chardonnay fruit includes some unique aromas due to the many different vineyard locations. Stuart keeps all lots separate during their fermentations and aging in French oak barrels. "I do as much barrel fermentation as possible, and aging on the lees," says Stuart.

Stuart's Cabernets are clearly his greatest achievements. They seem to avoid the vagaries of the vintage that are often evident in Napa Valley Cabernets. Starting with a spectacular 1981 Cabernet, Stuart hit it squarely on the head with his 1985 and 1986 wines. With the 1988 vintage, the winery began to use the designation "Stags Leap District" on the label, though nothing about the wine changed radically.

The Cabernets wowed wine lovers, especially for their prices. Most wineries were racing to price their wines near $25, but Silverado priced its Cabernet closer to half that.

"The only grapes I have never bought are Cabernet and Merlot," says Stuart. "That's because I feel the vineyard character is so important and I'm loath to blend anything with it." The grapes for these wines come from the Disney Ranch, where the winery is and where Lillian Disney lives when she's not at her home in Los Angeles. *DB*

Those who make reservations may visit Silverado. On good-weather days, the winery offers tables on a patio that rings the front and sides of the winery. From here there is a view of the winery's hillside vineyards.

SILVER OAK WINE CELLARS

This is a story of Cabernet, the whole Cabernet, and nothing but the Cabernet. Tune in your imagination and you can almost hear our Greek chorus — hired especially for this gig — just off stage, chanting, "Life is a Cabernet, old chum, life is . . ."

Fortunately, imaginary Greek choruses come cheap. Top quality Cabernet Sauvignons do not. But time and patience reward such expenditures with experiences that call simile and metaphor to the fore in what are usually vain attempts to record the sensory joy and pleasure unlocked by the conjoining of treasured, mature bottles and rare, aged meat.

Such experiences are for memories, not words.

This is the basis of Justin Meyer's vinous life. A former high school teacher, Meyer returned to school for a bachelor's degree in viticulture and enology and a master's degree in horticulture, which he put to good use first with The Christian Brothers (he was in the order then), and then for Franciscan Vineyards.

In 1972, Meyer and his partner in Franciscan (Colorado oil man Ray Duncan) spun off a smaller operation, dedicated to a single principle: well-matured Cabernet Sauvignon. "We wanted a Cabernet distinguished by its elegance and finesse, so we chose grapes from the

The white water tower to the left of Silver Oak's modern-day stone edifice appeared on the winery's label long before it existed in fact. "Yeah, we had to build it to keep everybody happy," laughs Justin Meyer.

Alexander Valley," says Meyer, whose smile beams between rosy cheeks and an angelic countenance that must be a carry-over from his days in the brotherhood.

"It is one of my profoundest beliefs that consumers drink too many great Cabernets well before they are mature," he continues with passion. "That's why we hold back our release date until the fifth year, and that's why we hold back a portion of each vintage for subsequent release in the tenth year.

"Alexander Valley Cabernets tend to be soft to start with, but they do hold age well. I've put away at least a case of magnums for

Justin Meyer takes the French admonition seriously: the first duty of a wine is to be red. At Silver Oak, Meyer assays the Cabernet, the whole Cabernet, and nothing but the Cabernet, so help us God.

each of my three kids, and I expect these wines to age at least 20 years."

Meyer is so taken by the beauty of mature Cabernets that he, Duncan, and ten other partners created Napa Valley Wines of Distinction, a company that buys up 200- to 500-case lots of other top California Cabernets, ages them for three years ("by which time the wineries will have been out of stock for two years"), and then re-releases them to the market. "They'll be six or seven years old by then, just at the beginning of their prime," he chortles. "It's so necessary to have older wines available, to show people how wonderful great Cabernets get to be after a little aging."

While several wineries have strayed from initial plans to be one-wine wineries, Meyer is content to remain dedicated to Cabernet alone. "To me, it's all pluses. People know exactly where we're coming from, they know exactly what we're about. I'm always asked, 'What's new?' Nothing is new! We're the same. It's the Great American Marketing Fallacy that you have to be all things to all people. If I want a Chardonnay, or a Zinfandel, I'll go out and buy it. I don't have to make it." *RPH*

Soft lighting and a low ceiling lend an air of romance to this wine "chai," a barrel cellar in which Silver Oak Cabernet Sauvignons spend about two years before being bottled. The wines are aged in bottle another year before release.

ROBERT SINSKEY VINEYARDS

The Robert Sinskey winery was built above the valley on a small knoll. Here, renowned cave designer Alf Burtleson created an underground chamber for the aging of the wines. The main winery uses natural rock for its wall facings.

D r. Robert Sinskey knew that starting a winery in the Napa Valley would be a venture fraught with pitfalls. But challenge was inherent in his profession. As an eye surgeon, he successfully pioneered an artifical lens that incorporated a technique for attaching the lens — a development that became an international standard.

As a lover of wine, Sinskey decided to make it commercially and, in 1980, he became one of the original investors in the Acacia Winery. A limited partnership based in the Carneros, Acacia specialized in production of Chardonnay and Pinot Noir — a kind of Burgundian house.

The wine quality was high and the venture successful, so the partners planned a second winery to specialize in Cabernet Sauvignon and other Bordeaux varieties. There was a falling-

out of the partnership in the mid-1980s and the property was eventually sold to Chalone Inc. Sinskey, however, was not discouraged.

"Dad wanted to do his own project right from the beginning," says Rob Sinskey, general manager of the Sinskey winery. "He learned a lot from his Acacia experience, and he had already bought some vineyard land in 1982 on Las Amigas Road in the Carneros." That 35-acre parcel was just up the street from Acacia. Sinskey then bought another 72 acres on Buhman Lane, also in the Carneros.

In 1986, soon after the Acacia sale, Sinskey proceeded with plans for his own winery. He acquired the 12-acre spot originally intended to be the site of Acacia's second winery, up off the Silverado Trail not far from Yountville.

In 1987 construction began on Sinskey's handsome winery, which sits carved into the

northern edge of the Stags Leap promontory. For barrel aging, a series of attractive caves was dug into the hillside.

A key to any wine is the man behind the grapes, so choosing the first winemaker for this project would be a critical task. Sinskey selected Joe Cafaro, who previously had set the styles of wine at Chappellet and Keenan. The style of wine Cafaro likes is lean, austere, with delicacy and wonderful acidity to permit the wines to age well. Cafaro wines also exhibit a marvelous, though delicate, after-taste. These are lean, sinewy wines that rarely show well early, but seem to age as well as any in the state.

The first Sinskey wines, from the 1986 and 1987 harvests, were made at Flora Springs. The Cafaro touch was seen in two of these wines — a crisp, lean Chardonnay and a mar-velously structured Pinot Noir. In 1987 Cafaro began making a Merlot that appeared destined to be a world-beater. Made from a combina-tion of three vineyards, the wine was amazing-ly complex and fruity without the heaviness of some warm-climate Merlots. Encouraged by this, Cafaro has since 1988 been focusing more heavily on red wines.

Construction of the winery was finished in 1988 and the first estate-bottled wines were made that year. Because of the relative reticence of the Sinskey wines when they are young, the winery holds the wines in the cellar a bit longer than some do before releasing them. *DB*

Sinskey, a former investor in Acacia Winery, founded Robert Sinskey Vineyards on the same spot where Acacia's second winery was planned — a hillside off the Silverado Trail. Sinskey winemaker Joe Cafaro has shown that the Merlot from the cool Carneros region is destined to be a star.

SMITH-MADRONE VINEYARDS

The winery, built by Stu and Charlie Smith, features a rooftop patio that overlooks the sloping vineyards at the top of Spring Mountain. Just down the hill from Smith-Madrone is the property of Stony Hill Vineyard.

S tarting a vineyard, Stu Smith felt in the early 1970s, would be fun and a little work. The property he found high atop Spring Mountain was perfect, just up the hill from world-famed Stony Hill, with soils and exposure that would surely make some of the greatest wine in the world.

There was only one problem. The 200-acre parcel was covered with trees. Big trees.

"It was heavily wooded, mostly Douglas firs with a smattering of oaks and madronas," says Charles Smith, Stuart's brother and a partner in the winery now called Smith-Madrone. (Madrona is a local oak tree.)

"We didn't own any land-clearing equipment, but there was a guy near here who drove a D-8 Caterpillar, and he traded work for logs. We paid him for the tractor time and he paid us

for the timber. There had to have been 250,000 board feet of Douglas fir hauled out of here. It's the kind of story that would cause some grief down in the Napa Valley these days because that's exactly what they're trying to prevent, cutting down the trees."

But clearing the wild land was the only way for Smith-Madrone to put in the vineyards that would be the heart of the winery project,

and Stu went at the project with more energy than knowledge. Another problem was that planting is harder on slopes than on flattland — and even worse for an academic with no formal training in tractor driving.

Stu, who sports one of the great walrus-style mustaches of all time, had gotten a degree in economics at the University of California at Berkeley, and then on weekends drove off to U.C. Davis to take courses in winemaking.

"We were both living in Berkeley at the time and we were both nuts about wine," recalls Charles. "I was in graduate school in English literature, but we both liked wine so much that after Stu bought this place, I came up to make the wine."

That first year, 1971, Stu Smith planted 20 acres of grapes, five each of Cabernet, Chardonnay, Pinot Noir, and Riesling. Over the years, 15 additional acres were added, the mix changed slightly, and the winery became mostly estate-bottled.

Charles joined his brother in 1973 and in 1977 the winery was built. "We wanted an underground wine cellar," says Stu, "so I got a tractor and just began digging into the hillside. Then when it was mostly dug out, we built the cellar and back-filled the earth." The cave-like environment proved to be ideal — too ideal — for aging Cabernet. There was little evaporation from the casks, and the wine developed slowly. Too slowly.

"We found out that the environment is too good down there," says Charles. "It is so good that it doesn't give the Cabernet any chance for development. We moved the Cabernet barrels upstairs and we're using the cellar for Chardonnay now."

Smith-Madrone Chardonnays are typically lean and delicate and age well, characteristic of the tightly compact, mountain-grown frui the wine is made from. The Cabernets offe deep, cassis-scented flavors; the later wines are more complex than the earlier ones, as addi tional vine age adds to the complexity of th product. *DB*

At the start of their Napa Valley adventure, the Smiths made Pinot Noir, but gave up that variety, retaining instead the other Burgundian variety, Chardonnay. The brothers' style for this wine is to make it lean and delicate, reminiscent of Chablis.

Casks in the Smith-Madrone underground wine cellar must be cleaned frequently because the high humidity inside the facility — which reduces evaporation — is also conducive to the creation of mold on the walls, ceiling, floor, and barrels.

SPOTTSWOODE WINERY

Incorporating a pair of Napa Valley's "ghost wineries," Spottswoode was founded by a Southern California general practitioner, Dr. Jack Novak. He and his wife, Mary, came to St. Helena in 1972, purchasing the Spottswoode estate on Hudson Avenue from descendants of the Spotts family, who had owned the property since 1910 and given it its present name.

The 46-acre estate, with its gravel-walked gardens, had been originally established in 1882 by George Schonewald, manager of Monterey's Del Monte Lodge, who called it Lyndenhurst. In the 1890s Schonewald built a stone winery next door at Hudson and Spring Streets, called Esmeralda, to supply wine to San Francisco's Palace Hotel.

These days the energetic head of sales for the winery is Beth Novak. "Dad was a doctor who wanted to be a farmer. So, from '73 to '75 we replanted the 40 acres of vineyard — which had Petite Sirah, Green Hungarian, and French Colombard — to mostly Cabernet Sauvignon and Sauvignon Blanc."

As his vines came closer to producing fruit, Dr. Novak sought the city's permission to restore winemaking to the former Esmeralda Winery. However, after a lengthy public discussion, the city council denied the necessary

The first Spottswoode wines were made in the basement of this century-old Victorian building. Once used to grow mushrooms, the basement today holds more than 200 oak barrels. A dining-room table on the first floor serves as winery office.

permits in the spring of 1977. Later that year, Novak suffered a heart attack and passed away, which placed any idea of a winery on hold.

For the next five years, grapes were sold to Duckhorn and Shafer and eventually permits were obtained. In 1982, a century after the estate's founding, Tony Soter was hired to oversee vines and wines. The Pomona College philosophy major produced the first 1,400 cases of Spottswoode Cabernet Sauvignon that year, barrel aging them in the basement of the estate's handsome Victorian home.

Upstairs is Beth, a former UCLA soccer player who graduated in 1983 with a degree in

Art and wine seem to be such a natural mix, as much of winemaking demands an intuitive, artistic touch. But the art of winemaking is also tempered by technical demands that are ignored with grave consequences. Spottswoode winemaker, Tony Soter, a philosopher by education, blends the best of both worlds.

German and economics. "But I wanted to get into the wine business, though I hadn't really thought of coming home to work," she says, speaking rapidly, as if she were in the Angwin hills riding her mountain bike in a race. "I did wine sales in San Francisco for four years, then spent a year in an ad agency there to learn computers before I came home in the fall of '87."

In the late '80s, the wines were produced at other wineries (Pepi and Rombauer), then aged in the cellar at the Novak home. But in 1990 the Novaks bought the old Kraft Winery, at the end of Hudson Avenue (on Madrona Street, across from the northeast corner of Spottswoode's vineyard). "Frank Kraft built it in 1883," says Beth. "It's 44 by 66 feet on the outside, and the sandstone walls are two-and-a-half feet thick." Kraft only operated the winery until the turn of the century, and in recent years the building had been used to store and repair farm equipment.

The larger part of Spottswoode's 6,000-case production is Cabernet. "We do blend in some of the Cabernet Franc we grow, which is aromatic, but don't use Merlot," notes Beth. "We want our wine to represent the Cabernet Sauvignon that our vineyard produces." Indeed, the Spottswoode Cabernets, which have earned rave reviews across the board, are invariably hardy wines, full of black currant fruit that is firm and lasting. *RPH*

The patio, palm trees, and swimming pool behind the house overlook the 40 acres of Spottswoode vinelands. Most are planted to Cabernet Sauvignon, with smaller amounts of Cabernet Franc, Merlot, Sauvignon Blanc, and Semillon.

SPRING MOUNTAIN VINEYARDS

Iowa native Mike Robbins is the rare being who, though cursed with lofty dreams, has been blessed with the ability to fulfill them. An Annapolis engineer who put himself through law school at night, Mike created a magnificent Victorian showplace on the lower reaches of Spring Mountain with all the energy that he once spent on sizable real estate deals.

Robbins made time to acquire the skills necessary so that stained-glass windows of his own creation could grace his restoration of the elegant Victorian mansion, which includes a special kitchen outfitted solely for the benefit of the dozen or so hurt and homeless dogs and cats that have long been adopted by the Robbins household.

This magnificent edifice — modeled after Beringer's Rhine House — was constructed a century ago by Tiburcio Parrott, a prosperous merchant and confidant of both Jacob and Frederick Beringer.

The illegitimate son of the U.S. consul at Mazatlán, Parrott was a patron of the arts and a lover of growing things. When he became interested in olive trees, Parrott had 5,000 planted on his 1,500-acre estate, known then as Miravalle. He grew tobacco, oranges, and

Miravalle, the Victorian beauty built by Beringer brothers' buddy Tiburicio Parrott, is best known as the home of the feuding owners of Falcon Crest, the prime-time soap that's been every bit as popular in Europe as in America. More visitors come to see "Falcon Crest" than Spring Mountain Vineyards.

lemons, and cultivated many rare flowers, shrubs, and trees. He was also a winegrower, and A.R. Morrow, considered one of the finest wine tasters in California history, said that "Miravalle Margaux" was the greatest wine produced in California prior to Prohibition.

When television's popular *Falcon Crest* was filmed at Spring Mountain, Parrott's stained-glass parrot on the landing became a falcon. "It was fun while we were doing it," reflects Robbins. "Overall, I'd have to say it was a plus. It generated a lot of revenue at a time when the wine business was sluggish, but there were a lot of negatives, too. The main

Handsome stained-glass windows are de rigueur in restored Victorian homes, and Spring Mountain is no exception. Parrott grew tobacco, oranges, and lemons; raised rare flowers and trees; and produced highly regarded wines prior to Prohibition.

thing was that our Spring Mountain wines were not taken as seriously. But life's sort of like golf: It's not meant to be fair!"

Robbins' own Napa Valley odyssey started in 1960 when he was, for a short time, a minor shareholder in Mayacamas Vineyards. In 1962, on a business trip to the valley, his fancy was captured by a stately Victorian home just north of Greystone Cellars. Stately, but in disrepair. The cellar of that vintage 1876 home became a bonded winery in 1968; two years later Robbins offered his first wines under the Spring Mountain label. (That home, and its since-expanded winery, is now known as St. Clement.)

In 1974 Robbins purchased part of Parrott's Miravalle estate and slowly began to move his operation there. He began building the south wing (the fermentation cellar) in 1976, having enough of it completed and outfitted with Mueller fermenters for that year's crush. The main level of the north wing (the barrel cellar), built in front of a 90-foot tunnel dug decades before, was completed early in 1977.

Spring Mountain's winemaker, Greg Vita, has been at the winery since 1980. He and his wife, Diana, have a tiny winery of their own south of Carmel; their label is Coastanoan. Diana, born in Rhodesia, is also a winemaker, having studied enology at Cornell University. *RPH*

Parrott planted more than 5,000 trees on his 1,500-acre estate. Mike Robbins bought only a part of Parrott's estate, and today has 34 acres planted to Cabernet Sauvignon, Sauvignon Blanc, and Semillon.

STAG'S LEAP WINE CELLARS

It is difficult for Stag's Leap Wine Cellars owner/winemaker Warren Winiarski to discuss wine without artistic interpolations. Every procedure, every decision in the wine-growing process, seems to have its artistic correlation at this estate.

Chardonnay is something of a new direction for Stag's Leap, a winery so known for its successes with Cabernet Sauvignon. Warren's thesis that relates Chardonnay to an artistic format derives from the supreme lesson of great art, from ancients to moderns: Hold something back, leave something to the imagination. It is, he suggests, akin to the difference between eroticism and pornography. With the former, there is tension, the act is incomplete, and future viewings will bring out new vistas, new complexities; with the latter, well, there's little

A gondola full of grapes — Cabernet, you'd have to guess — will be lined up with the receiving hopper just behind the tractor. After fermentation, juice will be separated from skins in one of a pair of presses behind the gondola.

left to say or see. Once is usually more than enough.

"It doesn't help Chardonnay to magnify its properties," the former University of Chicago lecturer in political science says by way of preface. "It's like trying to do better than well! Beyond a certain point, it becomes nothing more than a caricature. The real question, I think, has to do with appropriate magnitude."

Winiarski carries his artistic analogy still further: "Classic wines are always conceived with appropriate proportions. Every artist chooses a moment that represents what he wants the viewer to see, and in classic regimes that moment is always 'the moment before,' the moment prior to the completion or fulfillment of the action they wanted to portray. Therefore, there is always some tension, which engages the mind, the perceptions of the beholder. This engagement produces a sense of participation."

The primary tool of this mode is conspicuously missing from the palettes of many painters today, and rather rarer than it ought to be among winemakers' palates as well. In a word, restraint. "Look at the classical Greek sculpture *The Discus-Thrower*," argues Winiarski. "Because there has been no release, it overflows with tension. You know what's going to happen, but the piece still captures our attention and our thoughts. That's why it's classic. That's why it works."

It is, of course, quite natural to think first of Cabernet Sauvignon when the discussion turns to Stag's Leap Wine Cellars. The winery came bursting into the world's attention when the results of the May 24, 1976, wine tasting were trumpeted in *Time* magazine's article, "Judgment of Paris." There, in a tasting arranged by wine merchant Steven Spurrier and conducted by top French wine professionals, a pair of California wines topped their French classified counterparts in two categories: for White Burgundy/Chardonnay, it was Chateau Montelena 1973, and for Bordeaux/Cabernet Sauvignon, Stag's Leap 1973, only Warren's second vintage.

Ballyhoo aside, the kicker is that subsequent Stag's Leap Cabernets have only improved the breed, to the point that even a slightly-less-than-extraordinary Cabernet from Stag's Leap would be cause for consternation and concern throughout the industry.

Warren is almost forcefully certain about what he expects from his Cabernets. "We are looking for wines of enormous depth, with

Lobster and Stag's Leap Chardonnay is a perfectly lovely combination. But, as with all art, the matching of wine and food is as simple or as complex as you wish to make it. A simple soup would do as nicely as the lobster.

Warren Winiarski is convinced that the Stags Leap District is a special place to grow Cabernet Sauvignon. "There is a viticultural reality that supports the notion for Cabernet [here], from the soils to the climate to the wines themselves," he asserts.

great definition of varietal character and a graceful suppleness of fruit that is fleshy in texture. We are not, however, interested in making any 25-year wines, as such. We're not interested in making museum pieces, my art analogy notwithstanding."

That objective is no surprise once you analyze Warren's vinous background. First, he spent a two-year apprenticeship with the late Lee Stewart at Napa Valley's original Souverain Winery (now Burgess Cellars), and an equal time working with Robert Mondavi at his Oakville winery. Souverain Cabernets of the mid '60s, while distinctively varietal at core, were gloved with finesse.

The Mondavi Cabernets, though a bit more forceful, share similar finishing qualities, especially as they age. Combine that background with the fact that Warren's early consultant was Andre Tchelistcheff — the man who defined Rutherford Cabernet while at Beaulieu Vineyard from the '40s through the early '70s — and you've got a pedigree for Cabernet Sauvignon that is an eyelash short of perfection. (What fills the space of that "eyelash" is for you, the taster, to decide. Artistic restraint? Tension?)

Winiarski returns to the art analogy: "Art deals with human pleasures. If one is only quenching one's thirst, one drinks water. But if

Once a political science lecturer at the University of Chicago, Warren Winiarski broke through the wine barrier with his second vintage: at a tasting in Paris, top French wine professionals judged that Stag's Leap 1973 Cabernet Sauvignon outclassed all its counterparts -- French and otherwise!

one needs to quench one's appetite for pleasure, then you'd want wine. Wine is a useful, preservative art. Sort of like cheese making. With cheese, you've preserved milk. With wine, you've taken grape juice and preserved it in a different, more useful form."

As America's wine sophistication has grown in recent years, so too have winemakers become more specific in designating appellations of origin — the places their wines have been grown. The Stags Leap District was officially recognized in the late '80s ["Stags" plural to distinguish it from Winiarski's winery (singular possessive) and Carl Doumani's Stags' Leap Winery (plural possessive)].

If you have any doubt about the name of Winiarski's wine cellars, this barrel hammers home its apostrophe point clearly -- Stag's (singular possessive) Leap Wine Cellars. The District's appellation is Stags (just plain plural) Leap, while Carl Doumani owns and runs the Stags' (plural possessive) Winery. It's enough to drive a person to drink!

"Having our own appellation is part of an evolutionary process," says Winiarski. "The whole idea of having the appellation is that it implies a certain distinctiveness in the wines. Now, with regard to Cabernet Sauvignon in Stags Leap, I think that this is valid. There is a viticultural reality that supports the notion for Cabernet, from the soils to the climate to the wines themselves.

"To retain that distinctiveness requires regulation and restraint on our part. Otherwise, the appellation only becomes a freedom without restraint, and then we will have lost the distinctiveness that sets us apart and gives the Stags Leap District its meaning. That's why we name things, after all, because the names imply a specific meaning, a specific distinctiveness."

And that is what drives Warren Winiarski to produce these velvet-gloved, iron-fisted Cabernet Sauvignons and artistically restrained Chardonnays with great care and attention to detail.

"We make every effort to get down to minute considerations, from vineyard to winery," Winiarski always says. "When you spare no effort, the resulting wines live up to their price. I think that is what makes all this so attractive to me." *RPH*

STAGS' LEAP WINERY

A split-level road directs you east off the Silverado Trail, north of Napa, past olive trees and vines into a pocket valley. The straight walnut-lined drive, flanked by vineyards, gives way to the hillside, palm trees, an old stone winery, and the former Stags' Leap Manor.

The manor house was completed in 1891 or so by Chicago financier Horace Chase, who also planted 100 acres of grapes, built a 40,000-case winery, and is said to have bestowed the name Stags Leap on the rocky promontory that stands guard over this secluded section of the Napa Valley.

The three-story manor house was turned into a hotel in 1920 by its next owner, Clarence "Fred" Grange. It quickly became a popular hangout for those who pretended that Prohibi-

A forklift moves gondolas of grapes to the crusher-stemmer at Stags' Leap Winery. The stone winery in the background was restored in the late 1970s, and the new Stags' Leap quickly became famous for inky-black, thickly fruited Petite Sirahs.

tion did not exist and for whom "depression" had no economic meaning. The hotel remained open until 1953.

Carl Doumani had been a restaurateur in his native Los Angeles before he decided to show his four children a different way of life. So he and his wife, Joanne, bought the 400-acre estate in 1970 and began the seemingly endless job of restoration.

Over the years, constant attention has been paid to the 88 acres of vineyard, pulling out varieties unsuited to the microclimate of the Stags Leap District (Pinot Noir, Early Burgundy, Chenin Blanc) in favor of those which are suited (Petite Syrah, Cabernet Sauvignon, Cabernet Franc, Merlot, Petit Verdot, and Malbec).

The early Stags' Leap wines were fermented elsewhere, then aged in oak barrels in the 120-foot coolie-dug tunnel that bores into the hillside behind the stone winery Chase had constructed around the turn of the century. The main winery building later burned, but the stone walls remained, standing forlornly as a monument to past glories.

In the fall of 1978 a concrete interior floor was poured, the interior walls were rebuilt with redwood, an attic office space was carved out, and the 50-by-60-foot structure was roofed. Two stained-glass windows shine in the ornate window spaces flanking the arched front doorway. The south window represents spring with a lush green leaf, backed by blue sky; the north window has a red-orange autumn leaf.

For a number of years, the winery seemed merely to exist, its ageeable Petite Sirahs lost in the shadow of its hillside neighbor to the south, Stag's Leap Wine Cellars. But that seems to be changing since winemaker/viticulturist Robert Brittan came on board in early 1989.

Brittan has an eclectic vinous background. Leaving Oregon State's high-energy physics program in 1973, he took an off-the-cuff job as a lab technician at Bear Mountain Winery in his home town of Bakersfield. He liked the job so much that he eventually went back to school, earning his degree in fermentation science from U.C. Davis in 1980.

"Working in the central valley is an experience every winemaker should have," says the tall, bespectacled Brittan. "There, you really have to *make* the wines, you really have to stay on top of them. Here, I put vineyard development and winemaking together. If you're going to have world-class wines you have to pay close attention to the raw substrata. The vines." *RPH*

Stags' Leap Manor —
the Elizabethan
manor house built in
1890 by Chicago
financier Horace
Chase — boasts this
castle-like turret.
Chase had a 120-foot
cave dug in 1893 and
began producing
wine under the Stags'
Leap name the same
year. The manor was
turned into a vacation
resort at the onset of
Prohibition.

Olive and walnut
trees grow on the
border of 88 acres of
vines, nearly half of
which are Cabernet
Sauvignon. A rocky
tor rising in the east
gave life to the
legend of a magical
stag, able to leap
from crag to crag to
escape hunters and
predators.

STERLING VINEYARDS

Sterling Vineyards represents one of California's most successful and consistently great producers of a wide range of wines. It has achieved this lofty level because of the dedication of the original founders and their commitment to quality; the expertise of the original winemaker, Ric Forman, who established a house style that is followed to this day; and the faith of the new owner, The Seagram Classics Wine Co., which acquired superior vineyards, added new varieties, and supported the brand with vigor.

Sterling has never been under financial fire. It started life as a project of three wealthy businessmen from San Francisco — Peter Newton, Michael Stone, and Ned Skinner. The name the partners chose for the winery came from Sterling International, a paper company, of which Newton and Stone were executives. They first planted vineyards in 1964, and the first wines were made at a temporary cellar in 1968.

The winery was constructed in 1973 on a knoll in the center of the valley. The design was by Martin Waterfield, who selected a Mediterranean villa with monastery overtones as his theme. This is reflected in the archways over the windows and doorways, in the bell tower, and in the ascetic bleached-white exterior. The

Sterling Vineyards' barrel-aging room is well underground. Here winemaker Bill Dyer blends the wines into harmonious, age-worthy examples of their French counterparts. The winery's Reserve, a red wine blend of the classic Bordeaux varieties, is one of the most successful wines of its type in California.

hilltop location of the facility was not done for practical reasons. Grapes have to be trucked up to the top of a knoll on a narrow, serpentine road, and the crush pad is small and hard to expand. Parking for employees is nearly nil. The hilltop is excellent, however, for promotion. The winery is attractive and has a grand panoramic view of the valley; visitors love it.

To the south is the winery's own Larsen vineyard, followed by the sweeping greenery of vineyards stretching toward St. Helena and beyond. Mount St. Helena towers to the northeast; across the valley is Sterling's terraced Diamond Mountain vineyard; to the north is Calistoga.

Visitors to Sterling ride an aerial tram up the mountain to the alabastrine buildings that look more like a monastery than a winery. The flowers planted around the perimeter of the property soften its austerity, and the hospitality is warm.

One element of the construction was quite practical: the chai used for the aging of barrels was set into the mountainside, and that design keeps the barrels naturally cool. Today the winery houses an attractive demonstration kitchen for cooking classes, and it also is home to a hospitality school run by master sommelier Evan Goldstein. The winery has also added a cave for barrel aging. The Sterling hospitality center includes a large attractive dining room with a fireplace. Private groups often rent out the facility and cater parties there.

Newton and his partners sold Sterling and its vineyards in 1977 to The Wine Spectrum, a division of Coca-Cola, which added more vineyards. That corporation subsequently sold all its wine holdings to Seagram in 1984. Seagram expanded further with the acquisition of some of the best vineyard land in the Napa Valley, totaling more than 1,200 acres and stretching from the famed Winery Lake Vineyard in the cool Carneros far to the south, to the Diamond Mountain property high atop a canted ridge just southwest of Calistoga.

With vineyard manager Tucker Catlin as its implementing genius, Seagram planted a number of new vineyards with top Bordeaux varieties other than Cabernet Sauvignon and Merlot (notably Cabernet Franc and Petit Verdot) to have additional Bordeaux varieties that would be blended into the winery's top red wines.

Sterling's first winemaker, Ric Forman, was a brilliant technician and artist who employed classical French techniques and some of the latest California technology to craft wines of unique style. The Chardonnays were lean and delicate, but packed with a subtle undertone of richness, seen best in later years as the wines aged. The Cabernet Sauvignons, usually blended with Merlot and aged and treated in a Bordeaux manner, were rich, powerful, tannic, and long-lived. The 1974 Sterling Reserve Cabernet, tasted in 1991, showed amazing depth and richness and still had plenty of life left in it. Forman also developed a style for the Sauvignon Blanc, lean and austere, that reminded wine lovers of the great wines of Graves in Bordeaux.

Theo Rosenbrand, formerly a colleague of Andre Tchelistcheff, followed Forman as Sterling's winemaker. Then, for a brief stint,

Chilean-born Sergio Traverso joined Rosenbrand as a winemaking team.

In 1985, Seagram turned the winemaking reins over to Bill Dyer, a young assistant winemaker who had shown great understanding of the Sterling style. (Dyer's wife, Dawnine Sample Dyer, is winemaker at Domaine Chandon.) Dyer changed things only subtly, but his refinements made Sterling an even greater winery than it had been. Whereas a few of the Cabernets of an earlier era were a bit too tannic, Dyer's Cabernets had ample structure and were less astringent and seemed to have better aging potential. Where the Chardonnays may have been a tad too oaky at one stage, Dyer toned them down to become more graceful, showing more spice.

Sterling Chardonnays age well, but the wines are so luscious when young, with high acidity, that they are easy to consume, so some people who have the wines in their cellar don't keep any long enough to see what they are like

The classic, medieval-looking St. Dunstan's Room, located in the south wing of the winery, is used for private dinners where the wine trade may taste the new releases — and occasionally see some of the rare old treasures from the Sterling library.

with age. However, older bottlings are prized by knowledgeable collectors.

Sterling's Winery Lake Pinot Noirs were more of a struggle for Dyer. Long known as a temperamental grape variety, the Pinot Noir is notorious for changing after the winemaker is sure it won't. Although Dyer's first few Winery Lake Pinot Noirs were good wines, they seemed to carry a weight and a coarseness that great Pinot Noir usually lacks.

Dyer's greatest achievements have been with the Cabernet Sauvignons and Merlots, two wines similar in character. The Cabernet was made with a bit more finesse than it had been under previous regimes, and the wine took on a lovely, polished texture in the mouth compared with the previous coarse style. The Merlot was even more a wine of finesse, rich and round without the bite of so many other Merlots.

The best wine in the line, however, is called simply Reserve. It is Sterling's top-of-the-line red wine, a Cabernet Sauvignon-based wine that used to be called Sterling Reserve Cabernet Sauvignon. The varietal designation was removed in 1986 so Dyer could blend in more of the other Bordeaux varieties; the addition of Cabernet Franc and Petit Verdot into the Reserve made a major difference, adding complexity and additional nuances of fruit. *DB*

Sterling's winemaker Bill Dyer has a marvelous sense of style. He took over winemaking chores in 1985 and immediately the winery's efforts soared, even in mediocre vintages. Dyer is married to Dawnine Sample Dyer, sparkling winemaker at Domaine Chandon.

From a distance, Sterling might look a bit monastery-like, or even Tuscan in nature, but viewed close up, Martin Waterfield's architectural plan for this property is actually quite modern, with angular patterns to the design leading up to the bell tower.

STONEGATE

The stone archway though which guests pass as they enter the Stonegate winery wasn't constructed until well after the winery already had its name and the wine was in the marketplace. Today it can be seen from Dunaweal Lane, a familiar symbol to travelers.

Many of the finest wines come from steep hillside vineyards where soils are shallow and well-drained, and the vines must struggle to survive. It was such a vineyard that the Spauldings of Stonegate winery, founded in 1973, sought to create. Now, the Mayacamas Range hillside vineyards of the Spauldings and their neighbors produce all of Stonegate's Cabernet Sauvignon and Merlot, and much of their Chardonnay.

Despite the validity of the concept and the wines' quality and style — halfway between immediately enjoyable and lean/ageworthy — "we've never had a lot of press," says Spaulding. "We puzzle over that. Part of it is we were a new winery before it was fashionable to be new. There were two dozen wineries in the Napa Valley then and now there are well over 200. And later, when it *was* fashionable

to be new, we no longer were, so we had no story to tell."

Also, the style of Stonegate's wines has changed markedly since its first years of operation, leading to some consumer confusion. Stonegate's first wines came from grapes grown at various Napa Valley vineyards; the mountain-grown fruit that would become the Spauldings' hallmark was only barely perceptible in those early vintages. And the 1976 vintage saw a change in winemakers, too, from Robert Stemmler to David Spaulding, Jim and Barbara's son. Now, using mostly mountain-grown grapes, David can make the quality statement he wants to with Stonegate wines.

The vineyards are the key to the process. The main source of grapes is the Spauldings' own ranch high above the valley floor, off Kortum Canyon Road in Calistoga. The

neighboring Pershing vineyard provides Cabernet, Merlot, and Cabernet Franc. The Hayes ranch, a mile down the ridge to the west, is a major source of Chardonnay, as is Andy Beckstoffer's Carneros ranch. And a small vineyard adjacent to the Spauldings', owned by Sal Frasca, provides a small amount of top-quality Cabernet Franc for blending into the Cabernet Sauvignon.

The style of wine varies each year, especially the Chardonnay. Some years, it will undergo no malolactic fermentation, while other years and in some Reserve bottlings the wine is put through 65 to 75 percent malolactic. Also, in 1987 and 1989, the winery bottled a late-harvest Sauvignon Blanc. But that wine appears only when conditions warrant.

The name of the winery was hit upon by Barbara, almost the result of a series of coincidences. "Well, we had a lot of stones in the vineyard, and we had stone walls surrounding our vineyard," says Jim. "And when we lived in Berkeley we lived on Stonewall Road, and it was the era when [Richard] Nixon was stonewalling everything, but we couldn't use that term, so we just thought that Stonegate might be a nice name." Not until 1985 did the

family have a stone gate constructed in front.

Because Stonegate's sales are a bit slower than other wineries, often their tasting room has a number of older wines for sale. Some of these older vintages show how attractively the mountain-sourced Cabernets can age. *DB*

The Spaulding family's home vineyards, which were planted on steep, rocky soil halfway up Kortum Canyon Road above Calistoga, produce some of the top Cabernet Sauvignon and Merlot in the northern end of the Napa Valley.

STONY HILL VINEYARD

Fred and Eleanor McCrea of San Francisco originally bought this mountain-perched property on the west side of Highway 29 north of St. Helena for a summer home. The year was 1943. Neighbors suggested they plant grapes on their extra land, since the rock-strewn landscape wasn't suitable for much else. Except, perhaps, goats.

Dr. Richard Peterson, former winemaker at Beaulieu Vineyard to the south, tells a great story about Stony Hill's inauspicious beginning: "Fred and I were walking up his hill, through the vines one day, and we stopped at a point and he began talking.

"'This hill was all underbrush and boulders when I bought it,'" Peterson quotes McCrea as saying. "'And I had hired Andre Tchelistcheff to tell me how best to prepare the soil and plant the vineyard. Well, as we struggled through the brush here, Andre asked, 'Mr. McCrea, what business did you say you recently retired from?' Fred told Andre that he was in the advertising business. And Andre said, 'Well, Mr. McCrea, I seriously recommend that you remain in the advertising business.' That's how bad the soil was." But with Tchelistcheff's aid, McCrea eventually planted the rocky hillside vineyard and named it, appropriately, Stony Hill.

The weathered, wooden doors to the Stony Hill winery are rarely seen by visitors because the small-production winery is not open to the general public. Even the road on which the winery entrance is located is not identified by a sign at the base of the hill.

The winemaking operation was founded in 1953. Almost immediately, Stony Hill wines gained fame for their harmonies of flavor, their lean elegance, and their staying power. All of the wines are made with amazing delicacy; perfectly enjoyable when released, they change subtly over the years, taking on a charm and a bouquet unlike any other California wines.

Down through the years at Stony Hill, little has changed. When Fred McCrea died in 1977, Eleanor assumed the reins and, with Mike Chelini as winemaker, has continued to turn out a small quantity of exquisite wines.

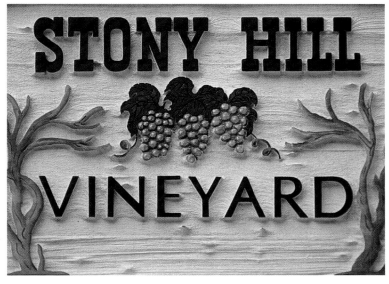

The familiar logo that has adorned the wine label for decades also is used as a sign on the property. The name reflects the soil in which the grapes grow — rocky and hard to farm, which gives the resulting wine a lean, austere character when just released.

The Chardonnay is the most sought wine in the line, though in the 1980s renown was obscured by the bigger, blowsier, and more unctuous styles of Chardonnay that the American palate was trained to like.

Stony Hill Chardonnays demand understanding. First of all, they are unlike almost any Chardonnays in the state when they are young. Some of them can be awkward, like the 13-year-old with braces, knock-knees, and pimples. The savvy sipper, however, will see the potential in the adolescent wine and will make allowances for what can only be hinted at.

Tasting back through decades of older Chardonnays reveals what the wines are about. They become lovely. The braces are removed, revealing straight, white teeth. The apple juice scent of youth is replaced by a clove-and-vanilla nuance wrapped around delicate pear and spice scents, and the aftertaste of even two-decade-old wine is sublime, still crisp and fresh.

The other wines in the line, the Riesling and Gewurztraminer, are wonderful, too, but also in that lean, delicate style. The wines are produced entirely from Stony Hill's vineyards. The family-owned winery is not open to the public, though appointments may be made to visit it. However, almost all wines are sold to a list of loyal mail subscribers, so rarely is there much of anything left over. *DB*

Winemaker Mike Chelini ages his Chardonnay in oak barrels, but uses little new oak, preferring instead to gain just a trace of wood flavor from older barrels. Stony Hill Chardonnays are known for their amazing staying power and ability to age decades.

STORYBOOK MOUNTAIN VINEYARDS

If you were to conjecture that Storybook Mountain was something out of the Brothers Grimm, you'd be quite close to the mark. You see, the winery's three connected caves were excavated in 1888 and 1889 by brothers named Grimm (Jacob and Adam), helped by their cousin Jacob. The winery, later connected with Grison's Steak House in San Francisco, operated well past the days of Prohibition.

The estate was overgrown and the caves neglected when former history professor Dr. J. Bernard "Jerry" Seps and his Franconia-born wife, Sigrid, acquired the property in 1976. Starting the next year, 37 acres of rolling hill-side were reclaimed and planted to Zinfandel, which Seps feels is the best match for his site. "Hey, when you've got Zinfandel, you don't need anything else," Jerry laughs.

Seps, who once taught at Stanford, says he came to the winegrowing life "to preserve the environment, not abuse it." Thus, he has not used insecticides or herbicides, but rather tries to achieve a natural balance on the land. "That means a lot of hand hoeing, but the results are worth it, so we'll continue to do it as long as we can. We've left trees standing simply because they were too beautiful to cut down, even though it makes our job more difficult."

Jerry Seps mostly employs smaller oak barrels to age and mature his full-flavored Zinfandels. This cellar cave was excavated in 1883 by brothers Jacob and Adam Grimm, who hailed from Mommenheim, Germany.

Seps continues, trying to verbalize more precisely the challenges of preservation farming. "When you've been on a tractor from dawn 'til dusk, you can look back and see exactly what you've accomplished. That is physically satisfying. Then there is the mental challenge of trying to understand what nature is giving us each vintage, and how best to change the fruit into wine.

"And there's that different, stimulating challenge of selling what you've made. It's nice to spend three days in Los Angeles when you know that you can return to this beautiful place."

This intricate ironwork, like the carved barrel head (below), replicates the Storybook Mountain label showing the fabled fox straining to reach a cluster of ripe grapes. (The fox pronounced them "sour" when unable to secure them.)

Storybook's "beautiful place" is the northernmost of the Napa Valley's 250-plus wineries, literally a stone's throw from Sonoma County. While some folks bridle at the bucolic life, Seps finds Napa's vine-filled valley as stimulating socially as it is physically and philosophically. "I don't think we're culturally deprived at all. Napa has a symphony orchestra, we're not all that far from the City [San Francisco], and the people up here are terrific. Everybody is so quick to offer help. Al Brounstein [Diamond Creek] was very helpful with marketing tips, and Rob Pecota took me along with him on a marketing trip and helped us make our first contacts out of state."

While others have given up on Zinfandel, Seps shows no signs of faltering. "The problems of Zinfandel were probably due to the wild diversity of the wines, from Beaujolais styles to the heavy, alcoholic late-harvest wines. I see that diversity as more of an asset, but it wasn't for consumers.

"I see Zinfandel making a comeback. We don't have much of a problem, because we're small and unique. I make wines that I like to drink, wines that are often compared to the clarets in their structure. Retailer Gerald Weisl once paid me a high compliment when he said, 'If Château Margaux made Zinfandel, this is what it would taste like.'" *RPH*

Seps is a purist when it comes to caring for his vines, the northernmost plantings in the Napa Valley. He hoes by hand, deploys neither herbicides nor insecticides, and hand harvests his fruit when it is mature. He is also a minimalist with regard to cellar treatments.

SUTTER HOME WINERY

It was an unlikely idea: the red Zinfandel would be made more like a white wine, converted into a pleasant, simple, pale-pink wine that would need no aging in a cellar and could be sipped on hot days as a "cooler-offer."

Sutter Home Winery initially made a small amount of the wine this way in the early 1970s. It took off. The American consumer, who talked dry, really drank sweet and liked this wine. People found this was the perfect wine for the upscaling times, the Yuppie wine if ever there was one, a wine that could be sipped as an aperitif or with lunch.

Small Sutter Home wound up by the mid-1980s as the largest winery in the Napa Valley — solely because of White Zinfandel.

Sutter Home had modest beginnings. John and Mario Trinchero acquired the barn-like

Sutter Home Winery's amazing success with White Zinfandel — without selling a single bottle of wine larger than 750 milliliters in size — included a sparkling White Zinfandel, called Sparkler. It was discontinued in 1989.

The second generation of Trincheros, Mario and Mary's sons, Bob and Roger, were the first to make White Zinfandel. It wasn't the first such wine ever made, but Bob, now CEO of the winery, had it made to fit a specific market — slightly sweet — and the wine took off like a rocket.

The White Zinfandel craze that swept the nation in the mid-1980s, entirely the work of Sutter Home, may actually have saved the Zinfandel grape from virtual extinction. By the late 1970s, many wine lovers had found red Zinfandels with high alcohol too difficult to drink, and there was a consumer backlash against the wine. Many producers toyed with the idea of ripping out old Zinfandel vineyards. Had not White Zinfandel come along to create demand for the old vines, they might have been lost.

Lost in all the hubbub over Sutter Home's amazing White Zinfandel sales is the fact that Sutter Home once made one of the top red Zinfandels in the state. In fact, it was red Zinfandel that gained the winery its first brush with greatness.

In the late 1960s, Charles Myers of Harbor Winery introduced Bob Trinchero to the superb Zinfandel grapes on a ranch owned by Ken Deaver in the Amador foothills. "I liked the fruit so much that we started buying from Ken's ranch," recounts Bob. Those grapes produced a string of fine, full-bodied red wines. The Sutter Home "Deaver Vineyard" Zinfandels of the early 1970s are, to this day, considered some of the best Zinfandels ever produced in California.

Shortly after the red Zinfandels of Sutter Home became popular, the winery began making a white wine from the same grapes by simply taking the juice off the skins earlier. The early versions of this wine were not pink, as so many White Zinfandels of the later years turned out, but barely salmon-colored. By 1980, Sutter Home was making a then-hefty 25,000 cases of White Zinfandel for a marketplace that seemed eager to pay $5 a bottle for it. The release each spring of the new White Zin, as it's called by devotees, was, for many

Sutter Home Winery on Highway 29 in the heart of the Napa Valley in 1941. They produced a number of good, inexpensive table wines, which represented some of the best values in the Napa Valley, including an herb-scented Vermouth and a sweet Muscat. Occasionally, some wines were bought in bulk from top-name producers, aged at Sutter Home, and bottled under its label.

Sutter Home Winery was a small, family-run operation until the mid-1970s, when the family discovered a niche in the market called White Zinfandel. By 1990, the winery was marketing more than three million cases of the product, representing one-quarter of the country's market!

wine merchants, as important an event as the release each November of French Beaujolais Nouveau.

By 1986, Sutter Home's growth in White Zinfandel reached 1.3 million cases and the small winery was stretched to capacity. At last the family acquired land and built a huge production facility at which it processed the grapes being brought in from other counties.

The demand for White Zinfandel that sparked Sutter Home's growth also motivated hundreds of other wineries to make it. (By 1990 more than 11 million cases were being produced in the U.S. — but Sutter Home was making 27 percent of it!) Sutter Home faced

an increasing demand for the top-quality fruit, which meant shortages as well as higher prices. To deal with this problem, the Trincheros acquired land in Glenn and Colusa counties, regions to the east where few if any wine grapes had been grown before. However, research showed the soil and climate would produce good Zinfandel for the winery's White Zin project. And the land was priced far below that of the Napa Valley, where an acre of vineyard land could sell for as much as $50,000.

The move was followed in December 1988 by the acquisition of the Montevina Winery in Amador County. Bob Trinchero's goal

Rare palm trees grace the front of the Sutter Home Winery tasting room, a former Victorian house that had been a bed and breakfast inn. The Trinchero Family acquired it after their White Zinfandel became a national success.

with Montevina was to convert that winery into one specializing in the Italian varieties of grapes, such as Barbera, Sangiovese, and Nebbiolo. Sutter Home moved more strongly in the direction of Italian varieties by planting additional acreage to those varieties.

In 1989, when Sutter Home made 360,000 cases of its first Chardonnay, it was sold out before release — so strong was the reputation of the winery in the marketplace. In addition, the winery broadened its base with large quantities of Sauvignon Blanc and Cabernet Sauvignon. Bob Trinchero points out by 1990 his winery was producing more than one million cases of wine in addition to its White Zinfandel.

As the Napa Valley has prospered, so have the local artisans. Often they are asked to recreate some of the art objects of the dim past, as in this hand-etched glass design of grapes and leaves hanging on the vine.

Meanwhile, the red Zinfandel program that started the winery off into a growth mode continued to progress. And Amador County remained the source of the grapes in the winery's best offering.

"We hit a flat spot in the middle of the 1980s," admits Trinchero. Because of great demand, his red Zinfandel wines were no longer solely from Amador grapes. The result was wines that showed thin, weak flavors and that didn't age as well in the bottle as had past vintages. "That taught us something," says Trinchero. He resumed making the Zinfandel entirely from Amador grapes, and again took the same kind of care once used for the wine. By the late 1980s, the wines began to receive the kind of plaudits they once had gotten, and Sutter Home was back on track.

It is ironic, of course, that Sutter Home's amazing growth to well past four million cases in total production by 1990 was fueled by non-Napa Valley grapes. And more ironic is that in connoisseur-conscious Napa, the wine that made Sutter Home famous appealed more to novices than collectors. Still, the wine remains a persistent reminder that when you make a consistently good product that is marketed well, success may be yours. *DB*

Sutter Home produces most of its White Zinfandel from grapes purchased from regions other than the Napa Valley. Also, the winery has planted more than 1,000 acres of vineyard land in counties well east of Napa to reduce the winery's dependence on outside grape sources.

SWANSON VINEYARD & WINERY

When someone hears that W. Clarke Swanson Jr. owns a Napa Valley vineyard and winery, the jokes begin: what wine goes with TV dinners?

It's true that Swanson's family owned and operated that food business when he was a youngster, but the firm was sold before Clarke graduated from Stanford University. What Swanson is deservedly noted for, in the business community, is being a successful developer of cable TV and publishing firms, and being owner and chairman of Averys of Bristol, one of England's most prestigious wine marketing companies.

But in the last few years, Swanson has spent more of his time carefully planning the first releases from his new winery west of Highway 29. And if auction results are any indication, Swanson Vineyards will be one of the great new wineries of the 1990s. The first wine brought to market, the 1988 Chardonnay, was so impressive that at a Napa Valley wine auction in 1990, three magnums sold for $2,300 — over $700 a bottle! (At the winery, the retail price of a 750 ml bottle is $15.)

Swanson himself is a focused man, dedicated to making the best wine imaginable. He is doing it from three vineyards, two of which

W. Clarke Swanson hired Marco Cappelli to be his winemaker. The first wines from this new property were stunning: a rich, complex Chardonnay with lively acid and deeply scented Cabernets that seemed as if they would age.

he acquired in the mid-1980s. The three properties are located in Oakville, along the Silverado Trail, and in Carneros, and are among the best in their respective regions.

The Oakville ranch is just east of the Napa River near Mondavi-Rothschild's Opus One vineyard and Silver Oak Cellars' Bonny's Vineyard. Clearly, the company is impressive. The red wines that winemaker Marco Cappelli has made show the character of this Oakville area, with startling intensity and almost mountain-grown qualities despite the fact that almost all the fruit is from valley floor property. Swanson's Carneros ranch provided the fruit for a

The winemaker's task: extracting wine from the barrel with the use of a thief -- a long, narrow tube that fits inside the bung hole of the barrel and with which he draws some of the wine, to be drained into a glass.

1988 Reserve Chardonnay that, when released in late 1990, wowed connoisseurs with its amazingly fresh fruit and overwhelming complexity for a wine so young.

The winery also had a spectacular Botrytis Semillon, made in 1988 following a rain that infected the grapes with the noble rot, *Botrytis cinerea.*

The Swanson winery was founded in 1986; it had been the old Cassayre-Forni winery, which closed in the early 1980s. The main Swanson property, 100 acres of prime terrain in the Oakville District, is planted to Merlot, Cabernet Sauvignon, Sangiovese, and Chardonnay. Swanson and vineyardist Jim Lincoln are eager to see what happens when their four acres of the Italian variety Sangiovese come into bearing. (Swanson is planning to make a premium blend of Cabernet and Sangiovese, similar to some of the super Tuscan wines of the later 1980s.)

The first wines in 1990 received rave reviews. Newer releases are rated as even better by Cappelli. One of those wines is a Reserve Red Blend, similar to the wines of Bordeaux, where Cappelli interned after U.C. Davis.

Swanson created his winery with domestic and international sales in mind. Averys will market the wines in Europe to a clientele that already has had a taste of what Swanson is shooting for. *DB*

Cappelli and vineyardist Jim Lincoln work as a team to create grapes that reach maturity and which have so much natural "vine-ripe" flavor that processing of the juice as it reaches its final state as wine is minimal.

TREFETHEN VINEYARDS

In 1978 the Trefethen family received one of five awards made by the Upper Napa Valley Associates for "excellence in the preservation or restoration of historic structures which symbolize the lifestyle of the valley in the 19th century." The award was for their restoration to useful service of the 1886 Eshcol Winery, the second oldest wooden winery in the valley. (Sutter Home is the oldest.)

Built to last with incredibly stout beams, the walls and ceilings of this Hamden W. McIntyre creation (he also built the stone fortresses of Greystone, Far Niente, and Chateau Montelena) are lined with tongue and groove redwood. Crushing and fermenting in redwood vats were accomplished on the top floor — now housing offices — the grapes hoisted there by means of an outdoor elevator on the west side. The wines were then racked to the second level for aging in barrels, from which they eventually flowed to the ground floor for bottling and shipment.

Napa bankers James and George Goodman named the property Eshcol, for the biblical brook (Numbers 13) where Moses's spys "cut down from thence a branch with one cluster of grapes, and they bare it between two upon a staff."

It is only fitting that an old wooden winery would age wines in wooden barrels. In the old days, the woods would have been the same: redwood. But redwood vats have given way to oak casks from French forests with names like Nevers, Allier Limousin, Troncais, and Vosges.

In 1895 a curious fellow by the name of J. Clark Fawver leased the property, purchasing it five years later. A beer drinker, Fawver wouldn't have wine served in his home. He was a farmer, though, and dearly loved the earth. He took pride in his vineyard, had wine made from his grapes, and sold the wine off in bulk. During Prohibition he actually enlarged the winery, which was leased to Beringer for storage after Fawver's death in 1940.

The 600-acre property was purchased in 1968 by Gene and Katie Trefethen (he, the former president of Kaiser Industries). They entrusted the vineyards to the care of award-

John and Janet Trefethen stand in the 600-acre vineyard that, under the management of Tony Baldini, provides quality fruit for the wines of Trefethen. While it is possible to make poor wines from good grapes, the opposite is quite impossible.

winning Tony Baldini, who instituted a program of replacing prune and walnut orchards and replanting parcels of older vines each year. "I spend a lot of time with my vines," says Baldini. "I try to monitor their development constantly. It's not hard. You just start at one end, walk to the other, and then walk back. Farming grapes is like any other industry. Survival is tied directly to quality."

With the handsome, pumpkin-colored winery building restored and the vineyard producing, the Trefethens turned their attention to winemaking in 1973. Gene's son, John, a former Navy lieutenant, is responsible for general winery and vineyard operations, ably assisted by Davis-trained winemaker David Whitehouse Jr. Janet Spooner Trefethen, John's wife, handles the marketing — usually on trips in a twin-engine Cessna Conquest 1 that John pilots.

"John actually made small lots of Chardonnay and Cabernet Sauvignon in 1970, just to see what we would get," recalls Janet. "He was in Stanford University's Graduate School of Business at the time, and those lots convinced us that we should be making wine, and not just selling grapes. So, at Stanford, John and four colleagues researched a project called 'A Business Plan for a Small Winery.' It thoroughly covered the financing, operations, winemaking criteria, and marketing for a small winery." *RPH*

Trefethen's century-old wooden winery has no difficulty being decorated at Halloween. The orange edifice looks like an over-sized, square pumpkin, all year long. The massive oak trees must predate the winery by a century or more.

TUDAL WINERY

Arnold Tudal was a row-crop farmer in Alameda who specialized in small, fast-growing vegetables that could be sold in the San Francisco and Oakland produce markets. As soon as one crop was harvested, Arnold, his father-in-law, and his brother-in-law would be back the next day, planting another. Thus did their wholesale produce firm prosper: a non-stop, year-around business.

But housing was encroaching and the residents opposed the agricultural enterprises. "Taxes were a thousand dollars per acre per year," says Arnold. "And the tractors made too much noise for the local gentry, so they com-

plained. And after a while I just said: 'Aw, let 'em have it.'"

So after 28 years in the produce business, Tudal sold his land and moved his family to a ten-acre plot that had a large walnut grove in the Napa Valley north of St. Helena. Here he intended to retire and sell his walnuts to a big company. One crop per year. That first year, he sold the walnuts to a big processor, and they sent him a check.

"It wasn't anything. I could have gotten two and a half times that amount in the produce district. So I got out my tractor and pushed the [walnut] trees over, and we cleaned

Arnold Tudal, a row-crop farmer from the Oakland area, planted his Cabernet vines without knowing much about viticulture.
A neighbor advised him that a wire trellising system wasn't necessary if he adopted a special pruning method, which he did, and the results turned out to be serendipitous: some of the best Cabernet in the Napa Valley.

up the land real good, and I decided to plant grapes. Well, I had never grown grapes before, just 20 different types of vegetables, so I went down to talk with Louis Martini, and he told me if I planted Cabernet he'd buy my grapes. So I went to get Cabernet stock."

Once his 7.6 acres were planted, however, Tudal didn't know how to train the vines. Many of his neighbors used wires in a trellissing system.

"But I had a neighbor at the time, a 75-year-old guy by the name of Vern March who was born and raised in the valley. Well, I looked at his place and his Cabernet was

An old hand press sits out in front of the Tudals' small winery. Tudal uses no high-tech equipment here, preferring to let gentle handling of the Cabernet and slow maturing of the wine in French oak casks make their mark.

pruned in what he called stepladder pruning." Tudal looked in his viticulture book and it wasn't there.

"Then all of a sudden it hit me: it was a vertical cordon and the book frowns on it. Says the grapes don't get enough sunlight in there." But Arnold figured if it was good enough for his neighbor, it would work for him — and it required no wires.

The first year after planting Tudal harvested 847 pounds of grapes. The next year tonnage remained small. "I told my kids, we're not about to take this small amount of grapes to Martini, so I bought a redwood tank, an open-top fermenter, two used barrels, and a book called *Fundamentals of Winemaking*, and I made some wine."

Three more harvests convinced Tudal that the work done by his kids, his wife, Alma, and himself was exhausting for the financial return. So in 1979 he decided to make wine. Tudal got a series of books, formed a company, gave 20 percent of the winery's "stock" to each member of the family, and the Tudal Winery was born.

Tudal makes the wine and the only wine made here is Cabernet — about 2,000 cases a year, all hand-sold. The wine is a prototype Napa Valley Cabernet, with the perfect herbal nuances, and ages beautifully, taking on a lush, burnished quality in time. *DB*

The Tudal vineyard and winery are located in the center of the Napa Valley, on dead-end Big Tree Road, off Highway 29. The entrance to Tudal is directly across the lane from the entrance to the Charles F. Shaw Vineyard & Winery.

VILLA MT. EDEN

The compound can be seen clearly from the Silverado Trail, nestled neatly in a small grove of trees north of the Oakville Cross Road, surrounded by open fields of grapevines. Its clean white buildings, glistening in the sunlight, are trimmed in teal blue.

A greenish-blue, nearly turquoise, teal blue was a favorite of Anne Giannini McWilliams, who owned Villa Mt. Eden with her financier husband, James, until the label was purchased by Washington State's dynamic Chateau Ste. Michelle in August 1986.

The blue-green theme is carried through in many aspects of ranch and winery. The soft color accents the Sebastian Titus drawing on the winery label; the boxed varietal name of each wine is likewise shaded in blue. Each bottle's lead foil capsule is a metallic shade of the color that originated with Anne's upright piano — a powder aqua-blue, ornately trimmed in white — which sits in the office.

A horse fancier, Anne McWilliams had been looking for a ranch in Pope Valley when Jim discovered Mt. Eden Ranch. They purchased the 57-acre property from Constantine Ramsay in 1969, later adding an adjacent 30-acre parcel.

Initially they sold their grapes, but three

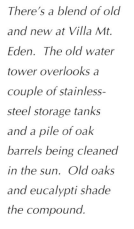

There's a blend of old and new at Villa Mt. Eden. The old water tower overlooks a couple of stainless-steel storage tanks and a pile of oak barrels being cleaned in the sun. Old oaks and eucalypti shade the compound.

vintages of Gewurztraminer vinified by Joe Heitz indicated the quality of the vineyard. McWilliams hired blue-eyed winemaker Nils Venge in February of Febrary 1973 to refurbish the vineyards, originally planted in 1881, and appoint the ancient buildings with stainless-steel fermenters, French casks, and German ovals.

A garage next to the guest quarters houses Anne's most prized possession, her father's 1911 Hupmobile. An original ad proclaims: "Exit the horse — enter the HUPMOBILE. 4 Cylinder, 20 H.P., $750." Dark blue, with black leather seats, the car is in mint condition. It was

Barrels need to be "topped" about once a month in summmertime, less often in winter. As wine evaporates, an air space ("ullage") forms at the top of each barrel. Too much air, and wine begins another transformation: into vinegar.

the first car owned by L.M. "Mario" Giannini, president of the Bank of America and son of its founder, A.P. Giannini, Anne's grandfather.

Even Villa Mt. Eden's present winemaker comes trimmed in blue, though Mike McGrath's eyes are a bit darker than the traditional teal. An angular young man, McGrath was born in Kansas City and raised in Argentina, where his father worked for Kaiser Jeep. (Curiously, two of the senior McGrath's co-workers at Kaiser, Gene Trefethen and Steven Girard Sr., are winegrowing neighbors of Villa Mt. Eden.)

A college all-American in the steeplechase and 5,000 meters, Mike now prefers windsurfing and tennis to serious running. "I ran the Napa Valley Marathon in 1979," he says with a mischievous grin. "It was my first and last marathon. I did pretty well, doing it in two hours 31 minutes, which was good enough to win. But that was definitely not my event."

If future marathons are not in McGrath's datebook, he does appreciate the necessity of staying active. "You know, physical activity really attunes the senses," he argues. "I know that wine tastes much, much better after a good run. You can also deduce that by the opposite. I know that when I take trips for marketing our wines, the lack of exercise dulls my senses. I go out to a nice dinner, with fine wines, and I can't appreciate them nearly enough." *RPH*

Quick hands at harvest strip clusters of Cabernet Sauvignon from vines that, from the color of the leaves, are beginning to show water stress — typical at the end of the growing season. A good picker can fill eight to twelve 30-pound lugboxes per hour.

VILLA ZAPU

Sometimes appearances are not reality, and this is certainly so in the case of Villa Zapu. Or is it?

On one hand, you see pictures in magazines of Thomas and Anna Lundstrom in and about their Villa Zapu villa. And you get the idea that this is a flamboyant millionaire's plaything, one of a half dozen homes they own from here to the Riviera, and a most absurd one at that. You get the feeling they're here only a few days a year, for the social season.

Then you meet the Lundstroms and you realize that (a) they are quiet, modest people who are anything but flamboyant; (b) they are

dedicated to making fine wine; (c) this is their only home; and (d) they don't consider it a curiosity. This is home.

Moreover, walking through the design of London architect David Connor, one gets a most amusing look at an almost literal definition of the word "eclectic." In the hallway is a "sculpture" of sorts — a couch made to look like the back end of a 1950s automobile. And within feet of it is a massive 17th-century tapestry.

The building is modernistic. Its sharp angles and bizarre nooks and crannies are fascinating, but shouldn't take the focus off the main point here: fine wines. And the Lundstroms have taken

Art and artifacts from the 1950s, including functional ones such as cars, are sprinkled around the Lundstrom home, side by side with classic furniture from the Swedish court. Lundstrom and his wife, Anna, and their two children now call this home.

steps to assure that this element is squared away. They hired experienced winemaker Bob Levy to make the wines; from the start, the efforts have been stunning. A 1988 Chardonnay won a number of gold medals at major competitions, including a sweepstakes award at one fair. And the 1987 and 1988 Cabernet Sauvignons are superb.

Without knowing any of this, one might look at the curious Villa Zapu label and think it's an affront to the Napa Valley. In fact, it happens to be a whimsical fun-poking at the stuffiness of the Napa Valley by pop artist Kenny Scharf — an Andy Warhol protégé.

The humorous painting above the fireplace at Villa Zapu was done by pop artist Kenny Scharf, a disciple of Andy Warhol. The Lundstroms had paid Warhol to create a label for their winery, but he died. Scharf's painting has been on the Villa Zapu label since the founding.

The name of the property might also prompt one to conclude that it's an "in" joke — for insiders only. In fact, the name is just another bit of whimsy. "The name doesn't mean anything," says Lundstrom. "Its just something I came up with because it sounded good."

Lundstrom is the scion of the family that owned Wasa crackerbread. The company was sold in 1982. He and Anna were living in London, managing investments, when they decided they liked the life to be found in the most un-London-like spot they could find — a remote plateau 1,300 feet above Oakville, California. Just up a rise from there is Mayacamas, the nearest neighboring winery.

Lundstrom bought more than 200 acres and began planting the 50 acres that were most feasible; the rest was pretty rugged. Even so, some acreage had to be terraced. He began to plant the five traditional Bordeaux grape varieties as well as some Sangiovese.

The project was just getting off the ground in 1990 when Villa Zapu was featured in a number of magazines. The image left by these articles was that the Lundstroms weren't for real.

Yet Villa Zapu's initial wines were exceptional; its upcoming wines are even better. And the plans to make still greater strides show that the Lundstroms have made a long-term commitment to the Napa Valley. *DB*

The Lundstroms, formerly of London, were intrigued by the architectural design of their building, including the pool and the tower that sits at the end of the property. The tower houses three guest bedrooms, one on top of another. "The county made us put in two staircases, for safety," notes Lundstrom.

WOLTNER ESTATES

At the Heublein Auction of Rare Wine in 1980, in San Francisco, Francis DeWavrin-Woltner was asked about California wine. "I love the Chardonnays, and I think it is possible to make very great Chardonnays, greater than have been made here already," he said. The answer was surprising because DeWavrin-Woltner was then co-proprietor of three of the top properties in Bordeaux — regions that produce no Chardonnay at all.

He then revealed that he was looking for land in California, in the Napa Valley, and hoped to make great wine there, though the variety he would make would be determined not by design, but by the soil he bought.

DeWavrin-Woltner and his wife, Françoise Woltner, were co-proprietors of Château La Mission Haut-Brion, Château Latour Haut-Brion, and Château Laville Haut-Brion. The properties made wonderful wine from Semillon, Sauvignon Blanc, and Cabernet Sauvignon.

"The properties were family-owned," says Francis, "and the family wanted to sell them, and we were not rich enough to buy them from the rest of the family." Knowing they'd be leaving the château, they moved to California to pursue wine. To fund their project, they sold a

Francis and Françoise DeWavrin-Woltner sold a forest in France to finance the reconstruction of the old Brux and Chaix winery on Howell Mountain, where they eventually planted Chardonnay vineyards.

1,500-acre forest of oak trees near Orléans in 1979, then hired winemaker Ric Forman to find them a Napa ranch.

The DeWavrins acquired the Howell Mountain property in 1981, renovated and reinforced the old winery against earthquakes, and put in a cellar two floors underground. Much of the 180 acres they bought was useless. To determine which grape varieties would thrive on the mountain, experiments were conducted. Chardonnay was best, so about 25 acres were planted.

In 1985, DeWavrin hired Ted Lemon as winemaker. The young American had attended

Winemaker Ted Lemon, a brilliant stylist, was hired to head up the Woltner Estates project. Lemon had studied winemaking and had worked in France, and he developed a style of wine that was delicate yet very complex.

the enology school at Dijon, France, and worked for two years in Burgundy. "I liked the wine he made," says DeWavrin. "The man was bright, and the man spoke French, which was good for me because my English is not so good."

"We didn't come in here with a style in mind," says Lemon, "just an outline. We didn't want to bend these wines into something they didn't want to be. I came in here thinking we'd do 100 percent malolactic fermentation, but that clearly was not appropriate. The wine wasn't as successful, so we decided against any malolactic."

Lemon says that when he arrived in California after French training, "I found all these wines with all this malolactic character, not wine character. And the ML character I saw here was not what I remember from Puligny and Chassagne. The ML aroma ought to be an aspect, but not the whole ball game. We found that the ML flattened the fruit and destroyed the finesse." Instead of ML, Lemon says he uses long lees contact, ten months in the barrel: "The flavor range of these wines when they are young is shy, but they age well."

Today 55 acres are in place, but the tiny production (just over one and a half tons per acre) helps explain why Woltner wines are so expensive — more than $50 a bottle for the Titus and Frederique wines, making them the most expensive Chardonnays in California. *DB*

Ted Lemon believes in handling Chardonnay grapes delicately, doing only a single fermentation and aging the wine in barrels only long enough to gain complexity. The result is wine that is creamy but not buttery.

ZD WINES

It was in 1969 that a pair of former Aerojet-General engineers — the late Gino Zepponi and Norman de Leuze — rented an empty farm building east of Sonoma and produced their first commercial wines. "We had originally intended to make only Chardonnay and Pinot Noir," recalls de Leuze, the "D" of ZD, "but these excellent lots of Gewurztraminer, Cabernet Sauvignon, Merlot, Zinfandel, and White Riesling kept coming our way. What could we do?"

They made the wines, and had a spot of fun doing it. They even made a few late-harvest wines, sometimes Gewurztraminer, sometimes Riesling. "A pain in the neck," says second-generation winemaker Robert de Leuze with a chuckle. "It's ridiculously hard to get much juice from those shriveled berries. But, hey,

Winemaking is a wonderful amalgam of science and technology, mysticism and art. The art of wine is expressed in many variations, functional and not, including this bronzed belt buckle.

they sure do taste good, don't they?"

In their tiny Sonoma Valley winery, de Leuze and Zepponi (Gino died in a 1985 auto accident) muddled along at some 2,000 cases each vintage, the wines aging in casks crammed into efficient barrel racks. Despite cramped quarters, the wines were never inhibited in style: invariably they were big and unabashed, of broadly defined varietal character.

After a decade of this crowded regime, ZD moved into a new, 5,800-square-foot, high-ceilinged structure a mile south of the Rutherford Cross Road on the west side of the Silverado Trail. At the ground-breaking ceremony in April 1979, Zepponi and de Leuze put a pair of sledge hammers to a barrel of their Pinot Noir 1976 — to properly baptize the site of their new winery.

Known for Chardonnay and Cabernet, ZD also makes dribbles and drabs of Pinot Noir, which come out of the Tori-Beth Vineyard (Carneros), Pickle Canyon (Mt. Veeder), and Tepusquet (Santa Barbara). "It's funny how Pinot Noir sells," says co-owner RosaLee de Leuze. "Sometimes it can be the hardest sell ever. Then you'll have a wine, like our '84 — which didn't win any competitions, and rated hardly any critical mention — which sells out so fast that you have to bring out the next vintage earlier than you'd like. The experts didn't like it, but the consumers sure did!"

Part of that may have been that American consumers are only recently recognizing the succulent, supple, juicy, fleshy, almost sinful glories that this variety brings to palate. Pinot Noir recalls Mae West's classic, "When I'm good I'm good; when I'm bad I'm better!"

The wood-fermented ZD Chardonnays are also sturdy, rich wines — chock-a-block full of exotic, tropical fruit (pineapple, papaya, grapefruit) — but often show a bit more elegance than their red brethren. ZD Chardonnays, which account for more than 80 percent of production, formerly came mostly from Tepusquet Vineyard, but now arrive from many different sources.

ZD has always been a family affair. Norm's son Robert handles the winemaking responsibilities, and also planted the three acres of Estate Cabernet Sauvignon on the south side of the winery. Norm's daughter, Julie Hice (who did the stained-glass work over the front entry), and wife, RosaLee (a superb cook), handle much of the paper glut that inevitably stalks artist winemakers, and son Brett heads the marketing team (which includes everybody.) *RPH*

A load of Pinot Noir grapes being dumped from gondolla to hopper, where they will be conveyed to a press. Pinot Noir is a major item at ZD, Where the de Leuze family have been successfully meeting that variety's special challenges for decades.

This lab sample of Chardonnay will undergo a range of testing procedures. While many will be chemical in nature -- measuring acidity and determining whether malolactic fermentation has been completed -- the most important is organoleptic: tasting.

GLOSSARY

BENCH: A slightly elevated plateau above a valley floor, which supposedly yields a better quality of fruit and thus better wine.

BOTRYTISED: Describes wine made from grapes that were infected with the beneficial mold Botrytis cinerea, or the condition affecting the grapes.

BRIX: The percentage of sugar by weight in grapes still on the vine, or, less often, the percentage of sugar remaining in wine.

BUNG: The wooden (or more recently neoprene) stopper for a cask.

CARBONIC MACERATION: A technique for fermenting wine. Whole grapes are put into a tank, the tank is sealed, and the fermentation is begun without air, until a small amount of alcohol is created inside the grapes.

CHAI: A barrel-aging cellar.

COOPERAGE: Barrels.

CRUSH: Used as a noun, the term refers to the harvest.

CUVÉE: The blend of various wines into a single wine.

EGG-WHITE FINED: The whites of eggs are commonly used to remove tiny matter from wine. The egg whites are removed before bottling.

EN TIRAGE: Bottles (usually of sparkling wine) left to age on the side, so the wine is in contact with the yeast.

ENOLOGY: The science of winemaking.

FINING: Removing tiny particles from wine.

GONDOLA: Large bin used for hauling grapes from the field to the winery.

IMPERIAL: A large bottle, holding six liters.

LACTIC ACID: An acid found in wines, said to cause a milky or buttery aroma.

LEES CONTACT: Leaving the wine in contact with the lees, the spent yeast cells.

LUGBOX: A small box for hauling grapes, usually from the vines to gondolas.

MAGNUM: A double-size bottle, holding 1.5 liters.

MALIC ACID: An acid found in grapes, supposedly yielding an aroma like apples.

MALOLACTIC FERMENTATION: The process of converting the stronger malic acid into the weaker lactic acid, using malolactic yeast.

MÉTHODE CHAMPENOISE: The fermentation process, used after the primary fermentation, that gives sparkling wine its bubbles.

MUST: Unfermented or partially fermented grape juice.

NÉGOCIANT: A person who buys wines in bulk, bottles them, and sells them under a proprietary or company name.

NON-VINTAGE: In California, a wine that does not carry a vintage date.

PHYLLOXERA: The root louse Phylloxera vastatrix, which devastated the vineyards of California and France in the late 1800s and which reappeared in California in the late 1980s. The problem is controlled by replanting vines onto resistant rootstocks.

PIERCE'S DISEASE: A systemic disease that can rapidly destroy a vine.

POT STILL: A small copper device used to distil liquids slowly, usually wine into brandy.

PUNCHEON: A barrel about 2.5 times bigger than the standard 55-gallon wine barrels.

REPEAL: The 21st Amendment to the U.S. Constitution, which went into effect on Dec. 1933, repealing the 13-year Prohibition on the manufacture, transportation, or sale of alcoholic beverages.

ROOTSTOCK: Vine roots that may be "budded" with a specific variety of grape after planting.

SUR LIE: The process in which wine is left in contact with the spent yeast cells, usually in barrel.

U.C. DAVIS: The University of California campus at Davis, which has one of the world's finest schools of viticulture and enology.

UCLA: University of California at Los Angeles.

VITICULTURE: The science of grape growing.

TANNIN: The polyphenols that give wine roughness and astringency; also found in tea.

VINIFY: To ferment.

WINE TRAIN: A controversial tourist attraction that began operating in the Napa Valley in late 1980s in spite of very strong, unified opposition by most residents of the valley.

INDEX

PHOTO CREDITS

All photographs in this book are by Eric Sander, except for those listed below.

(T = top, B = bottom, R = right, L = left)

p. 6	T	Gamma
p. 11	L	Gamma
p. 23	BL, BR	Beringer Vineyards
p. 51	T	Clos Du Val Wine Company
p. 69	T	Richard Gillette
p. 92	B	Freemark Abbey
p. 94	B	Freemark Abbey
p. 95	all	Freemark Abbey
p. 138	B	Faith Echtermeyer
p. 139	all	Faith Echtermeyer
p. 167	T	Faith Echtermeyer
p. 192	B	V. Sattui Winery
p. 194	B	V. Sattui Winery
p. 195	T, M	V. Sattui Winery
p. 209	T	Faith Echtermeyer
p. 219		Jean-Paul Paireault
p. 220		Faith Echtermeyer
p. 221	T	Stag's Leap Wine Cellars
	B	Jean-Paul Paireault
p. 227	T	Faith Echtermeyer
p. 241	T	Faith Echtermeyer
p. 252		Jean-Paul Paireault

ACKNOWLEDGMENTS

The publisher acknowledges with gratitude the cooperation and support given by the companies listed below during the preparation of this book:

Balloons Above the Valley, Napa, California
Beltane Ranch, Glen Ellen, California
California Visitors Review, El Verano, California
Faith Echtermeyer, St. Helena, California
Meadowood Resort, St. Helena, California
The New Lab, San Francisco, California
Sonoma Mission Inn & Spa, Sonoma, California